OTHER BOOKS BY PETER ANDREI

How Highly Effective People Speak

Eloquence

How Legendary Leaders Speak

Influential Leadership

Public Speaking Mastery

The 7 Keys to Confidence

Trust is Power

Influence

Decoding Human Nature

The Psychology of Persuasion

How Visionaries Speak

The Eloquent Leader

The Language of Leadership

The Psychology of Communication

The Charisma Code

Available on Amazon

Claim These Free Resources that Will Help You Unleash the Power of Your Words and Speak with Confidence. Visit www.speakforsuccesshub.com/toolkit for Access.

18 Free PDF Resources

30 Free Video Lessons

2 Free Workbooks

Claim These Free Resources that Will Help You Unleash the Power of Your Words and Speak with Confidence. Visit www.speakforsuccesshub.com/toolkit for Access.

18 Free PDF Resources

12 Iron Rules for Captivating Story, 21 Speeches that Changed the World, 341-Point Influence Checklist, 143 Persuasive Cognitive Biases, 17 Ways to Think On Your Feet, 18 Lies About Speaking Well, 137 Deadly Logical Fallacies, 12 Iron Rules For Captivating Slides, 371 Words that Persuade, 63 Truths of Speaking Well, 27 Laws of Empathy, 21 Secrets of Legendary Speeches, 19 Scripts that Persuade, 12 Iron Rules For Captivating Speech, 33 Laws of Charisma, 11 Influence Formulas, 219-Point Speech-Writing Checklist, 21 Eloquence Formulas

30 Free Video Lessons

We'll send you one free video lesson every day for 30 days, written and recorded by Peter D. Andrei. Days 1-10 cover authenticity, the prerequisite to confidence and persuasive power. Days 11-20 cover building self-belief and defeating communication anxiety. Days 21-30 cover how to speak with impact and influence, ensuring your words change minds instead of falling flat. Authenticity, self-belief, and impact – this course helps you master three components of confidence, turning even the most high-stakes presentations from obstacles into opportunities.

2 Free Workbooks

We'll send you two free workbooks, including long-lost excerpts by Dale Carnegie, the mega-bestselling author of *How to Win Friends and Influence People* (5,000,000 copies sold). *Fearless Speaking* guides you in the proven principles of mastering your inner game as a speaker. *Persuasive Speaking* guides you in the time-tested tactics of mastering your outer game by maximizing the power of your words. All of these resources complement the Speak for Success collection.

HOW HIGHLY EFFECTIVE PEOPLE

SPEAK

HOW HIGH PERFORMERS USE PSYCHOLOGY TO INFLUENCE WITH EASE

HOW HIGHLY
EFFECTIVE PEOPLE
SPEAK

SPEAK FOR SUCCESS COLLECTION BOOK

I

↑
SPEAK
TRUTH
WELL
PRESS

A SUBSIDIARY OF SPEAK TRUTH WELL LLC
800 Boylston Street
Boston, MA 02199

↑
SPEAK
TRUTH
WELL LLC

SPEAK FOR SUCCESS COLLECTION

Printed in the United States of America
40 39 38 37 36 35 34 33 32 31

While the author has made every effort to provide accurate internet addresses at the time of publication, neither the publisher nor the author assumes any responsibility for errors, or for changes that occur after publication. Further, the publisher does not have any control over and does not assume any responsibility for author or third-party websites or their content.

www.speakforsuccesshub.com/toolkit

FREE RESOURCES FOR OUR READERS

We believe in using the power of the internet to go above and beyond for our readers. That's why we created the free communication toolkit: 18 free PDF resources, 30 free video lessons, and even 2 free workbooks, including long-lost excerpts by Dale Carnegie, the mega-bestselling author of *How to Win Friends and Influence People*. (The workbooks help you put the most powerful strategies into action).

We know you're busy. That's why we designed these resources to be accessible, easy, and quick. Each PDF resource takes just 5 minutes to read or use. Each video lesson is only 5 minutes long. And in the workbooks, we bolded the key ideas throughout, so skimming them takes only 10 minutes each.

Why give so much away? For three reasons: we're grateful for you, it's useful content, and we want to go above and beyond. Questions? Feel free to email Peter directly at pandreibusiness@gmail.com.

www.speakforsuccesshub.com/toolkit

WHY DOES THIS HELP YOU?

I

The PDF resources cover topics like storytelling, logic, cognitive biases, empathy, charisma, and more. You can dig deeper into the specific topics that interest you most.

II

Many of the PDF resources are checklists, scripts, example-compilations, and formula-books. With these practical, step-by-step tools, you can quickly create messages that work.

III

With these free resources, you can supplement your reading of this book. You can find more specific guidance on the areas of communication you need to improve the most.

IV

The two workbooks offer practical and actionable guidance for speaking with complete confidence (*Fearless Speaking*) and irresistible persuasive power (*Persuasive Speaking*).

V

You can even learn from your phone with the free PDFs and the free video lessons, to develop your skills faster. The 30-lesson course reveals the secrets of building confidence.

VI

You are reading this because you want to improve your communication. These resources take you to the next level, helping you learn how to speak with power, impact, and confidence. We hope these resources make a difference. They are available here:

www.speakforsuccesshub.com/toolkit

From the desk of Peter Andrei
Speak Truth Well LLC
800 Boylston Street
Boston, MA 02199
pandreibusiness@gmail.com

May 15, 2021

What is Our Mission?

To whom it may concern:

The Wall Street Journal reports that public speaking is the world's biggest fear – bigger than being hit by a car. According to Columbia University, this pervasive, powerful, common phobia can reduce someone's salary by 10% or more. It can reduce someone's chances of graduating college by 10% and cut their chances of attaining a managerial or leadership position at work by 15%.

If weak presentation kills your good ideas, it kills your career. If weak communication turns every negotiation, meeting, pitch, speech, presentation, discussion, and interview into an obstacle (instead of an opportunity), it slows your progress. And if weak communication slows your progress, it tears a gaping hole in your confidence – which halts your progress.

Words can change the world. They can improve your station in life, lifting you forward and upward to higher and higher successes. But they have to be strong words spoken well: rarities in a world where most people fail to connect, engage, and persuade; fail to answer the question "why should we care about this?"; fail to impact, inspire, and influence; and, in doing so, fail to be all they could be.

Now zoom out. Multiply this dynamic by one thousand; one million; one billion. The individual struggle morphs into a problem for our communities, our countries, our world. Imagine the many millions of paradigm-shattering, life-changing, life-saving ideas that never saw the light of day. Imagine how many brilliant convictions were sunk in the shipyard. Imagine all that could have been that failed to be.

Speak Truth Well LLC solves this problem by teaching ambitious professionals how to turn communication from an obstacle into an engine: a tool for converting "what could be" into "what is." There is no upper limit: inexperienced speakers can become self-assured and impactful; veteran speakers can master the skill by learning advanced strategies; masters can learn how to outperform their former selves.

We achieve our mission by producing the best publications, articles, books, video courses, and coaching programs available on public speaking and communication, and at non-prohibitive prices. This combination of quality and accessibility has allowed Speak Truth Well to serve over 70,000 customers in its year of launch alone (2021). Grateful as we are, we hope to one day serve millions.

Dedicated to your success,

Peter Andrei
President of Speak Truth Well LLC
pandreibusiness@gmail.com

PROLOGUE:

This three-part prologue reveals my story, my work, and the practical and ethical principles of communication. It is not a mere introduction. It will help you get more out of the book. It is a preface to the entire 15-book Speak for Success collection. It will show you how to use the information with ease, confidence, and fluency, and how to get better results faster. If you want to skip this, flip to page 42, or read only the parts of interest.

I

page XIII

MY STORY AND THE STORY OF THIS COLLECTION

how I discovered the hidden key to successful communication, public speaking, influence, and persuasion

page XXI

THE 15-BOOK SPEAK FOR SUCCESS COLLECTION

confidence, leadership, charisma, influence, public speaking, eloquence, human nature, credibility - it's all here

II

III

page XXIV

THE PRACTICAL TACTICS AND ETHICAL PRINCIPLES

how to easily put complex strategies into action and how to use the power of words to improve the world

MY STORY AND THE STORY OF THIS COLLECTION

how I discovered the hidden key to successful communication, public speaking, influence, and persuasion (by reflecting on a painful failure)

HOW TO GAIN AN UNFAIR ADVANTAGE IN YOUR CAREER, BUSINESS, AND LIFE BY MASTERING THE POWER OF YOUR WORDS

I WAS SITTING IN MY OFFICE, TAPPING A PEN against my small wooden desk. My breaths were jagged, shallow, and rapid. My hands were shaking. I glanced at the clock: 11:31 PM. "I'm not ready." Have you ever had that thought?

I had to speak in front of 200 people the next morning. I had to convince them to put faith in my idea. But I was terrified, attacked by nameless, unreasoning, and unjustified terror which killed my ability to think straight, believe in myself, and get the job done.

Do you know the feeling?

After a sleepless night, the day came. I rose, wobbling on my tired legs. My head felt like it was filled with cotton candy. I couldn't direct my train of thoughts. A rushing waterfall of unhinged, self-destructive, and meaningless musings filled my head with an uncompromising cacophony of anxious, ricocheting nonsense.

"Call in sick."

"You're going to embarrass yourself."

"You're not ready."

I put on my favorite blue suit – my "lucky suit" – and my oversized blue-gold wristwatch; my "lucky" wristwatch.

"You're definitely not ready."

"That tie is ugly."

"You can't do this."

The rest went how you would expect. I drank coffee. Got in my car. Drove. Arrived. Waited. Waited. Waited. Spoke. Did poorly. Rushed back to my seat. Waited. Waited.

Waited. Got in my car. Drove. Arrived home. Sat back in my wooden seat where I accurately predicted "I'm not ready" the night before.

Relieved it was over but disappointed with my performance, I placed a sheet of paper on the desk. I wrote "MY PROBLEMS" at the top, and under that, my prompt for the evening: "What did I do so badly? Why did everything feel so off? Why did the speech fail?"

"You stood in front of 200 people and looked at... a piece of paper, not unlike this one. What the hell were you thinking? You're not fooling anyone by reading a sentence and then looking up at them as you say it out loud. They know you're reading a manuscript, and they know what that means. You are unsure of yourself. You are unsure of your message. You are unprepared. Next: Why did you speak in that odd, low, monotone voice? That sounded like nails on a chalkboard. And it was inauthentic. Next: Why did you open by talking about yourself? Also, you're not particularly funny. No more jokes. And what was the structure of the speech? It had no structure. That, I feel, is probably a pretty big problem."

I believed in my idea, and I wanted to get it across. Of course, I wanted the tangible markers of a successful speech. I wanted action. I wanted the speech to change something in the real world. But my motivations were deeper than that. I wanted to see people "click" and come on board my way of thinking. I wanted to captivate the audience. I wanted to speak with an engaging, impactful voice, drawing the audience in, not repelling them. I wanted them to remember my message and to remember me. I wanted to feel, for just a moment, the thrill of power. But not the petty, forceful power of tyrants and dictators; the justified power – the earned power – of having a good idea and conveying it well; the power of Martin Luther King and John F. Kennedy; a power harnessed in service of a valuable idea, not the personal privilege of the speaker. And I wanted confidence: the quiet strength that comes from knowing your words don't stand in your way, but propel you and the ideas you care about to glorious new mountaintops.

Instead, I stood before the audience, essentially powerless. I spoke for 20 painful minutes – painful for them and for me – and then sat down. I barely made a dent in anyone's consciousness. I generated no excitement. Self-doubt draped its cold embrace over me. Anxiety built a wall between "what I am" and "what I could be."

I had tried so many different solutions. I read countless books on effective communication, asked countless effective communicators for their advice, and consumed countless courses on powerful public speaking. Nothing worked. All the "solutions" that didn't really solve my problem had one thing in common: they treated communication as an abstract art form. They were filled with vague, abstract pieces of advice like "think positive thoughts" and "be yourself." They confused me more than anything else. Instead of illuminating the secrets I had been looking for, they shrouded the elusive but indispensable skill of powerful speaking in uncertainty.

I knew I had to master communication. I knew that the world's most successful people are all great communicators. I knew that effective communication is the bridge between "what I have" and "what I want," or at least an essential part of that bridge. I knew that without effective communication – without the ability to influence, inspire, captivate, and move – I would be all but powerless.

I knew that the person who can speak up but doesn't is no better off than the person who can't speak at all. I heard a wise man say "If you can think and speak and write, you are absolutely deadly. Nothing can get in your way." I heard another wise man say "Speech is power: speech is to persuade, to convert, to compel. It is to bring another out of his bad sense into your good sense." I heard a renowned psychologist say "If you look at people who are remarkably successful across life, there's various reasons. But one of them is that they're unbelievably good at articulating what they're aiming at and strategizing and negotiating and enticing people with a vision forward. Get your words together... that makes you unstoppable. If you are an effective writer and speaker and communicator, you have all the authority and competence that there is."

When I worked in the Massachusetts State House for the Department of Public Safety and Homeland Security, I had the opportunity to speak with countless senators, state representatives, CEOs, and other successful people. In our conversations, however brief, I always asked the same question: "What are the ingredients of your success? What got you where you are?" 100% of them said effective communication. There was not one who said anything else. No matter their field – whether they were entrepreneurs, FBI agents, political leaders, business leaders, or multimillionaire donors – they all pointed to one skill: the ability to convey powerful words in powerful ways. Zero exceptions.

Can you believe it? It still astonishes me.

My problem, and I bet this may be your obstacle as well, was that most of the advice I consumed on this critical skill barely scratched the surface. Sure, it didn't make matters worse, and it certainly offered some improvement, but only in inches when I needed progress in miles. If I stuck with the mainstream public speaking advice, I knew I wouldn't unleash the power of my words. And if I didn't do that, I knew I would always accomplish much less than I could. I knew I would suffocate my own potential. I knew I would feel a rush of crippling anxiety every time I was asked to give a presentation. I knew I would live a life of less fulfillment, less success, less achievement, more frustration, more difficulty, and more anxiety. I knew my words would never become all they could be, which means that I would never become all I could be.

To make matters worse, the mainstream advice – which is not wrong, but simply not deep enough – is everywhere. Almost every article, book, or course published on this subject falls into the mainstream category. And to make matters worse, it's almost impossible to know that until you've spent your hard-earned money and scarce time with the resource. And even then, you might just shrug, and assume that shallow, abstract advice is all there is to the "art" of public speaking. As far as I'm concerned, this is a travesty.

I kept writing. "It felt like there was no real motive; no real impulse to action. Why did they need to act? You didn't tell them. What would happen if they didn't? You didn't tell them that either. Also, you tried too hard to put on a formal façade; you spoke in strange, twisted ways. It didn't sound sophisticated. And your mental game was totally off. You let your mind fill with destructive, doubtful, self-defeating thoughts. And your preparation was totally backward. It did more to set bad habits in stone than it did to set you up for success. And you tried to build suspense at one point but revealed the final point way too early, ruining the effect."

I went on and on until I had a stack of papers filled with problems. "That's no good," I thought. I needed solutions. Everything else I tried failed. But I had one more idea: "I remember reading a great speech. What was it? Oh yeah, that's right: JFK's inaugural address. Let me go pull it up and see why it was so powerful." And that's when everything changed.

I grabbed another sheet of paper. I opened JFK's inaugural address on my laptop. I started reading. Observing. Analyzing. Reverse-engineering. I started writing down what I saw. Why did it work? Why was it powerful? I was like an archaeologist, digging through his speech for the secrets of powerful communication. I got more and more excited as I kept going. It was late at night, but the shocking and invaluable discoveries I was making gave me a burst of energy. It felt like JFK – one of the most powerful and effective speakers of all time – was coaching me in his rhetorical secrets, showing me how to influence an audience, draw them into my narrative, and find words that get results.

"Oh, so that's how you grab attention."

"Aha! So, if I tell them this, they will see why it matters."

"Fascinating – I can apply this same structure to my speech."

Around 3:00 in the morning, an epiphany hit me like a ton of bricks. That night, a new paradigm was born. A new opportunity emerged for all those who want to unleash the unstoppable power of their words. This new opportunity changed everything for me and eventually, tens of thousands of others. It is now my mission to bring it to millions, so that good people know what they need to know to use their words to achieve their dreams and improve the world.

Want to hear the epiphany?

The mainstream approach: Communication is an art form. It is unlike those dry, boring, "academic" subjects. There are no formulas. There are no patterns. It's all about thinking positive thoughts, faking confidence, and making eye contact. Some people are naturally gifted speakers. For others, the highest skill level they can attain is "not horrible."

The consequences of the mainstream approach: Advice that barely scratches the surface of the power of words. Advice that touches only the tip of the tip of the iceberg. A limited body of knowledge that blinds itself to thousands of hidden, little-known communication strategies that carry immense power; that blinds itself to 95% of what great communication really is. Self-limiting dogmas about who can do what, and how great communicators become great. Half the progress in twice the time, and everything that entails: missed opportunities, unnecessary and preventable frustration and anxiety, and confusion about what to say and how to say it. How do I know? Because I've been there. It's not pretty.

My epiphany, the new Speak for Success paradigm: Communication is as much a science as it is an art. You can study words that changed the world, uncover the hidden secrets of their power, and apply these proven principles to your own message. You can discover precisely what made great communicators great and adopt the same strategies. You can do this without being untrue to yourself or flatly imitating others. In fact, you can do this while being truer to yourself and more original than you ever have been before. Communication is not unpredictable, wishy-washy, or abstract. You can apply predictable processes and principles to reach your goals and get results. You can pick and choose from thousands of little-known speaking strategies, combining your favorite to create a unique communication approach that suits you perfectly. You can effortlessly use the same tactics of the world's most transformational leaders and speakers, and do so automatically, by default, without even thinking about it, as a matter of effortless habit. That's power.

The benefits of the Speak for Success paradigm: Less confusion. More confidence. Less frustration. More clarity. Less anxiety. More courage. You understand the whole iceberg of effective communication. As a result, your words captivate others. You draw them into a persuasive narrative, effortlessly linking your desires and their motives. You know exactly what to say. You know exactly how to say it. You know exactly how to keep your head clear; you are a master of the mental game. Your words can move mountains. Your words are the most powerful tools in your arsenal, and you use them to seize opportunities, move your mission forward, and make the world a better place. Simply put, you speak for success.

Fast forward a few years.

I was sitting in my office at my small wooden desk. My breaths were deep, slow, and steady. My entire being – mind, body, soul – was poised and focused. I set my speech manuscript to the side. I glanced at the clock: 12:01 AM. "Let's go. I'm ready."

I had to speak in front of 200 people the next morning. I had to convince them to put faith in my idea. And I was thrilled, filled with genuine gratitude at the opportunity to do what I love: get up in front of a crowd, think clearly, speak well, and get the job done.

I slept deeply. I dreamt vividly. I saw myself giving the speech. I saw myself victorious, in every sense of the word. I heard applause. I saw their facial expressions. I rose. My head was clear. My mental game was pristine. My mind was an ally, not an obstacle.

"This is going to be fun."

"I'll do my best, and whatever happens, happens."

"I'm so lucky that I get to do this again."

I put on my lucky outfit: the blue suit and the blue-gold watch.

"Remember the principles. They work."

"You developed a great plan last night. It's a winner."

"I can't wait."

The rest went how you would expect. I ate breakfast. Got in my car. Drove. Arrived. Waited. Waited. Waited. Spoke. Succeeded. Walked back to my seat. Waited. Waited. Waited. Got in my car. Drove. Arrived home. Sat back in my wooden seat where I accurately predicted "I'm ready" the night before.

I got my idea across perfectly. My message succeeded: it motivated action and created real-world change. I saw people "click" when I hit the rhetorical peak of my speech. I saw them leaning forward, totally hushed, completely absorbed. I applied the proven principles of engaging and impactful vocal modulation. I knew they would remember me and my message; I engineered my words to be memorable. I felt the thrilling power of giving a great speech. I felt the quiet confidence of knowing that my words carried weight; that they could win hearts, change minds, and help me reach the heights of my potential. I tore off the cold embrace of self-doubt. I defeated communication anxiety and broke down the wall between "what I am" and "what I could be."

Disappointed it was over but pleased with my performance, I placed a sheet of paper on the desk. I wrote "Speak Truth Well" and started planning what would become my business.

To date, we have helped tens of thousands of people gain an unfair advantage in their career, business, and life by unleashing the power of their words. And they experienced the exact same transformation I experienced when they applied the system.

If you tried to master communication before but haven't gotten the results you wanted, it's because of the mainstream approach; an approach that tells you "smiling at the audience" and "making eye contact" is all you need to know to speak well. That's not exactly a malicious lie – they don't know any better – but it is completely incorrect and severely harmful.

If you've been concerned that you won't be able to become a vastly more effective and confident communicator, I want to put those fears to rest. I felt the same way. The people I work with felt the same way. We just needed the right system. One public speaking book written by the director of a popular public speaking forum – I won't name names – wants you to believe that there are "nine public speaking secrets of the world's top minds." Wrong: There are many more than nine. If you feel that anyone who would boil down communication to just nine secrets is either missing something or holding it back, you're right. And the alternative is a much more comprehensive and powerful system. It's a system that gave me and everyone I worked with the transformation we were looking for.

Want to Talk? Email Me:

PANDREIBUSINESS@GMAIL.COM

This is My Personal Email.
I Read Every Message and
Respond in Under 12 Hours.

Visit Our Digital Headquarters:

WWW.SPEAKFORSUCCESSHUB.COM

See All Our Free Resources,
Books, Courses, and Services.

THE 15-BOOK SPEAK FOR SUCCESS COLLECTION

confidence, leadership, charisma, influence, public speaking, eloquence, human nature, credibility – it's all here, in a unified collection

....A Brief Overview.......................................

- I wrote *How Highly Effective People Speak* to reveal the hidden patterns in the words of the world's most successful and powerful communicators, so that you can adopt the same tactics and speak with the same impact and influence.

- I wrote *Eloquence* to uncover the formulas of beautiful, moving, captivating, and powerful words, so that you can use these exact same step-by-step structures to quickly make your language electrifying, charismatic, and eloquent.

- I wrote *How Legendary Leaders Speak* to illuminate the little-known five-step communication process the top leaders of the past 500 years all used to spread their message, so that you can use it to empower your ideas and get results.

- I wrote *Influential Leadership* to expose the differences between force and power and to show how great leaders use the secrets of irresistible influence to develop gentle power, so that you can move forward and lead with ease.

- I wrote *Public Speaking Mastery* to shatter the myths and expose the harmful advice about public speaking, and to offer a proven, step-by-step framework for speaking well, so that you can always speak with certainty and confidence.

- I wrote *The 7 Keys to Confidence* to bring to light the ancient 4,000-year-old secrets I used to master the mental game and speak in front of hundreds without a second of self-doubt or anxiety, so that you can feel the same freedom.

- I wrote *Trust is Power* to divulge how popular leaders and career communicators earn our trust, speak with credibility, and use this to rise to new heights of power, so that you can do the same thing to advance your purpose and mission.

- I wrote *Decoding Human Nature* to answer the critical question "what do people want?" and reveal how to use this knowledge to develop unparalleled influence, so that people adopt your idea, agree with your position, and support you.

- I wrote *Influence* to unearth another little-known five-step process for winning hearts and changing minds, so that you can know with certainty that your message will persuade people, draw support, and motivate enthusiastic action.

- I wrote *The Psychology of Persuasion* to completely and fully unveil everything about the psychology behind "Yes, I love it! What's the next step?" so that you can use easy step-by-step speaking formulas that get people to say exactly that.

- I wrote *How Visionaries Speak* to debunk common lies about effective communication that hold you back and weaken your words, so that you can boldly share your ideas without accidentally sabotaging your own message.

- I wrote *The Eloquent Leader* to disclose the ten steps to communicating with power and persuasion, so that you don't miss any of the steps and fail to connect, captivate, influence, and inspire in a crucial high-stakes moment.

- I wrote *The Language of Leadership* to unpack the unique, hidden-in-plain-sight secrets of how presidents and world-leaders build movements with the laws of powerful language, so that you use them to propel yourself forward.

- I wrote *The Psychology of Communication* to break the news that most presentations succeed or fail in the first thirty seconds and to reveal proven, step-by-step formulas that grab, hold, and direct attention, so that yours succeeds.

- I wrote *The Charisma Code* to shatter the myths and lies about charisma and reveal its nature as a concrete skill you can master with proven strategies, so that people remember you, your message, and how you electrified the room.

You Can Learn More Here:
www.speakforsuccesshub.com/series

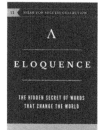

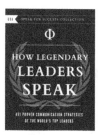

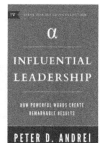

I SPEAK FOR SUCCESS COLLECTION

ψ

HOW HIGHLY
EFFECTIVE PEOPLE
SPEAK

HOW HIGH PERFORMERS USE
PSYCHOLOGY TO INFLUENCE WITH EASE

PETER D. ANDREI

II SPEAK FOR SUCCESS COLLECTION

Λ

ELOQUENCE

THE HIDDEN SECRET OF WORDS
THAT CHANGE THE WORLD

PETER D. ANDREI

III SPEAK FOR SUCCESS COLLECTION

Φ

HOW LEGENDARY
**LEADERS
SPEAK**

451 PROVEN COMMUNICATION STRATEGIES
OF THE WORLD'S TOP LEADERS

PETER D. ANDREI

IV SPEAK FOR SUCCESS COLLECTION

α

**INFLUENTIAL
LEADERSHIP**

HOW POWERFUL WORDS CREATE
REMARKABLE RESULTS

PETER D. ANDREI

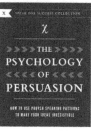

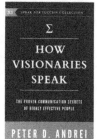

V SPEAK FOR SUCCESS COLLECTION

λ

**PUBLIC
SPEAKING
MASTERY**

HOW TO SPEAK WITH CONFIDENCE,
IMPACT, AND INFLUENCE

PETER D. ANDREI

VI SPEAK FOR SUCCESS COLLECTION

Ω

THE **7 KEYS**
TO
CONFIDENCE

HOW TO LEAD, SPEAK, AND
LIVE WITH COURAGE

PETER D. ANDREI

VII SPEAK FOR SUCCESS COLLECTION

Θ

**TRUST IS
POWER**

HOW TO COMMUNICATE IN A WORLD
THAT DOUBTS EVERYTHING

PETER D. ANDREI

VIII SPEAK FOR SUCCESS COLLECTION

φ

**DECODING
HUMAN
NATURE**

THE UNDERGROUND GUIDE TO
EMOTIONAL INTELLIGENCE

PETER D. ANDREI

IX SPEAK FOR SUCCESS COLLECTION

Δ

INFLUENCE

THE PSYCHOLOGY OF WORDS THAT
WIN HEARTS AND CHANGE MINDS

PETER D. ANDREI

X SPEAK FOR SUCCESS COLLECTION

χ

>>>> THE >>>>
PSYCHOLOGY
<<<< OF <<<<
PERSUASION

HOW TO USE PROVEN SPEAKING PATTERNS
TO MAKE YOUR IDEAS IRRESISTIBLE

PETER D. ANDREI

XI SPEAK FOR SUCCESS COLLECTION

Σ

**HOW
VISIONARIES
SPEAK**

THE PROVEN COMMUNICATION SECRETS
OF HIGHLY EFFECTIVE PEOPLE

PETER D. ANDREI

XII SPEAK FOR SUCCESS COLLECTION

σ

**THE
ELOQUENT
LEADER**

10 STEPS TO COMMUNICATION THAT
PROPELS YOU FORWARD

PETER D. ANDREI

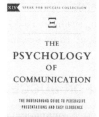

XIII SPEAK FOR SUCCESS COLLECTION

Π

THE
LANGUAGE
OF
LEADERSHIP

HOW GREAT LEADERS USE THE LAWS OF
POWERFUL LANGUAGE TO GET RESULTS

PETER D. ANDREI

XIV SPEAK FOR SUCCESS COLLECTION

Ξ

THE
PSYCHOLOGY
OF
COMMUNICATION

THE UNDERGROUND GUIDE TO PERSUASIVE
PRESENTATIONS AND EASY ELOQUENCE

PETER D. ANDREI

XV SPEAK FOR SUCCESS COLLECTION

ζ

THE
**CHARISMA
CODE**

MASTERING INFLUENCE, PUBLIC SPEAKING,
AND THE ART OF COMMUNICATION

PETER D. ANDREI

III

PRACTICAL TACTICS AND ETHICAL PRINCIPLES

how to easily put complex strategies into action and how to use the power of words to improve the world in an ethical and effective way

MOST COMMUNICATION BOOKS

HAVE YOU READ ANOTHER BOOK ON COMMUNICATION? If you have, let me remind you what you probably learned. And if you haven't, let me briefly spoil 95% of them. "Prepare. Smile. Dress to impress. Keep it simple. Overcome your fears. Speak from the heart. Be authentic. Show them why you care. Speak in terms of their interests. To defeat anxiety, know your stuff. Emotion persuades, not logic. Speak with confidence. Truth sells. And respect is returned."

There you have it. That is most of what you learn in most communication books. None of it is wrong. None of it is misleading. Those ideas are true and valuable. But they are not enough. They are only the absolute basics. And my job is to offer you much more.

Einstein said that "if you can't explain it in a sentence, you don't know it well enough." He also told us to "make it as simple as possible, but no simpler." You, as a communicator, must satisfy both of these maxims, one warning against the dangers of excess complexity, and one warning against the dangers of excess simplicity. And I, as someone who communicates about communication in my books, courses, and coaching, must do the same.

THE SPEAK FOR SUCCESS SYSTEM

The Speak for Success system makes communication as simple as possible. Other communication paradigms make it even simpler. Naturally, this means our system is more complex. This is an unavoidable consequence of treating communication as a deep and concrete science instead of a shallow and abstract art. If you don't dive into learning communication at all, you miss out. I'm sure you agree with that. But if you don't dive *deep*, you still miss out.

THE FOUR QUADRANTS OF COMMUNICATION

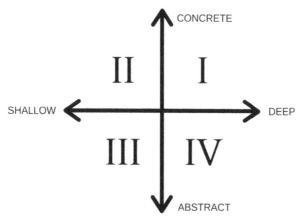

FIGURE VIII: There are four predominant views of communication (whether it takes the form of public speaking, negotiation, writing, or debating is irrelevant). The first view is that communication is concrete and deep. The second view is that communication is concrete and shallow. The third view is that communication is shallow and abstract. The fourth view is that communication is deep and abstract.

WHAT IS COMMUNICATION?

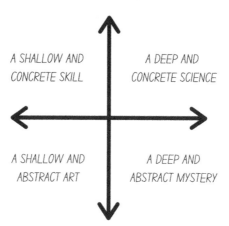

FIGURE VII: The first view treats communication as a science: "There are concrete formulas, rules, principles, and strategies, and they go very deep." The second view treats it as a skill: "Yes, there are concrete formulas, rules, and strategies, but they don't go very deep." The third view treats it as an art: "Rules? Formulas? It's not that complicated. Just smile and think positive thoughts." The fourth view treats it as a mystery: "How are some people such effective communicators? I will never know..."

WHERE WE STAND ON THE QUESTION

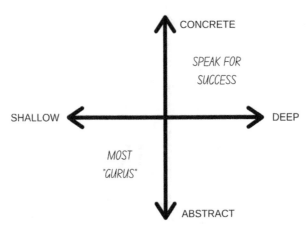

FIGURE VI: Speak for Success takes the view that communication is a deep and concrete science. (And by "takes the view," I mean "has discovered.") Most other writers, thought-leaders, public speaking coaches, and individuals and organizations in this niche treat communication as a shallow and abstract art.

This doesn't mean the Speak for Success system neglects the basics. It only means it goes far beyond the basics, and that it doesn't turn simple ideas into 200 pages of filler. It also doesn't mean that the Speak for Success system is unnecessarily complex. It is as simple as it can possibly be. In this book, and in the other books of the Speak for Success collection, you'll find simple pieces of advice, easy formulas, and straightforward rules. You'll find theories, strategies, tactics, mental models, and principles. None of this should pose a challenge. But you'll also find advanced, complicated tactics. These might.

What is the purpose of the guide on the top of the next page? To reveal the methods that make advanced strategies easy. When you use the tactics revealed in this guide, the difficulty of using the advanced strategies drops dramatically. If the 15-book Speak for Success collection is a complete encyclopedia of communication, to be used like a handbook, then this guide is a handbook for the handbook.

A SAMPLING OF EASY AND HARD STRATEGIES

Easy and Simple	Hard and Complicated
Use Four-Corner Eye Contact	The Fluency-Magnitude Matrix
Appeal to Their Values	The VPB Triad
Describe the Problem You Solve	The Illusory Truth Effect
Use Open Body Language	Percussive Rhythm
Tell a Quick Story	Alliterative Flow
Appeal to Emotion	Stacking and Layering Structures
Project Your Voice	The Declaratory Cascade
Keep it as Simple as Possible	Alternating Semantic Sentiments

THE PRACTICAL TACTICS

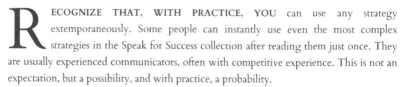

R ECOGNIZE THAT, WITH PRACTICE, YOU can use any strategy extemporaneously. Some people can instantly use even the most complex strategies in the Speak for Success collection after reading them just once. They are usually experienced communicators, often with competitive experience. This is not an expectation, but a possibility, and with practice, a probability.

CREATE A COMMUNICATION PLAN. Professional communication often follows a strategic plan. Put these techniques into your plan. Following an effective plan is not harder than following an ineffective one. Marshall your arguments. Marshall your rhetoric. Stack the deck. Know what you know, and how to say it.

DESIGN AN MVP. If you are speaking on short notice, you can create a "minimum viable plan." This can be a few sentences on a notecard jotted down five minutes before speaking. The same principle of formal communication plans applies: While advanced strategies may overburden you if you attempt them in an impromptu setting, putting them into a plan makes them easy.

MASTER YOUR RHETORICAL STACK. Master one difficult strategy. Master another one. Combine them. Master a third. Build out a "rhetorical stack" of ten strategies you can use fluently, in impromptu or extemporaneous communication. Pick strategies that come fluently to you and that complement each other.

PRACTICE THEM TO FLUENCY. I coach a client who approached me and said he wants to master every strategy I ever compiled. That's a lot. As of this writing, we're 90 one-hour sessions in. To warm up for one of our sessions, I gave him a challenge: "Give an impromptu speech on the state of the American economy, and after you stumble, hesitate, or falter four times, I'll cut you off. The challenge is to see how long you can go." He spoke for 20 minutes without a single mistake. After 20 minutes, he brought the impromptu speech to a perfect, persuasive, forceful, and eloquent conclusion. And he naturally and fluently used advanced strategies throughout his impromptu speech. After he closed the speech (which he did because he wanted to get on with the session), I asked him if he thought deeply about the strategies he used. He said no. He used them thoughtlessly. Why? Because he practiced them. You can too. You can practice them on your own. You don't need an audience. You don't need a coach. You don't even need to speak. Practice in your head. Practice ones that resonate with you. Practice with topics you care about.

KNOW TEN TIMES MORE THAN YOU INTEND TO SAY. And know what you do intend to say about ten times more fluently than you need to. This gives your mind room to relax, and frees up cognitive bandwidth to devote to strategy and rhetoric in real-time. Need to speak for five minutes? Be able to speak for 50. Need to read it three times to be able to deliver it smoothly? Read it 30 times.

INCORPORATE THEM IN SLIDES. You can use your slides or visual aids to help you ace complicated strategies. If you can't remember the five steps of a strategy, your slides can still follow them. Good slides aren't harder to use than bad slides.

USE THEM IN WRITTEN COMMUNICATION. You can read your speech. In some situations, this is more appropriate than impromptu or extemporaneous speaking. And if a strategy is difficult to remember in impromptu speaking, you can write it into your speech. And let's not forget about websites, emails, letters, etc.

PICK AND CHOOSE EASY ONES. Use strategies that come naturally and don't overload your mind. Those that do are counterproductive in fast-paced situations.

TAKE SMALL STEPS TO MASTERY. Practice one strategy. Practice it again. Keep going until you master it. Little by little, add to your base of strategies. But never take steps that overwhelm you. Pick a tactic. Practice it. Master it. Repeat.

MEMORIZE AN ENTIRE MESSAGE. Sometimes this is the right move. Is it a high-stakes message? Do you have the time? Do you have the energy? Given the situation, would a memorized delivery beat an impromptu, in-the-moment, spontaneous delivery? If you opt for memorizing, using advanced strategies is easy.

USE ONE AT A TIME. Pick an advanced strategy. Deliver it. Now what? Pick another advanced strategy. Deliver it. Now another. Have you been speaking for a while? Want to bring it to a close? Pick a closing strategy. For some people, using advanced strategies extemporaneously is easy, but only if they focus on one at a time.

MEMORIZE A KEY PHRASE. Deliver your impromptu message as planned, but add a few short, memorized key phrases throughout that include advanced strategies.

CREATE TALKING POINTS. Speak from a list of pre-written bullet-points; big-picture ideas you seek to convey. This is halfway between fully impromptu speaking and using a script. It's not harder to speak from a strategic and persuasively-advanced list of talking points than it is to speak from a persuasively weak list. You can either memorize your talking points, or have them in front of you as a guide.

TREAT IT LIKE A SCIENCE. At some point, you struggled with a skill that you now perform effortlessly. You mastered it. It's a habit. You do it easily, fluently, and thoughtlessly. You can do it while you daydream. Communication is the same. These tactics, methods, and strategies are not supposed to be stuck in the back of your mind as you speak. They are supposed to be ingrained in your habits.

RELY ON FLOW. In fast-paced and high-stakes situations, you usually don't plan every word, sentence, and idea consciously and deliberately. Rather, you let your subconscious mind take over. You speak from a flow state. In flow, you may flawlessly execute strategies that would have overwhelmed your conscious mind.

LISTEN TO THE PROMPTS. You read a strategy and found it difficult to use extemporaneously. But as you speak, your subconscious mind gives you a prompt: "this strategy would work great here." Your subconscious mind saw the opportunity and surfaced the prompt. You execute it, and you do so fluently and effortlessly.

FOLLOW THE FIVE-STEP CYCLE. First, find truth. Research. Prepare. Learn. Second, define your message. Figure out what you believe about what you learned. Third, polish your message with rhetorical strategies, without distorting the precision with which it conveys the truth. Fourth, practice the polished ideas. Fifth, deliver them. The endeavor of finding truth comes before the rhetorical endeavor. First, find the right message. Then, find the best way to convey it.

CREATE YOUR OWN STRATEGY. As you learn new theories, mental models, and principles of psychology and communication, you may think of a new strategy built around the theories, models, and principles. Practice it, test it, and codify it.

STACK GOOD HABITS. An effective communicator is the product of his habits. If you want to be an effective communicator, stack good communication habits (and break bad ones). This is a gradual process. It doesn't happen overnight.

DON'T TRY TO USE THEM. Don't force it. If a strategy seems too difficult, don't try to use it. You might find yourself using it anyway when the time is right.

KNOW ONLY ONE. If you master one compelling communication strategy, like one of the many powerful three-part structures that map out a persuasive speech, that can often be enough to drastically and dramatically improve your impact.

REMEMBER THE SHORTCOMING OF MODELS. All models are wrong, but some are useful. Many of these complex strategies and theories are models. They represent reality, but they are not reality. They help you navigate the territory, but they are not the territory. They are a map, to be used if it helps you navigate, and to be discarded the moment it prevents you from navigating.

DON'T LET THEM INHIBIT YOU. Language flows from thought. You've got to have something to say. And *then* you make it as compelling as possible. And *then* you shape it into something poised and precise; persuasive and powerful; compelling and convincing. Meaning and message come first. Rhetoric comes second. Don't take all this discussion of "advanced communication strategies," "complex communication tactics," and "the deep and concrete science of communication" to suggest that the basics don't matter. They do. Tell the truth as precisely and boldly as you can. Know your subject-matter like the back of your hand. Clear your mind and focus on precisely articulating exactly what you believe to be true. Be authentic. The advanced strategies are not supposed to stand between you and your audience. They are not supposed to stand between you and your authentic and spontaneous self – they are supposed to be integrated with it. They are not an end in themselves, but a means to the end of persuading the maximum number of people to adopt truth. Trust your instinct. Trust your intuition. It won't fail you.

MASTERING ONE COMMUNICATION SKILL

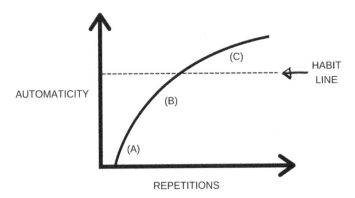

FIGURE V: Automaticity is the extent to which you do something automatically, without thinking about it. At the start of building a communication habit, it has low automaticity. You need to think about it consciously (A). After more repetitions, it gets easier and more automatic (B). Eventually, the behavior becomes more automatic than deliberate. At this point, it becomes a habit (C).

MASTERING COMMUNICATION

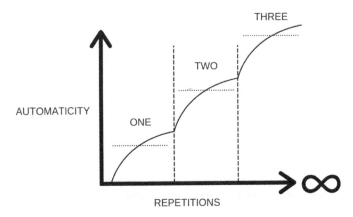

FIGURE IV: Layer good communication habits on top of each other. Go through the learning curve over and over again. When you master the first good habit, jump to the second. This pattern will take you to mastery.

THE FOUR LEVELS OF KNOWING

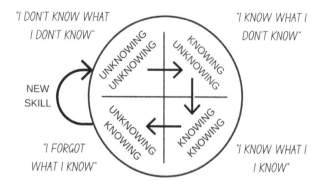

FIGURE III: First, you don't know you don't know it. Then, you discover it and know you don't know it. Then, you practice it and know you know it. Then, it becomes a habit. You forget you know it. It's ingrained in your habits.

REVISITING THE LEARNING CURVE

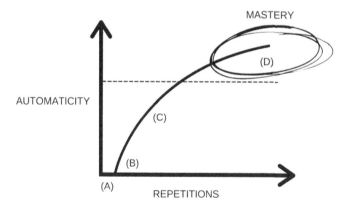

FIGURE II: Note the stages of knowing on the learning curve: unknowing unknowing (A), knowing unknowing (B), knowing knowing (C), unknowing knowing (D).

WHAT'S REALLY HAPPENING?

Have you ever thought deeply about what happens when you communicate? Let's run through the mile-high view.

At some point in your life, you bumped into an experience. You observed. You learned. The experience changed you. Your neural networks connected in new ways. New rivers of neurons began to flow through them.

The experience etched a pattern into your neurobiology representing information about the moral landscape of the universe; a map of *where we are, where we should go, and how we should make the journey.* This is meaning. This is your message.

Now, you take the floor before a crowd. Whether you realize it or not, you want to copy the neural pattern from your mind to their minds. You want to show them where we are, where we should go, and how we should make the journey.

So, you speak. You gesture. You intone. Your words convey meaning. Your body language conveys meaning. Your voice conveys meaning. You flood them with a thousand different inputs, some as subtle as the contraction of a single facial muscle, some as obvious as your opening line. Your character, your intentions, and your goals seep into your speech. Everyone can see them. Everyone can see you.

Let's step into the mind of one of your audience members. Based on all of this, based on a thousand different inputs, based on complex interactions between their conscious and nonconscious minds, the ghost in the machine steps in, and by a dint of free will, acts as the final arbiter and makes a choice. A mind is changed. You changed it. And changing it changed you. You became more confident, more articulate, and deeper; more capable, more impactful, and stronger.

Communication is connection. One mind, with a consciousness at its base, seeks to use ink or pixels or airwaves to connect to another. Through this connection, it seeks to copy neural patterns about the present, the future, and the moral landscape. Whatever your message is, the underlying connection is identical. How could it not be?

IS IT ETHICAL?

By "it," I mean deliberately using language to get someone to do or think something. Let's call this rhetoric. We could just as well call it persuasion, influence, communication, or even leadership itself.

The answer is yes. The answer is no. Rhetoric is a helping hand. It is an iron fist. It is Martin Luther King's dream. It is Stalin's nightmare. It is the "shining city on the hill." It is the iron curtain. It is "the pursuit of happiness." It is the trail of tears. It is "liberty, equality, and brotherhood." It is the reign of terror. Rhetoric is a tool. It is neither good nor evil. It is a reflection of our nature.

Rhetoric can motivate love, peace, charity, strength, patience, progress, prosperity, common sense, common purpose, courage, hope, generosity, and unity. It can also sow the seeds of division, fan the flames of tribalism, and beat back the better angels of our nature.

Rhetoric is the best of us and the worst of us. It is as good as you are. It is as evil as you are. It is as peace-loving as you are. It is as hate-mongering as you are. And I know what you are. I know my readers are generous, hardworking people who want to build a better future for themselves, for their families, and for all humankind. I know that if you have these tools in your hands, you will use them to achieve a moral mission. That's why putting them in your hands is my mission.

Joseph Chatfield said "[rhetoric] is the power to talk people out of their sober and natural opinions." I agree. But it is also the power to talk people out of their wrong and harmful opinions. And if you're using rhetoric to talk people out of their sober opinions, the problem isn't rhetoric, it's you.

In the *Institutes of Rhetoric*, Roman rhetorician Quintilian wrote the following: "The orator then, whom I am concerned to form, shall be the orator as defined by Marcus Cato, a good man, skilled in speaking. But above all he must possess the quality which Cato places first and which is in the very nature of things the greatest and most important, that is, he must be a good man. This is essential not merely on account of the fact that, if the powers of eloquence serve only to lend arms to crime, there can be nothing more pernicious than eloquence to public and private welfare alike, while I myself, who have labored to the best of my ability to contribute something of the value to oratory, shall have rendered the worst of services to mankind, if I forge these weapons not for a soldier, but for a robber."

Saint Augustine, who was trained in the classical schools of rhetoric in the 3rd century, summed it up well: "Rhetoric, after all, being the art of persuading people to accept something, whether it is true or false, would anyone dare to maintain that truth should stand there without any weapons in the hands of its defenders against falsehood; that those speakers, that is to say, who are trying to convince their hearers of what is untrue, should know how to get them on their side, to gain their attention and have them eating out of their hands by their opening remarks, while these who are defending the truth should not? That those should utter their lies briefly, clearly, plausibly, and these should state their truths in a manner too boring to listen to, too obscure to understand, and finally too repellent to believe? That those should attack the truth with specious arguments, and assert falsehoods, while these should be incapable of either defending the truth or refuting falsehood? That those, to move and force the minds of their hearers into error, should be able by their style to terrify them, move them to tears, make them laugh, give them rousing encouragement, while these on behalf of truth stumble along slow, cold and half asleep?"

THE ETHICS OF PERSUASION

R EFER BACK TO THIS ETHICAL GUIDE as needed. I created this in a spirit of humility, for my benefit as much as for the benefit of my readers. And you don't have to choose between efficacy and ethics. When I followed these principles, my words became more ethical *and* more powerful.

FOLLOW THESE TWELVE RULES. Do not use false, fabricated, misrepresented, distorted, or irrelevant evidence to support claims. Do not intentionally use specious, unsupported, or illogical reasoning. Do not represent yourself as informed or as an "expert" on a subject when you are not. Do not use irrelevant appeals to divert attention from the issue at hand. Do not cause intense but unreflective emotional reactions. Do not link your idea to emotion-laden values, motives, or goals to which it is not related. Do not hide your real purpose or self-interest, the group you represent, or your position as an advocate of a viewpoint. Do not distort, hide, or misrepresent the number, scope, or intensity of bad effects. Do not use emotional appeals that lack a basis of evidence or reasoning or that would fail if the audience examined the subject themselves. Do not oversimplify complex, gradation-laden situations into simplistic two-valued, either/or, polar views or choices. Do not pretend certainty where tentativeness and degrees of probability would be more accurate. Do not advocate something you do not believe (Johannesen et al., 2021).

APPLY THIS GOLDEN HEURISTIC. In a 500,000-word book, you might be able to tell your audience everything you know about a subject. In a five-minute persuasive speech, you can only select a small sampling of your knowledge. Would learning your entire body of knowledge result in a significantly different reaction than hearing the small sampling you selected? If the answer is yes, that's a problem.

SWING WITH THE GOOD EDGE. Rhetoric is a double-edged sword. It can express good ideas well. It can also express bad ideas well. Rhetoric makes ideas attractive; tempting; credible; persuasive. Don't use it to turn weakly-worded lies into well-worded lies. Use it to turn weakly-worded truths into well-worded truths.

TREAT TRUTH AS THE HIGHEST GOOD. Use any persuasive strategy, unless using it in your circumstances would distort the truth. The strategies should not come between you and truth, or compromise your honesty and authenticity.

AVOID THE SPIRIT OF DECEIT. Wrong statements are incorrect statements you genuinely believe. Lies are statements you know are wrong but convey anyway. Deceitful statements are not literally wrong, but you convey them with the intent to mislead, obscure, hide, or manipulate. Hiding relevant information is not literally lying (saying you conveyed all the information would be). Cherry-picking facts is not literally lying (saying there are no other facts would be). Using clever innuendo to twist reality without making any concrete claims is not literally lying (knowingly making a false accusation would be). And yet, these are all examples of deceit.

ONLY USE STRATEGIES IF THEY ARE ACCURATE. Motivate unified thinking. Inspire loving thinking. These strategies sound good. Use the victim-perpetrator-benevolence structure. Paint a common enemy. Appeal to tribal psychology. These strategies sound bad. But when reality lines up with the strategies that sound bad, they become good. They are only bad when they are inaccurate or move people down a bad path. *But the same is true for the ones that sound good.* Should Winston Churchill have motivated unified thinking? Not toward his enemy. Should he have avoided appealing to tribal psychology to strengthen the Allied war effort? Should he have avoided painting a common enemy? Should he have avoided portraying the victimization of true victims and the perpetration of a true perpetrator? Should he have avoided calling people to act as the benevolent force for good, protecting the victim and beating back the perpetrator? Don't use the victim-perpetrator-benevolence structure if there aren't clear victims and perpetrators. This is demagoguery. Painting false victims disempowers them. But if there are true victims and perpetrators, stand up for the victims and stand against the perpetrators, calling others to join you as a benevolent force for justice. Don't motivate unified thinking when standing against evil. Don't hold back from portraying a common enemy when there is one. Some strategies might sound morally suspect. Some might sound inherently good. But it depends on the situation. Every time I say "do X to achieve Y," remember the condition: "if it is accurate and moves people up a good path."

APPLY THE TARES TEST: truthfulness of message, authenticity of persuader, respect for audience, equity of persuasive appeal, and social impact (TARES).

REMEMBER THE THREE-PART VENN DIAGRAM: words that are authentic, effective, and true. Donald Miller once said "I'm the kind of person who wants to present my most honest, authentic self to the world, so I hide backstage and rehearse honest and authentic lines until the curtain opens." There's nothing dishonest or inauthentic about choosing your words carefully and making them more effective, as long as they remain just as true. Rhetoric takes a messy marble brick of truth and sculpts it into a poised, precise, and perfect statue. It takes weak truths and makes them strong. Unfortunately, it can do the same for weak lies. But preparing, strategizing, and sculpting is not inauthentic. Unskillfulness is no more authentic than skillfulness. Unpreparedness is no more authentic than preparedness.

APPLY FITZPATRICK AND GAUTHIER'S THREE-QUESTION ANALYSIS. For what purpose is persuasion being employed? Toward what choices and with what consequences for individual lives is it being used? Does the persuasion contribute to or interfere with the audience's decision-making process (Lumen, 2016)?

STRENGTHEN THE TRUTH. Rhetoric makes words strong. Use it to turn truths strong, not falsities strong. There are four categories of language: weak and wrong, strong and wrong, weak and true, strong and true. Turn weak and true language into strong and true language. Don't turn weak and wrong language into strong and wrong language, weak and true language into strong and wrong language, or strong and true language into weak and true language. Research. Question your assumptions. Strive for truth. Ensure your logic is impeccable. Defuse your biases.

START WITH FINDING TRUTH. The rhetorical endeavor starts with becoming as knowledgeable on your subject as possible and developing an impeccable logical argument. The more research you do, the more rhetoric you earn the right to use.

PUT TRUTH BEFORE STYLE. Rhetorical skill does not make you correct. Truth doesn't care about your rhetoric. If your rhetoric is brilliant, but you realize your arguments are simplistic, flawed, or biased, change course. Let logic lead style. Don't sacrifice logic to style. Don't express bad ideas well. Distinguish effective speaking from effective rational argument. Achieve both, but put reason and logic first.

AVOID THE POPULARITY VORTEX. As Plato suggested, avoid "giving the citizens what they want [in speech] with no thought to whether they will be better or worse as a result of what you are saying." Ignore the temptation to gain positive reinforcement and instant gratification from the audience with no merit to your message. Rhetoric is unethical if used solely to appeal rather than to help the world.

CONSIDER THE CONSEQUENCES. If you succeed to persuade people, will the world become better or worse? Will your audience benefit? Will you benefit? Moreover, is it the best action they could take? Or would an alternative help more? Is it an objectively worthwhile investment? Is it the best solution? Are you giving them all the facts they need to determine this on their own?

CONSIDER SECOND- AND THIRD-ORDER IMPACTS. Consider not only immediate consequences, but consequences across time. Consider the impact of the action you seek to persuade, as well as the tools you use to persuade it. Maybe the action is objectively positive, but in motivating the action, you resorted to instilling beliefs that will cause damage over time. Consider their long-term impact as well.

APPLY THE FIVE ETHICAL APPROACHES: seek the greatest good for the greatest number (utilitarian); protect the rights of those affected and treat people not as means but as ends (rights); treat equals equally and nonequals fairly (justice); set the good of humanity as the basis of your moral reasoning (common good); act consistently with the ideals that lead to your self-actualization and the highest potential of your character (virtue). Say and do what is right, not what is expedient, and be willing to suffer the consequences of doing so. Don't place self-gratification, acquisitiveness, social status, and power over the common good of all humanity.

APPLY THE FOUR ETHICAL DECISION-MAKING CRITERIA: respect for individual rights to make choices, hold views, and act based on personal beliefs and values (autonomy); the maximization of benefits and the minimization of harms, acting for the benefit of others, helping others further their legitimate interests; taking action to prevent or remove possible harms (beneficence); acting in ways that cause no harm, avoid the risk of harm, and assuring benefits outweigh costs (non-maleficence); treating others according to a defensible standard (justice).

USE ILLOGICAL PROCESSES TO GET ETHICAL RESULTS. Using flawed thinking processes to get good outcomes is not unethical. Someone who disagrees should stop speaking with conviction, clarity, authority, and effective paralanguage. All are irrelevant to the truth of their words, but impact the final judgment of the audience. You must use logic and evidence to figure out the truth. But this doesn't mean logic and evidence will persuade others. Humans have two broad categories of cognitive functions: system one is intuitive, emotional, fast, heuristic-driven, and generally illogical; system two is rational, deliberate, evidence-driven, and generally logical. The best-case scenario is to get people to believe right things for right reasons (through system two). The next best case is to get people to believe right things for wrong reasons (through system one). Both are far better than letting people believe wrong things for wrong reasons. If you don't use those processes, they still function, but lead people astray. You can reverse-engineer them. If you know the truth, have an abundance of reasons to be confident you know the truth, and can predict the disasters that will occur if people don't believe the truth, don't you have a responsibility to be as effective as possible in bringing people to the truth? Logic and evidence are essential, of course. They will persuade many. They should have persuaded you. But people can't always follow a long chain of reasoning or a complicated argument. Persuade by eloquence what you learned by reason.

HELP YOUR SELF-INTEREST. (But not at the expense of your audience or without their knowledge). Ethics calls for improving the world, and you are a part of the world – the one you control most. Improving yourself is a service to others.

APPLY THE WINDOWPANE STANDARD. In Aristotle's view, rhetoric reveals how to persuade and how to defeat manipulative persuaders. Thus, top students of rhetoric would be master speakers, trained to anticipate and disarm the rhetorical tactics of their adversaries. According to this tradition, language is only useful to the extent that it does not distort reality, and good writing functions as a "windowpane," helping people peer through the wall of ignorance and view reality. You might think this precludes persuasion. You might think this calls for dry academic language. But what good is a windowpane if nobody cares to look through it? What good is a windowpane to reality if, on the other wall, a stained-glass window distorts reality but draws people to it? The best windowpane reveals as much of reality as possible while drawing as many people to it as possible.

RUN THROUGH THESE INTROSPECTIVE QUESTIONS. Are the means truly unethical or merely distasteful, unpopular, or unwise? Is the end truly good, or does it simply appear good because we desire it? Is it probable that bad means will achieve the good end? Is the same good achievable using more ethical means if we are creative, patient, and skillful? Is the good end clearly and overwhelmingly better than any bad effects of the means used to attain it? Will the use of unethical means to achieve a good end withstand public scrutiny? Could the use of unethical means be justified to those most affected and those most impartial? Can I specify my ethical criteria or standards? What is the grounding of the ethical judgment? Can I justify the reasonableness and relevancy of these standards for this case? Why are these the best criteria? Why do they take priority? How does the communication succeed or fail by these standards? What judgment is justified in this case about the degree of ethicality? Is it a narrowly focused one rather than a broad and generalized one? To whom is ethical responsibility owed – to which individuals, groups, organizations, or professions? In what ways and to what extent? Which take precedence? What is my responsibility to myself and society? How do I feel about myself after this choice? Can I continue to "live with myself?" Would I want my family to know of this choice? Does the choice reflect my ethical character? To what degree is it "out of character?" If called upon in public to justify the ethics of my communication, how adequately could I do so? What generally accepted reasons could I offer? Are there precedents which can guide me? Are there aspects of this case that set it apart from others? How thoroughly have alternatives been explored before settling on this choice? Is it less ethical than some of the workable alternatives? If the goal requires unethical communication, can I abandon the goal (Johannesen et al., 2007)?

VIEW YOURSELF AS A GUIDE. Stories have a hero, a villain who stands in his way, and a guide who helps the hero fulfill his mission. If you speak ineffectively, you are a nonfactor. If you speak deceitfully, you become the villain. But if you convey truth effectively, you become the guide in your audience's story, who leads them, teaches them, inspires them, and helps them overcome adversity and win. Use your words to put people on the best possible path. And if you hide an ugly truth, ask yourself this: "If I found out that *my* guide omitted this, how would I react?"

KNOW THAT THE TRUTH WILL OUT. The truth can either come out in your words, or you can deceive people. You can convince them to live in a fantasy. And that might work. Until. Until truth breaks down the door and storms the building. Until the facade comes crashing down and chaos makes its entry. Slay the dragon in its lair before it comes to your village. Invite truth in through the front door before truth burns the building down. Truth wins in the end, either because a good person spreads, defends, and fights for it, or because untruth reveals itself as such by its consequences, and does so in brutal and painful fashion, hurting innocents and perpetrators alike. Trust and reputation take years to create and seconds to destroy.

MAXIMIZE THE TWO HIERARCHIES OF SUCCESS: honesty *and* effectiveness. You could say "Um, well, uh, I think that um, what we should… should uh… do, is that, well… let me think… er, I think if we are more, you know… fluid, we'll be better at… producing, I mean, progressing, and producing, and just more generally, you know, getting better results, but… I guess my point is, like, that, that if we are more fluid and do things more better, we will get better results than with a bureaucracy and, you know how it is, a silo-based structure, right? I mean… you know what I mean." Or, you could say "Bravery beats bureaucracy, courage beats the status quo, and innovation beats stagnation." Is one of those statements truer? No. Is one of them more effective? Is one of them more likely to get positive action that instantiates the truth into the world? Yes. Language is not reality. It provides signposts to reality. Two different signposts can point at the same truth – they can be equally and maximally true – and yet one can be much more effective. One gets people to follow the road. One doesn't. Maximize honesty. Then, insofar as it doesn't sacrifice honesty, maximize effectiveness. Speak truth. And speak it well.

APPLY THE WISDOM OF THIS QUOTE. Mary Beard, an American historian, author, and activist, captured the essence of ethical rhetoric well: "What politicians do is they never get the rhetoric wrong, and the price they pay is they don't speak the truth as they see it. Now, I will speak truth as I see it, and sometimes I don't get the rhetoric right. I think that's a fair trade-off." It's more than fair. It's necessary.

REMEMBER YOUR RESPONSIBILITY TO SOCIETY. Be a guardian of the truth. Speak out against wrongdoing, and do it well. The solution to evil speech is not less speech, but more (good) speech. Create order with your words, not chaos. Our civilization depends on it. Match the truth, honesty, and vulnerable transparency of your words against the irreducible complexity of the universe. And in this complex universe, remember the omnipresence of nuance, and the dangers of simplistic ideologies. (Inconveniently, simplistic ideologies are persuasive, while nuanced truths are difficult to convey. This is why good people need to be verbally skilled; to pull the extra weight of conveying a realistic worldview). Don't commit your whole mind to an isolated fragment of truth, lacking context, lacking nuance. Be precise in your speech, to ensure you are saying what you mean to say. Memorize the logical fallacies, the cognitive biases, and the rules of logic and correct thinking. (Conveniently, many rhetorical devices are also reasoning devices that focus your inquiry and help you explicate truth). But don't demonize those with good intentions and bad ideas. If they are forthcoming and honest, they are not your enemy. Rather, the two of you are on a shared mission to find the truth, partaking in a shared commitment to reason and dialogue. The malevolent enemy doesn't care about the truth. And in this complex world, remember Voltaire's warning to "cherish those who seek the truth but beware of those who find it," and Aristotle's startling observation that "the least deviation from truth [at the start] is multiplied a thousandfold." Be cautious in determining what to say with conviction. Good speaking is not a substitute for good thinking. The danger zone is being confidently incorrect. What hurts us most is what we know that just isn't so. Remember these tenets and your responsibility, and rhetoric becomes the irreplaceable aid of the good person doing good things in difficult times; the sword of the warrior of the light.

KNOW THAT DECEPTION IS ITS OWN PUNISHMENT. Knowingly uttering a falsehood is a spoken lie of commission. Having something to say but not saying it is a spoken lie of omission. Knowingly behaving inauthentically is an acted-out lie of commission. Knowingly omitting authentic behavior is an acted-out lie of omission. All these deceptions weaken your being. All these deceptions corrupt your own mind, turning your greatest asset into an ever-present companion you can no longer trust. Your conscience operates somewhat autonomously, and it will call you out (unless your repeated neglect desensitizes it). You have a conscious conscience which speaks clearly, and an unconscious conscience, which communicates more subtly. A friend of mine asked: "Why do we feel relieved when we speak truth? Why are we drawn toward it, even if it is not pleasant? Do our brains have something that makes this happen?" Yes, they do: our consciences, our inner lights, our inner north stars. And we feel relieved because living with the knowledge of our own deceit is often an unbearable burden. You live your life before an audience of one: yourself. You cannot escape the observation of your own awareness; you can't hide from yourself. Everywhere you go, there you are. Everything you do, there you are. Some of the greatest heights of wellbeing come from performing well in this one-man theater, and signaling virtue to yourself; being someone you are proud to be (and grateful to observe). Every time you lie, you tell your subconscious mind that your character is too weak to contend with the truth. And this shapes your character accordingly. It becomes true. And then what? Lying carries its own punishment, even if the only person who catches the liar is the liar himself.

BE A MONSTER (THEN LEARN TO CONTROL IT). There is nothing moral about weakness and harmlessness. The world is difficult. There are threats to confront, oppressors to resist, and tyrants to rebuff. (Peterson, 2018). There are psychopaths, sociopaths, and Machiavellian actors with no love for the common good. There is genuine malevolence. If you are incapable of being an effective deceiver, then you are incapable of being an effective advocate for truth: it is the same weapon, pointed in different directions. If you cannot use it in both directions, can you use it at all? Become a monster, become dangerous, and become capable of convincing people to believe in a lie... and then use this ability to convince them to believe in the truth. The capacity for harm is also the capacity for harming harmful entities; that is to say, defending innocent ones. If you can't hurt anyone, you can't help anyone when they need someone to stand up for them. Words are truly weapons, and the most powerful weapons in the world at that. The ability to use them, for good *or* for bad, is the prerequisite to using them for good. There is an archetype in our cultural narratives: the well-intentioned but harmless protagonist who gets roundly defeated by the villain, until he develops his monstrous edge and integrates it, at which point he becomes the triumphant hero. Along similar lines, I watched a film about an existential threat to humanity, in which the protagonist sought to convey the threat to a skeptical public, but failed miserably because he lacked the rhetorical skill to do so. The result? The world ended. Everyone died. The protagonist was of no use to anyone. And this almost became a true story. A historical study showed that in the Cuban Missile Crisis, the arguments that won out in the United States mastermind group were not the best, but those argued with the most conviction. Those with the best arguments lacked the skill to match. The world (could have) ended. The moral? Speak truth... well.

MASTERING COMMUNICATION, ONE SKILL AT A TIME

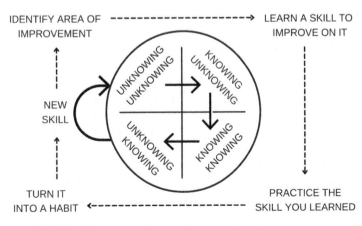

FIGURE I: The proven path to mastery.

highly

....

adverb
>   in or to a high place, level, or rank

effective

....

adjective
>   producing a decided, decisive, or desired effect

CONTENTS

BASE RATE NEGLECT: 261

HOW TO USE THE PSYCHOLOGY OF NUMERICAL INCOMPETENCY

BEFORE YOU GO...

Rhetoric, Motivated by Love, Guided by Reason, and Aimed at Truth, Is a Powerful Force for the Greatest Good.

POLITICAL DISCLAIMER

Throughout this book, and throughout all my books, I draw examples of communication strategies from the political world. I quote from the speeches of many of America's great leaders, like JFK and MLK, as well as from more recent political figures of both major parties. Political communication is ideal for illustrating the concepts revealed in the books. It is the best source of examples of words that work that I have ever found. I don't use anything out of the political mainstream. And it is by extensively studying the inaugural addresses of United States Presidents and the great speeches of history that I have discovered many of the speaking strategies I share with you.

My using the words of any particular figure to illustrate a principle of communication is not necessarily an endorsement of the figure or their message. Separate the speaker from the strategy. After all, the strategy is the only reason the speaker made an appearance in the book at all. Would you rather have a weak example of a strategy you want to learn from a speaker you love, or a perfect example of the strategy from a speaker you detest?

For a time, I didn't think a disclaimer like this was necessary. I thought people would do this on their own. I thought that if people read an example of a strategy drawn from the words of a political figure they disagreed with, they would appreciate the value of the example as an instructive tool and set aside their negative feelings about the speaker. "Yes, I don't agree with this speaker or the message, but I can clearly see the strategy in this example and I now have a better understanding of how it works and how to execute it." Indeed, I suspect 95% of my readers do just that. You probably will, too. But if you are part of the 5% who aren't up for it, don't say I didn't warn you, and please don't leave a negative review because you think I endorse this person or that person. I don't, as this is strictly a book about communication.

HOW HIGHLY EFFECTIVE PEOPLE

SPEAK

HOW HIGH PERFORMERS USE PSYCHOLOGY TO INFLUENCE WITH EASE

SPEAK FOR SUCCESS COLLECTION BOOK

I

HOW HIGHLY EFFECTIVE PEOPLE SPEAK CHAPTER

I

THE BIG SECRET:

What Is the Foundation of All
Influence and Persuasion?

EVERYTHING WAS PERFECT. BUT SOMETHING STILL TROUBLED ME...

I T WAS A BEAUTIFUL DAY. It was also a New England winter. Believe it or not: Those two can both be true at the same time. It's rare, but possible, and it happened on this fateful day many years ago.

It was the day my life changed.

Golden sunshine poured through the floor-to-ceiling windows of my workplace. I gazed across the landscape sprawling for miles below me: idyllic and humble suburbia interspersed with office parks, a landscape ending where the mountains begin.

High-noon's smiling sunshine sparkled on a distant lake's surface. The light danced on its gentle ripples, mesmerizing me as I watched it from my perch on the sixth floor. It's not a tall building, but it's on a big hill, affording me a great view. No snow yet. Just sunshine and warmth in the middle of winter.

I viciously consumed an extra-extra-large iced coffee (which doesn't officially exist, but we have an arrangement) and a warm chocolate chip muffin from Dunkin Donuts. The air was fresh and crisp. Everything was as I wanted it. My personal projects were advancing at a pace I thought impossible a few short months ago. Tomorrow marked the start of a much-needed vacation.

In short: Everything was perfect.

But something still troubled me.

What? What gave me pause on such a remarkably perfect day? What bubbled this anxiety within me when I had absolutely nothing to be anxious about?

The feeling passed the next day. But my curiosity – my deep desire to figure out what caused it – did not. A year later, I had my answer...

My eyes shot open. It was 4:00 AM. I turned on my lamp. In a daze, I grabbed a pen from my night-stand, and scribbled some words on the only paper I could reach.

A sigh of relief, and back to sleep.

It was the best sleep I had in months, knowing the next few years of my life would be extremely exciting because of what I wrote. And it was the best sleep I had in months because, at long last, I figured out what troubled me a year ago, and on frequent occasion since...

WHAT DID I WRITE?

Two words, a symbol, and another word. They defined the nature of my work for the next three years. They changed everything I thought I knew about my area of expertise: communication. They can change the world, bring you success, and turn you into a highly effective leader.

Let's rewind back to the sunny winter day.

The golden sunshine illuminated my laptop, my legal pad, my iPhone, and a book.

The book? *Thinking, Fast and Slow*, by Daniel Kahneman: my first foray into a revolutionary subject.

The subject? Behavioral economics: the study of human irrationality; the search for hidden, little-known functions of human psychology that govern decision-making, belief-formation, and information-interpretation; the subject challenging everything we think we know about the world, the economy, and ourselves.

Why did it trouble me so much? Because it blew a massive hole in my area of expertise. And it wasn't the hole bothering me, but the unsatisfied potential it represented. I knew it would weigh on me until I did something about it.

Let's fast-forward, back to my 4:00 AM scribbling session.

Why did the two words, the symbol, and the other word put me at ease? Why did they excite me beyond description? Why did they change the nature of my work for the next three years, and culminate in the book you're reading now? Because they filled the hole.

What did I write?

"Behavioral economics + communication."

And now, I'll answer all your questions: What does behavioral economics have to do with communication? What does it have to do with high performance? How can this help you actualize your ambitions and strive for success, becoming a highly effective leader?

Let's talk about the two puzzle-pieces, how they connect, and what it means for you.

LET'S TALK ABOUT COMMUNICATION FIRST...

Want to succeed? Learn to speak. The world's highly effective people are highly effective communicators. They can take an idea existing in their minds, replicate it in other minds, and build a mass movement devoted to manifesting it. They can subtly compel others to think a certain way, act a certain way, and live a certain way. They can immediately earn trust, portray credibility, and achieve authority.

They can argue well, present proposals well, and persuade well. They can instantly influence nearly anyone, in nearly any situation, to believe nearly anything. They can speak with complete confidence in themselves, their ideas, and their visions for the future. They are visionaries and true leaders. They are those who ask not "why?" but "why not?" and inspire others to perform incredible feats, like putting a man on the moon, or defeating Nazi Germany.

They are empaths: They understand how others feel, and how to communicate to those feelings. They are powerful: They are deadly effective because they are severely well-equipped to reign in the only important battleground, the battleground of ideas. They win under the weight of the burdens buckling others. They are bold and brave, capable and competent, persuasive and powerful. They match good intentions with an ability to make a difference. Their presence is a gift to everyone around them.

And here's my question to you: Will you be one of them?

If your bad presentation kills your good ideas, it also kills your career. If your proposals fall flat, failing to inspire others, you miss opportunities daily. If your communication doesn't convey complete self-confidence, you might falter at a critical moment, undermine your professional image, and accidentally pull a premature hand-break on your career, grinding it to a frustrating halt.

Communication creates reality. Highly effective people shape our world. How? By communicating big ideas in big ways; by inspiring passion for a key proposal on a grand scale. Or on a miniscule scale. Big or small, grand or humble, a goal demands a team. Nobody succeeds alone. Nobody builds anything worth building without the contribution of other people, and sometimes, a lot of them. And nobody gets this contribution – a key to high performance – without effective communication. That's why all highly effective people are highly effective communicators. That's why they play a role in shaping our world.

And here's my follow-up question: Do you want to claim your rightful stake in this ongoing project, this never-finished mission of building the world? Or do you want to cede it to someone else? Someone with weaker ideas but stronger communication? If you accept the challenge of changing our world, you'll need to develop many qualities. The most important? Effective communication.

HOW DOES BEHAVIORAL ECONOMICS REVOLUTIONIZE POWERFUL COMMUNICATION?

Behavioral economics is the surprising key to effortlessly effective communication. It changes everything you think you know about communication, influence, and persuasion, breaking it down into a proven and predictable science, not an arcane art.

The most incredible part? Behavioral economists don't even realize it. They focus on public policy, social science, and economics, without realizing the tremendous impact of their research on communication.

Let me make one promise: 99% of people will not know what you when you finish this book. Why? Because behavioral economics is a new field. Some people might know a modicum as the field grows mainstream. But nobody – not even behavioral economists – will know how to apply the insights of behavioral economics to communication. This can be your competitive advantage.

How do the two puzzle pieces fit together? How do behavioral economics and communication connect? Behavioral economics and communication meet in one mantra: Convey information how the human mind is wired to receive it.

This will give you influence, power, persuasion, empathy, and insight into how human beings make decisions and form beliefs. It will teach you how to turn little-known, hidden, and I'll go so far as to say *secret* cognitive functions into persuasive assets for advancing your agenda, presenting your proposals, and forming your future.

And this is powerful. The wiring (and occasionally miswiring) of psychology, a complex web of biases and heuristics behavioral economics untangles, has motivated history's wars, mass movements, and incomprehensibly incredible feats.

THE LITTLE-KNOWN SECRET OF IRRESISTIBLE INFLUENCE

YOU CONVEYING YOUR MESSAGE

YOUR LISTENERS RECEIVING IT

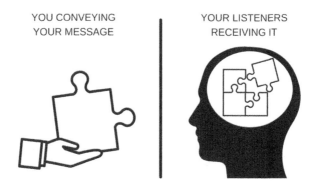

FIGURE 1: All effective influence relies on conveying a message that conforms to (and / or minimizes the clash with) the contents, processes, biases, heuristics, and functions of the mind receiving it. Or, put simply, all effective influence relies on conveying information how the human mind is wired to receive it.

How did cigarettes become mainstream prior to government crackdowns? Why did countless militants in countless conflicts perform countless abhorrent act at the direction of countless despotic dictators, despite their own moral intuitions? How did we manage to send a man to the moon amidst the anxious confusion of the Cold War? And why do we vehemently support some policies while viciously despising others?

Why do we think what we think, think we know what we think we know, believe what we believe, like what we like, and do what we do? Why do others trust or distrust us? Respect or disrespect us? Listen to or ignore us? Reach out to or neglect us? Like or dislike us? Praise or slander us? Believe or doubt us?

Why do others follow our lead or stand in our way? Give us opportunities or send them elsewhere? Support our striving for success and appreciate our message or toss it – and us – aside?

Why, why, why, ad infinitum. The answer is often the same: because our psychological wiring exerts tremendous influence on everything about us.

Want to untangle the wiring? Want to learn how to use it to help, not hurt your journey to success? Want to learn how to activate it in your communication for instant influence and easy persuasion, like all highly effective people do? Read further.

IT'S TRAGIC...

Too many would-be leaders turn the wiring against themselves, and wonder why nothing goes their way. It's like an army firing its artillery on its own trenches, and then wondering why it's losing ground. This book is a firing manual, teaching you how to aim the wiring correctly, and avoid the inevitable self-destruction befalling if you don't.

WHAT HAPPENS IF YOU TRY TO FIGHT THE SECRET?

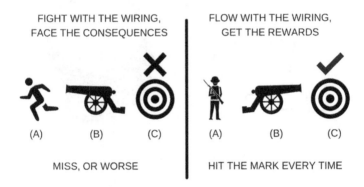

FIGURE 2: Your (A) relationship with the wiring (B) impacts your success (C). The same psychological process can be activated both in the service of your goal or against you. Improve your chances by learning the prevalent psychological processes and how to flow with them rather than counteracting them.

As a student of history, the ubiquity of communication rooted in behavioral economics is shockingly self-evident. Every single legendary leader who produced legendary results unknowingly followed our mantra in communicating a vision.

The framers of the United States Constitution. John F. Kennedy. Nearly every single President with an approval rating above 57% and nearly no president with one below 47%. Business leaders praised around the world for their vision, efficiency, and leadership. They all follow our mantra.

These highly effective people don't always know they follow our mantra. But it works wonders nonetheless. And if almost every single highly effective person in human history produced legendary results by accidentally using behavioral economics in communication, I have a final follow-up question for you: Why not use it in your communication, and why not on purpose?

ABOUT THIS BOOK

Allow me to outline my thought process governing the composition of this book. While the response has been overwhelmingly positive, a subset of readers was perplexed by the unorthodox approach.

How Highly Effective People Speak takes a different approach than most business books. It is designed to be eminently practical. You can act on every strategy revealed in the book. And it is designed to be thoroughly comprehensive, offering you as many of these practical strategies as possible and as quickly as possible. While this book does offer compelling anecdotes to illustrate the strategies, it does not follow the approach of most business books; it does not oversaturate you with prolonged and unnecessary stories to fill a page count. Would you rather have ten chapters centered around ten long stories to illustrate ten watered-down strategies stretched out to a length of 300 pages? Or would you rather would you rather master 174 different strategies for activating 12 different cognitive heuristics in your favor? Would you rather master the subject or gain only a specious understanding of it, an understanding so shallow it fools you into thinking you know the subject matter sufficiently well? Unfortunately, this is what most books on this subject offer: the veneer of knowledge. And as you may know, it's not what you don't know that hurts you, but what you don't know that you think you know.

The book may feel crammed. But this is the necessary byproduct of hyper-saturation with the knowledge you seek. It is dense. It does not waste my words or your time. It gets to the point, and does so 174 times, revealing 174 little-known strategies even the world's top communicators don't understand. It reveals the raw material for the discipline of persuasive communication – the "what," the cognitive heuristics governing judgement – and then the "how," showing you the strategies you can use to activate the heuristic in your favor. This book has often been described as a "course" by readers. This tells me I achieved my principal goal in writing it. I sought not to write a "book," so to speak, but to develop a manual, a codebook, an input-output system to the psychology of influential communication. If it entertains you, this is a happy accident. Regardless, it will bring you stunningly close to mastery of a subject 99% of people don't know exists.

You will master this subject in two steps. First, you learn the strategies. Second, the strategies become you. This second step is often called "practice," but this confuses the means with the end. It demands practice, but the goal is to ingrain the strategies so deep in yourself that you can execute them perfectly and thoughtlessly. This is mastery. This is fluency. And it is deadly effective. Though step two is your burden, I am here to help you with step one. And I am here to help you with step one in such a way that it facilitates an easier step two. To that end, I incorporated several composition strategies proven to help you "become" the knowledge.

First, I repeat the essential mantra – speak how humans are wired to listen – multiple times throughout. This is to root it in your subconscious mind. I also repeat some essential truths of the subject that you absolutely cannot forget, so that you absolutely do not forget them. And some repetition of the cognitive biases or psychological processes is unavoidable, simply because of the nature of the subject. The biases twist in and out of each other. They cause each other. One bias will crop up in reference to all the others; all the others will potentially loop back into it. Every time you learn a bias, do not expect it to be a one-and-done meeting. You will see it again in connection to some other bias later on.

HOW THE BIASES CONNECT TO ONE ANOTHER

THE COGNITIVE BIASES
DO NOT CONNECT LINEARLY

THE COGNITIVE BIASES
ARE ALL INTERCONNECTED

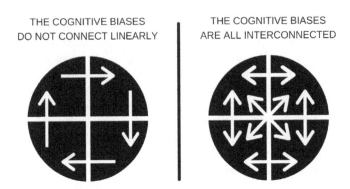

FIGURE 3: While it is tempting to treat each cognitive bias or psychological process as a discrete, self-contained unit, they all interlink in complex webs of causation. For example, a bias causes a bias which causes another bias that further enflames the first bias. Throughout the book, we cover many examples of these interconnections.

Second, I apply the strategy of chunking. I "chunk" the information into multiple smaller segments. The benefits of this are well-known and scientifically proven. It lowers cognitive load, allowing you to read for longer periods of time without reaching a point of mental fatigue. It drastically improves your memory of the material. It breaks down the subject into discrete, short, concentrated, focused, and manageable units of meaning, instead of a sequence of long, uninterrupted segments. This book follows the mantra of this book: By presenting information how you are wired to remember it – in chunks – this book facilitates your mastery of the subject.

Third, I use diagrams and images throughout. The benefits of doing so are much like the benefits of chunking. It aids memory. It allows me to present information verbally and visually, which assists a broader range of cognitive profiles. It offers a more intuitive frame of reference through which to view the concepts. And it functions as a form of repetition, cementing the core ideas in your mind such that you never forget them in a moment when you need them.

Fourth, I use an extensive array of examples. This goes beyond the norm. I use a superabundance of examples. Each example is another lesson, another chance to set the stage for the strategies to become you, thereby bringing you closer to mastery.

Fifth, I structure the book in a manner scientifically proven to raise comprehension and recall while lowering cognitive load, making the information easier to absorb. Everything flows from the core mantra. Each of the chapters represents another way to achieve the core mantra; another cognitive bias. Each of the sections is structured in a parallel format. They mirror their organization. Within each chapter, I introduce a legendary speaker using the bias, then define the bias, then provide a real-world example of the bias, then break down the most illustrative portions of the scientific literature on the bias, then show you how to overcome the bias in your own thinking, then offer a broad directive for how to use it in communication, then describe the specific and practical strategies for doing so. In short: legendary speaker, definition, example, scientific literature, how to overcome the bias, how to use the bias, and the strategies. The example of the legendary speaker is a preview, drawn from American presidents and other historical heads of state. It does not reveal the strategy; rather, it hints at it, allowing it to emerge from your own consciousness and pre-framing the rest of the section. It is designed so that at the beginning of the section, you don't know exactly why the example represents a compelling strategy in action, but that by the end, you are able to explain both the strategy and the psychology of why it works, as well as how to use it yourself. We draw these introductory examples from Ronald Reagan, Bill Clinton, John F. Kennedy, Barack Obama, Lyndon B. Johnson, and Winston Churchill. Throughout the sections themselves, we draw countless examples from the world's greatest leaders.

HOW THIS BOOK IS STRUCTURED TO HELP YOU

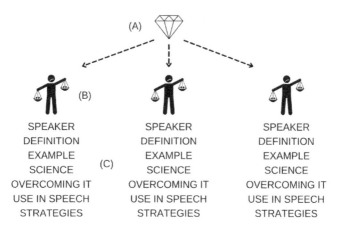

FIGURE 4: Everything flows from the core mantra (A). The core mantra is to present information how the human mind is wired to receive it – how biases will interpret the information in such a way that it garners maximum influence. We cover several different biases (B), and within each of those sections, we examine how a legendary speaker used it, the definition, an example, analysis of the science, how to overcome the bias, a broad directive for how to use it in speech, and then multiple specific strategies (C).

Sixth, I structure parts of the books as lists. The benefits of this are the same as the benefits of chunking.

Seventh, I follow each of the chapters with a grid revealing the framework, which I update after each chapter. The final chapter completes it. Each chapter also includes a chapter summary.

Truth lies at the bottom of a very muddy well. This book, while not predominantly story-driven, draws anecdotes from a wide range of subjects, including politics, history, marketing, and neuroscience. You will learn the surprising connection between cognitive heuristics in psychology, the phrase "rule of thumb," and nuclear mushroom clouds. You will learn how the moniker of "welfare queen" was born, and how it activates powerful components of human cognition. You will learn how real estate agents use the contrast effect to get drastically higher prices for the same homes. You will learn how the famous Milgram experiment reveals the dirty edge of the sword of cognitive biases. You will learn how base rate neglect makes people unaware of their own proclivity for evil. You will learn the connection between stories and fear, and why people drastically overestimate the risks of shark attacks and terrorist attacks. You will learn the psychology behind first impressions and why they are so hard to shake later on. And this is just a small sampling.

Of course, the book is not fundamentally story-driven. Many business books fall into the trap of allowing the available stories to supply the message. In this book, the message supplies the stories. All of these anecdotes may seem like tangents; they may seem unconnected to one another and to the rest of the book. On a superficial level of analysis, this is true. But on a deeper level of analysis – on the level of analysis of the book – they are all meaningfully connected. They all reveal the deep and beautiful connection between psychology and communication. They all exemplify the core mantra: Deliver your message how the human mind is wired to receive it. Every single chapter, paragraph, sentence, and word flows from this theme. This theme unites the entirety of the book into one coherent compilation of (a large part of) communication theory. If you forget the mantra, you lose the coherence and unity of the book. If you remember it, you see the natural connection between every single anecdote, story, example, quote, and strategy; between every single unit of meaning. This is another reason why I repeat it so often. If you are ever wondering what the purpose of a strategy is, recall the essential mantra. The purpose is to do what it says.

The first edition of *How Highly Effective People Speak* received a very positive response, and for that, I am grateful. Of course, as with all books, there were some critical reviews. Of the book that thousands said illuminated a missing piece of the puzzle for them, one reviewer wrote that "it is a bag of tips and tricks... mostly common sense." My response is, at first, a resounding agreement. This book most certainly is, in part, a bag of tips and tricks. But it is most certainly not common sense. If it were common sense, would the vast majority of communicators fail to heed its directives? If it were common sense, would it take a decade of experience and years of research to uncover the little-known principles and strategies? If it were common sense, would top CEOs and world-leaders continuously make the deleterious mistakes it warns against? Perhaps part of it is common sense. Perhaps most people do have some vague sense that highly effective people and successful leaders communicate in certain ways, and that there is some link between psychology and communication. But this is about as far as their knowledge goes. And the vast extent to which the content of this book is not common sense is both a blessing and a curse; a blessing because it offers unique value to readers, but a curse because it is not always simple. It can be complex and difficult material at times. Just know that I did everything I could possibly do to simplify it.

Another reviewer called it "psychobabble." I am willing to offer my agreement, provided that we agree on the definition of "psychobabble." If drawing out the most communication-relevant psychological components revealed by 100 years of rigorous research is psychobabble, I agree. If synthesizing modern, ground-breaking studies conducted by teams of researchers around the world with 2,000-year-old psychological fables is psychobabble, I agree. If drawing together personal experience, historical examples, and empirical evidence to outline a proven communication framework based in the science of psychology qualifies as psychobabble, I agree. If citing an incontrovertible mountain of iron-clad psychological evidence in support of my claims qualifies as psychobabble, I agree. If drawing together all this with extensive supporting evidence from other authors who identified the connection between cognitive biases and communication qualifies as psychobabble, I agree.

Finally, one critical reviewer alleged that the book could be summarized in five pages, but was artificially stretched to hundreds. I would go even further: The book could be summarized in one sentence. If you need five pages, you missed the whole point. And you've heard the sentence multiple times already. Now go take that sentence and, based on that sentence alone, speak in front of 1,000 people; develop a "plan of persuasion" for a new product targeting a customer base of 1,000,000; decode high-stakes communication situations with millions of dollars on the line and reengineer them in your favor. That one sentence – or, for the more inefficient summarizers out there, those five pages – is the "what." The other 260-odd pages? That is the "how."

THE ICEBERG EFFECT OF EFFECTIVE COMMUNICATION

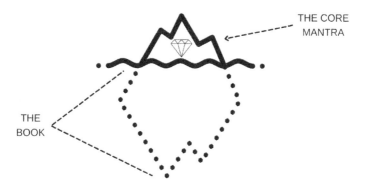

FIGURE 5: The core mantra is only the tip of the iceberg. Don't make the mistake of thinking it floats alone. It requires significant "underwater" support to peak above the surface of the ocean. The mantra is the end; it is the goal. The book is the means; it is the

plan for hitting the goal. You don't need me to only tell you the goal, but how to achieve it as well.

The strategies are not ethical. They are not unethical. They are tools. Their moral nature is not inherent; it depends on you. Indeed, you can use these principles for great evil. This has happened before. You can also use them to manifest the highest goods. They are as good as you are. I know some people will misuse them. But I refuse to allow this to stop me from helping what I believe is the vast majority of my readers: good people who will use these strategies to do good things. Martin Luther King used them. Mahatma Gandhi used them. Abraham Lincoln used them. Don't fall for the trap of thinking you are turning on the cognitive biases. They were on to begin with. You are just channeling them toward the truth; you are just using them to persuade people to do the best possible thing; you are just using them to communicate in the most effective way you possibly can.

If you believe that truth is a fundamental moral good, a principle that is the foundation of Western philosophy, then you must also believe that you have a moral duty to bring people to the truth. And if the principles revealed in this book influence human judgement with uncanny precision, and you know the truth, then you have an ethical duty to use them to show people the truth. Truth is good. You know the truth. You must show it to others. You must do everything you can possibly do while remaining within ethical boundaries – no lying, no coercion – to bring people to the truth as effectively as you can. These strategies do so better than nearly anything else. And if a particular strategy calls for something that doesn't hold true for the subject of your communication, pick a different one. For example, don't use the "reject randomness" directive revealed in chapter seven if the phenomenon you are addressing really is random. Do not tolerate a little lie to persuade someone to adopt the big truth. None of these strategies calls for grasping the thorns to reach the rose.

And this brings us to a concise definition of highly effective people. A highly effective person is someone who gets what they want and wants what is good; a highly effective person is someone who "makes things happen" as effectively as possible without straying into unethical grounds.

Some people find the breakdown of the psychology of human judgement to be unsettling. I understand this. If we are really just a bundle of conditioned responses – and flawed conditioned responses at that – what are we really? If our minds are really just bundles of pseudo-random, semi-guided cognitive biases, what does that say about our free will or about our ability to find truth? What does that say about the existence of epistemological truth in the first place?

We have a paradoxical nature. It is with our flawed minds that we discover the flaws of our minds. It is with our flawed minds that we discover truth, and it is with our flawed minds that we seek to persuade other flawed minds of that truth by using their flaws. But out of all this emerges something flawless. If our understanding of these biases brings us to the conclusion that we cannot find truth and that we lack free will and that reason is a myth, then we must also deny the truth of these biases. If it is true that an understanding of this part of our psychology shows us that we are unable to find truth, then we must also deny our understanding of this part of our psychology and what it supposedly shows us. I like the term the critical reviewer used: "psychobabble." I think I will apply it to those who seek to use an understanding of our psychological biases to deny the deeper elements of humanity: our ability to find truth as well as our ceaseless thirst for it; our reason, without which we would not be able to find the biases that supposedly deny our reason; our free will, without which we would not have the willful, consciously-directed reason required to thirst for and find truth.

HOW STUDYING THESE BIASES PRODUCES METACOGNITION

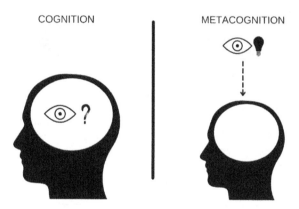

COGNITION   METACOGNITION

FIGURE 6: Metacognition is "seeing from above the mind." It is a form of mind-transcendence, of looking down onto the mind and its processes as opposed to being wrapped up in them. Metacognition is thinking about thoughts. It is observing thoughts, and identifying as the observer of the thoughts, as opposed to identifying as the thoughts themselves.

KEY INSIGHT:

Metacognition is Mindfulness. Mindfulness is Metacognition. The Two Are Inextricably Interlinked. Knowing the Biases Produces Both.

GETTING YOURSELF IN ORDER WITH METACOGNITION

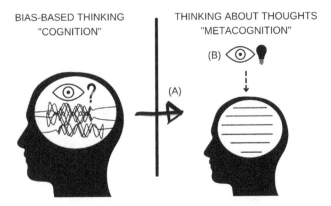

FIGURE 7: Instead of being wrapped up in a tangled web of bias-driven thoughts, and instead of identifying with this tangle, when you understand the biases (A) and attain metacognition (B), you are able to straighten out the tangle and set your mental world in order. You are able to look down onto the mind, think about the thoughts you are observing, and see when biases produce erroneous thinking and false conclusions.

KEY INSIGHT:

The Antidote to Bad Thinking is Understanding Plus Awareness.

Understanding: "I Know the Thinking Errors I Am Prone To."

Awareness: "I Am Present, And I Catch Myself in the Act."

Communication is complex. These strategies are models. They are not reality. They are good models, but they do not catch all. They are not the thing they point at, just signposts. Conceive of them as a lossy field, as shown in the image below. This is what James Clear, author of *Atomic Habits*, has to say about mental models:

> Mental models help you understand life. For example, supply and demand is a mental model that helps you understand how the economy works. Game theory is a mental model that helps you understand how relationships and trust work. Entropy is a mental model that helps you understand how disorder and decay work. Mental models also guide your perception and behavior. They are the thinking tools that you use to understand life, make decisions, and solve problems. Learning a new mental model gives you a new way to see the world—like Richard Feynman learning a new math technique. Mental models are imperfect, but useful. There is no single mental model from physics or engineering, for example, that provides a flawless explanation of the entire universe, but the best mental models from those disciplines have allowed us to build bridges and roads, develop new technologies, and even travel to outer space. As historian Yuval Noah Harari puts it, "Scientists generally agree that no theory is 100 percent correct. Thus, the real test of knowledge is not truth, but utility." ("Mental Models," Clear)

HOW THESE MODELS OF COMMUNICATION MAP TO REALITY

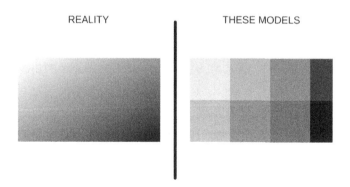

REALITY   THESE MODELS

FIGURE 8: Reality is virtually infinitely complex. Truth is deeply granular. We form mental models that explain reality sufficiently well sufficiently often. These mental models map onto reality, rendering it understandable and usable. Some sets of mental models map onto reality better than others; those that map on poorly are "pixelated," while those that map on with greater accuracy are "high-resolution." No set of mental models is perfect.

THESE MENTAL MODELS BEAT THE COMMON MODELS

HOW MOST PEOPLE SEE
COMMUNICATION

HOW THESE MODELS
ALLOW YOU TO SEE IT

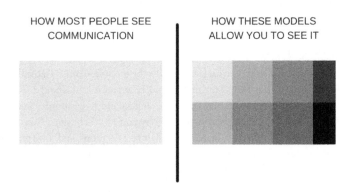

FIGURE 9: While these models are not perfect, they are drastically and dramatically more granular and "higher-resolution" than most people's communication and psychological models.

Some of the strategies are best suited for extemporaneous delivery. Others require planning. Regardless, they all contribute to your rhetorical stack. Do you need to master each and every secret in this book? Or in all of my books? No. You need to develop a rhetorical stack: master ten or so strategies. But I mean really master them. Master them to the point of complete impromptu fluency. Select strategies that come easily to you and strategies that complement each other.

WHY THE RHETORICAL STACK IS THE KEY TO MASTERY

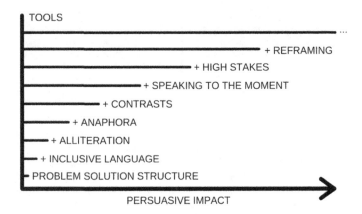

FIGURE 10: Stacking rhetorical tools, particularly rhetorical tools that complement each other, produces non-linear increases in your persuasive impact. You don't need to master every single

strategy in this book; you simply need to master ten fluently to be more persuasive than 99% of people.

LET'S PULL BACK THE CURTAIN FOR A BRIEF PREVIEW...

Behavioral economics uncovers hundreds of cognitive biases: systematic, repetitive, predictable judgement-making processes that often act as "short-cuts" to conserve mental energy while producing "good-enough" judgements.

Biases often lead to systematic thinking errors. I teach you how to avoid the systematic thinking errors in short snippets after I present a bias, but the book centers on strategies to present information in a way that activates these biases in your favor.

The result? People will find your message psychologically irresistible. Why? Because deeply-rooted cognitive processes and inherent, evolutionary features of the human mind basically force them to agree with you.

SYSTEM ONE, SYSTEM TWO, AND WHICH ONE TO USE

COMPLEX, DIFFICULT, COGNITIVELY-DEMANDING THINKING

EASY, FAST, BIAS- AND HEURISTIC-DRIVEN THINKING

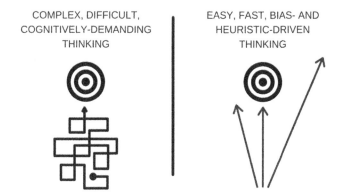

FIGURE 11: While humans are capable of complex, difficult, slow, cognitively-demanding thinking processes (which behavioral economists define as "system two" thinking), we typically operate in the fast-paced, cognitively inexpensive "system one," which is the home of biases and heuristics.

For example, humans have an "availability bias." We overweigh available information; information coming quickly to mind. This is an unfathomably powerful bias. If you can engineer your communication to be available, people will systematically, reliably, and predictably overweigh what you say. This is what we discuss in the first chapter: the availability bias, how it works, what it is, and how to use it for instant influence and easy persuasion in a professional setting.

Let's start a journey everyone else will regret missing.

......................Chapter Summary...........................

- The field of behavioral economics studies the psychology of human judgement and decision-making.
- Behavioral economics empirically proves systematic, predictable, and universal thinking processes.
- These processes exert a tremendous amount of influence over us, and most of us don't know it.
- By adjusting your communication to work with these processes, you increase your psychological influence.
- By neglecting these processes, you miss out on potential influence; by countering them, you harm your prospects.
- This book reveals 12 of these processes and proven, time-tested, concrete strategies for allying yourself with them

---

KEY INSIGHT:

System One: Instinct, Reflex, Nonconscious Impulse, Speed. Home of the Cognitive Biases.

System Two: Deliberation, Reason, Conscious Consideration, Slow and Methodical Thought.

It's Instinct Versus Insight, Reflex Versus Reason, and Nonconscious Versus Conscious Processing.

Claim These Free Resources that Will Help You Unleash the Power of Your Words and Speak with Confidence. Visit www.speakforsuccesshub.com/toolkit for Access.

18 Free PDF Resources

12 Iron Rules for Captivating Story, 21 Speeches that Changed the World, 341-Point Influence Checklist, 143 Persuasive Cognitive Biases, 17 Ways to Think On Your Feet, 18 Lies About Speaking Well, 137 Deadly Logical Fallacies, 12 Iron Rules For Captivating Slides, 371 Words that Persuade, 63 Truths of Speaking Well, 27 Laws of Empathy, 21 Secrets of Legendary Speeches, 19 Scripts that Persuade, 12 Iron Rules For Captivating Speech, 33 Laws of Charisma, 11 Influence Formulas, 219-Point Speech-Writing Checklist, 21 Eloquence Formulas

Claim These Free Resources that Will Help You Unleash the Power of Your Words and Speak with Confidence. Visit www.speakforsuccesshub.com/toolkit for Access.

30 Free Video Lessons

We'll send you one free video lesson every day for 30 days, written and recorded by Peter D. Andrei. Days 1-10 cover authenticity, the prerequisite to confidence and persuasive power. Days 11-20 cover building self-belief and defeating communication anxiety. Days 21-30 cover how to speak with impact and influence, ensuring your words change minds instead of falling flat. Authenticity, self-belief, and impact – this course helps you master three components of confidence, turning even the most high-stakes presentations from obstacles into opportunities.

Claim These Free Resources that Will Help You Unleash the Power of Your Words and Speak with Confidence. Visit <u>www.speakforsuccesshub.com/toolkit</u> for Access.

2 Free Workbooks

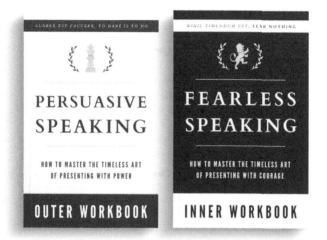

We'll send you two free workbooks, including long-lost excerpts by Dale Carnegie, the mega-bestselling author of *How to Win Friends and Influence People* (5,000,000 copies sold). *Fearless Speaking* guides you in the proven principles of mastering your inner game as a speaker. *Persuasive Speaking* guides you in the time-tested tactics of mastering your outer game by maximizing the power of your words. All of these resources complement the Speak for Success collection.

SPEAK FOR SUCCESS COLLECTION BOOK

I

HOW HIGHLY EFFECTIVE PEOPLE SPEAK CHAPTER

II

THE AVAILABILITY BIAS:

How to Be Memorable

(And Why It Matters)

"AND IN THAT SENTENCE HE TOLD US THE ENTIRE STORY..."

R ONALD REAGAN VIRTUALLY LAUNCHED his entire political career with one speech. This speech was a major pivot-point for his political career and, as a result, for the life of the nation. It was so vastly important to the trajectory of his life that he called it "the speech." He had delivered it time and again on a public speaking circuit, and word of the powerful speech and its compelling delivery reached the 1964 Republican Presidential campaign. California party officials asked him to televise the speech, using it to support the candidacy of Barry Goldwater. After the immensely positive reception, the party sought Reagan as a candidate. He served two terms as the governor of California and then two terms as the President. The influence of this speech quite literally propelled Reagan to the White House. And it was an influence based, in large part, on the availability bias.

As for the peace that we would preserve, I wonder who among us would like to approach the wife or mother whose husband or son has died in South Vietnam and ask them if they think this is a peace that should be maintained indefinitely. Do they mean peace, or do they mean we just want to be left in peace? There can be no real peace while one American is dying some place in the world for the rest of us. We're at war with the most dangerous enemy that has ever faced mankind in his long climb from the swamp to the stars, and it's been said if we lose that war, and in so doing lose this way of freedom of ours, history will record with the greatest astonishment that those who had the most to lose did the least to prevent its happening. Well I think it's time we ask ourselves if we still know the freedoms that were intended for us by the Founding Fathers. Not too long ago, two friends of mine were talking to a Cuban refugee, a businessman who had escaped from Castro, and in the midst of his story one of my friends turned to the other and said, "We don't know how lucky we are." And the Cuban stopped and said, "How lucky you are? I had someplace to escape to." And in that sentence he told us the entire story. If we lose freedom here, there's no place to escape to. This is the last stand on earth. And this idea that government is beholden to the people, that it has no other source of power except the sovereign people, is still the newest and the most unique idea in all the long history of man's relation to man. This is the issue of this election: Whether we believe in our capacity for self-government or whether we abandon the American revolution and confess that a little intellectual elite in a far-distant capitol can plan our lives for us better than we can plan them ourselves.

Stories are memorable. Due to the availability bias, memorable messages are influential. By telling the story of his Cuban friend, Reagan tied his complex message to an unforgettable narrative. The story revealed an epiphany; the epiphany emerged out of the story. People reached the conclusion before Reagan stated the conclusion. People thought "this is the last stand on Earth" before Reagan said "this is the last stand on Earth."

In this section, we explore the psychology of the availability bias, as well as proven strategies for activating it. Doing so systematically makes your message seem more important to listeners. Communication activating the availability bias played a crucial role in bringing Reagan to the White House. Where might it bring you?

WHAT IS THE AVAILABILITY BIAS?

The availability bias is overweighing evidence we easily remember; evidence that is available. A bias or heuristic is a systematic, predictable, scientifically-proven mental operation that acts as a "short-cut." It can give us correct judgements faster, but also lead us to false conclusions.

THE AVAILABILITY BIAS VISUALIZED

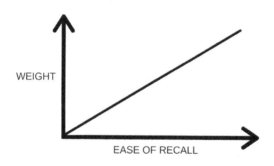

FIGURE 12: As the ease of recall of a piece of information rises, so does the weight decision-makers afford to it.

WHAT IS AN EXAMPLE OF THE AVAILABILITY BIAS?

Availability is ease of recall. What is ease of recall? A piece of information has ease of recall if it is remembered quickly, confidently, completely, and fluently. Thus, the availability bias is overweighing information that we remember quickly, confidently, completely, and fluently.

Cognitive substitution helps explain the availability bias. What is cognitive substitution? When we replace a difficult question with an easier one, substituting a simpler operation for a complicated one. And the availability bias operates on substitution.

For example, we replace the difficult question "how representative of reality is this piece of evidence?" with the easier question "how available is it to me?" And why do we do this? Why do we have any biases and heuristics? To conserve mental resources, and keep cognitive load down.

HOW COGNITIVE SUBSTITUTION PRODUCES AVAILABILITY

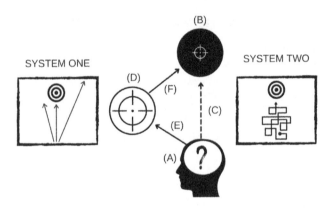

FIGURE 13: Cognitive substitution is foundational to many of these cognitive processes, both producing them and flowing from them. We cover it more deeply in a later section. When someone is prompted (A) to form an evaluation about a "target question" (B), they can either approach it logically, deliberately, and slowly with system two (C) or perform "attribute substitution," which is a system one process. They "substitute" a "substitute question" (D) for the target question, evaluate this substitute question (E), and transfer the answer to the target question (F). This occurs in part because the substituted question is easier to evaluate than the target question.

What is an example of the availability bias? We drastically overestimate the likelihood of certain disasters, like shark attacks, plane crashes, or terrorist attacks.

Why? Because examples of these disasters are highly available to us, so we overweigh them when considering a question like "how likely is a shark attack?"

And here's the important part: By understanding the availability bias, you can drastically and dramatically improve the accuracy of your judgements. Moreover, you can apply a proven set of communication strategies to activate the availability bias in your favor, so people overweigh the evidence you want them to overweigh.

Needless to say, this is huge if you need to convince people to think or act a certain way to succeed in your profession. But we're getting a little ahead of ourselves.

What is the step-by-step availability bias process? First, we consider a question: "How likely is a shark attack?" Second, we start an associative cascade, digging up anything related to the question: "What do I remember about shark attacks?" Third, we dig up a piece of information quickly: "That's right! I remember seeing the movie Jaws."

Fourth, we overweigh the available information: "Yes, shark attacks are quite frequent. I remembered an example quickly."

THE FOUR-STEP AVAILABILITY BIAS PROCESS

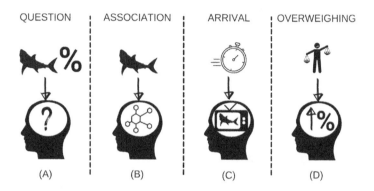

FIGURE 14: When people are asked to, for example, estimate the probability of a shark attack (A), they launch an associative cascade to search for information that can provide an answer (B). This associative cascade yields some pieces of information faster than others (C), and the availability bias causes people to overweigh this easy-to-recall information (D). This is all a subconscious process.

The decision-lab – an organization devoted to revealing the cognitive biases that influence our judgments – provides the following example:

Other events leave a lasting impression, which primes their chance of recall when we make decisions. Tversky and Kahneman exposed this tendency in a study conducted in 1983, in which half of the participants were asked to guess the chance that a massive flood would occur somewhere in North America, while the other half were asked the likelihood of a massive flood occurring due to an earthquake in California. By definition, the chance of a flood in California is necessarily smaller than that of a flood for all of North America. Participants said, nonetheless, that the chance of the flood in California, provoked by an earthquake, is higher than that in all of North America. An explanation is that an earthquake in California is easier to imagine. There is a coherent story, which begins with a familiar event (the earthquake) that causes the flood, in a context that creates a vivid picture in one's head. A large, ambiguous area like all of North America does not create a clear picture, so the prediction has no lasting mental imprint to draw on.

HOW DO YOU OVERCOME THE AVAILABILITY BIAS?

Stories persuade us, but carry little information; statistics inform us, but carry little persuasion. How do you overcome the availability bias? Gather all related statistics telling you the frequency of relevant events instead of relying on the ease of recall heuristic. In other words, interrupt the four-step availability-bias process before step two: Don't run the associative cascade. Instead, search for reliable measures of frequency.

HOW TO OVERCOME THE FOUR-STEP AVAILABILITY PROCESS

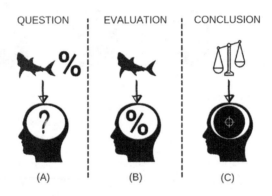

FIGURE 15: To overcome the four-step availability process, after the prompt (A), give yourself enough time to supplant the associative cascade and instead seek more infallible sources of information (B). This allows you to accurately evaluate the target question directly (C).

HOW DO YOU USE THE AVAILABILITY BIAS IN COMMUNICATION?

We know what availability is, but how does something become available? When people remember it quickly. And what do people remember quickly? Information packaged to be emotionally arousing, simple, vivid, detail-oriented, repeatedly-encountered, memorable, visual, and high-stakes.

What do the following communication strategies do? They make your message available by creating the qualities producing availability.

HOW THESE STRATEGIES CREATE IMMENSE INFLUENCE

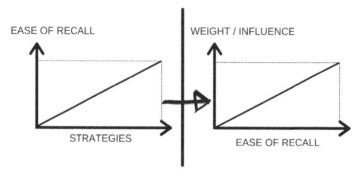

FIGURE 16: As you apply these strategies, you raise ease of recall. As you raise ease of recall, you raise the cognitive weight of your statement as well as its influence.

But why do that at all? What's the benefit? How can it advance your career and help you succeed in life? Let's say you're persuading a decision-maker to pick one option out of two options. Maybe you're a salesperson. Don't you want them to overweigh your evidence when it's decision-time? Don't you want them to remember the arguments supporting your option? Don't you want the availability bias to act in your favor, making your proposal look better by overweighing positive evidence supporting it? That's the massive power of availability-activating communication strategies.

STRATEGY #1: TELL STORIES

Stories are incredibly memorable tools for conveying information. We love stories. For thousands of years, our species used stories as vehicles for passing down wisdom to following generations. And if you want people to easily remember your message, and thus overweigh what you said when it's decision-time, embed your evidence in a story.

But don't neglect statistics and quantitative proof. Provide a statistic, lending your message authority, and then follow-up with a compelling story, lending your message availability.

How do you tell a compelling story? According to Donald Miller, CEO of StoryBrand, and author of *Building a StoryBrand*, a story follows this model:

A character has a problem, then meets a guide who gives them a plan and calls them to action. That action either results in a success or failure. (Miller, 2017)

He also states that answering these questions can help you define a story:

Who were you and what did you want?
What was the problem you encountered? How did it feel?
Who did you meet or what did you read that helped you?
What plan did you come up with after meeting the guide?
What did it feel like to take action on that plan?
What could have been lost if you'd have failed?
What was the happy ending you experienced? (Miller, 2017)

By using this simple strategy to activate the availability bias, you can guarantee decision-makers remember your words, people enthusiastically do what you want, and you bring more opportunity into your professional life.

THE EVOLUTIONARY-PRACTICAL WORLDVIEW

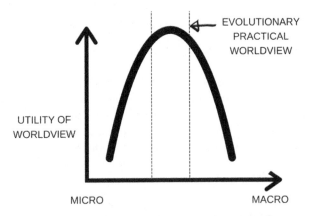

FIGURE 17: Stories also appeal to our evolutionary-practical worldview. This is how we evolved to see the world. If our perception inundates us with the micro-view, we lose the forest for the trees. If our perception inundates us for the macro-view, we see the forest, but not the trees. The middle-ground offers us the most utility, and evolution selected for this kind of perception. As you move toward the middle ground between a micro- and macro-oriented worldview, the utility of your worldview rises. As you move away from the middle ground between a micro- and macro-oriented worldview, the utility of your worldview falls. Stories appeal to our evolutionary worldview because they naturally lend themselves not to macro-oriented information or micro-oriented information but information combining the macro with the micro.

THE COMPLEX PSYCHOLOGY OF STORIES

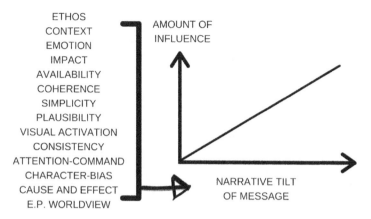

FIGURE 18: Stories appeal to many psychological features. Stories produce ethos. They offer context. They appeal to emotion. They produce impact, which is about how your subject hurts or helps people. They are available. They are coherent, simple, plausible, visual, and consistent. We overweigh these qualities. They command our attention, appealing to our bias to see the world through the lens of characters and cause and effect.

THE FIRST STORY FORMULA

FIGURE 19: This story formula has reoccurred millions of times – perhaps tens of millions of times – over the past ten thousand years. It is an archetype, which is discussed further in the section titled "Use Archetypal Personalities." As such, it is innately influential.

THE SECOND STORY FORMULA

FIGURE 20: This second story formula appears to be equally ubiquitous. A hero – who is not always particularly heroic at the beginning – is called to action. Perhaps after ignoring the all for some time, he leaps to action after some external or internal impetus compels him. This action leads to a momentary success followed by a string of failures which ultimately lead to a truer success in the end.

KEY INSIGHT:

Our Psyches, On Some Deep Level, View the World as a Grand Stage Filled with Stories.

On this Level, the World Isn't Made of Matter, But of Meaning. (Peterson, 2018).

STRATEGY #2: USE PATHOS

In his groundbreaking book *Contagious*, author Jonah Berger identified what makes a message go viral. One of the key components? Emotional arousal (Berger, 2016). According to Berger, messages that make people feel something go viral.

But here's the key: Berger often writes that "top of mind equals tip of tongue," describing how what stays on our mind is what we talk about (and thus what goes viral). And he suggests that emotionally arousing equals top of mind.

Do you see what this means? Emotionally arousing equals tip of tongue, tip of tongue equals top of mind, top of mind equals easily recalled, easily recalled equals overweighed.

People remember messages that make them feel. It's called pathos. It's one third of Aristotle's rhetorical triad (the other two thirds are logos, or logic, and ethos, or evidence and authority).

ARISTOTLE'S 2,000-YEAR-OLD PERSUASIVE FRAMEWORK

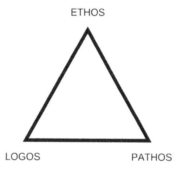

FIGURE 21: Thousands of years ago, Aristotle conveyed a timeless persuasive framework. He argued that all effective persuasion and impactful rhetoric was the result of successfully appealing to pathos (emotion), logos (logic), and ethos (evidence). Ethos has also been understood as a characteristic of the speaker: his credibility, character, and the extent to which he has the audience's interests at heart. This definition is valuable as well.

How do you create emotional arousal? Stories are, in general, emotionally arousing. But a particular kind of story is especially emotionally arousing: A story that circumvents compassion fade, another cognitive bias, will beat a story that falls victim to compassion fade.

Joseph Stalin once said the following: "The death of one man is a tragedy, the death of millions is a statistic." And, unfortunately, he is correct from a psychological perspective. In a paper by authors Daniel Västfjäll, Paul Slovic, Marcus Mayorga and

Ellen Peters, titled *Compassion Fade: Affect and Charity Are Greatest for a Single Child in Need*, we uncover a compelling feature of cognition:

> Charitable giving in 2013 exceeded $300 billion, but why do we respond to some life-saving causes while ignoring others? In our first two studies, we demonstrated that valuation of lives is associated with affective feelings (self-reported and psychophysiological) and that a decline in compassion may begin with the second endangered life. In Study 3, this fading of compassion was reversed by describing multiple lives in a more unitary fashion. Study 4 extended our findings to loss-frame scenarios. Our capacity to feel sympathy for people in need appears limited, and this form of compassion fatigue can lead to apathy and inaction, consistent with what is seen repeatedly in response to many large-scale human and environmental catastrophes. (Västfjäll et al., 2014)

Why does this happen? Maybe it's because we can't sympathize with a massive group of people; maybe it's just harder to place ourselves in their shoes. Maybe we can't comprehend such a large amount of suffering. Or maybe we can't simulate the suffering of groups like we can with individuals. Regardless, three key elements of compassion fade emerge, summarized well by the Wikipedia article on compassion fade:

> The singularity effect, whereby single victims receive more compassion than those in a group. Identified victim effect, whereby identified victims receive more compassion than unidentified ones. The proportion dominance effect, whereby people show more compassion and a willingness to help when the proportion of lives saved is higher even if the number of lives saved is the same. ("Compassion Fade," n.d.)

THE THREE COMPONENTS OF COMPASSION FADE

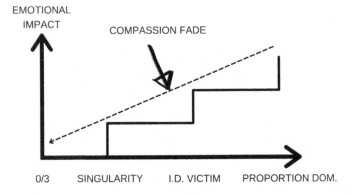

FIGURE 22: When you do not appeal to singularity, the identified victim effect, or proportion dominance, you have zero of the three

"empathy triggers." As you press the empathy triggers, your emotional impact rises. Compassion fade refers to the drop in emotional impact and compassion that occurs as you move from hitting the three triggers to lacking them.

And the following strategy emerges from these findings: Activate the availability bias by telling an emotionally arousing story of a single identified person. Why? To activate the singularity and identified victim effects.

But don't just tell any story: Tell one that embeds within itself the evidence you want people to easily recall and thus overweigh at decision-time.

A historical example of this strategy in action? In an article on Slate titled *The Welfare Queen* by Josh Levin, he writes the following:

> Ronald Reagan loved to tell stories. When he ran for president in 1976, many of Reagan's anecdotes converged on a single point: The welfare state is broken, and I'm the man to fix it. On the trail, the Republican candidate told a tale about a fancy public housing complex with a gym and a swimming pool. There was also someone in California, he'd explain incredulously, who supported herself with food stamps while learning the art of witchcraft. And in stump speech after stump speech, Reagan regaled his supporters with the story of an Illinois woman whose feats of deception were too amazing to be believed. "In Chicago, they found a woman who holds the record," the former California governor declared at a campaign rally in January 1976. "She used 80 names, 30 addresses, 15 telephone numbers to collect food stamps, Social Security, veterans' benefits for four nonexistent deceased veteran husbands, as well as welfare. Her tax-free cash income alone has been running $150,000 a year." As soon as he quoted that dollar amount, the crowd gasped. ("The Welfare Queen," Levin)

Reagan could have cited statistic upon statistic regarding Welfare fraud. Instead, he identified a single person, activating the singularity and identified victim – or in this case, identified perpetrator – effect. And he described her vivid, emotionally arousing story in memorable terms.

The impact? The story was memorable. When voters considered questions like "is Welfare fraud a big problem?" and "who should I vote for?" they easily recalled the story, the availability-bias fired up, and they overweighed the evidence. The result? They answered "Yes, Welfare fraud is a huge problem," and "I should vote for Ronald Reagan and the entire Republican ticket, because they'll fix it." Reagan lost this election. But he lost it by a smaller margin than he would have if he didn't use this strategy.

Why was the story memorable? Because compassion fade didn't dull its emotional impact. Reagan packaged the evidence in an emotionally arousing way, which made it memorable. He guaranteed that it would be memorable because he guaranteed that it would be emotionally arousing. How? By ensuring compassion fade didn't weaken its impact.

UNLOCKING THE PSYCHOLOGY OF MEMORABLE STORIES

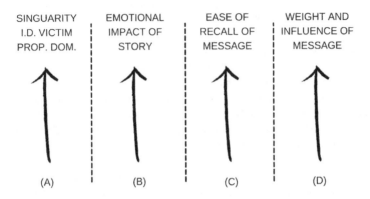

FIGURE 23: As you hit the three empathy triggers – as you achieve singularity, the identified victim effect, and proportion dominance (A) – the emotional impact of your story rises (B). As the emotional impact of your story rises, the ease of recall of your message rises (C). As the ease of recall of your message rises, so does its weight and influence (D).

One more point: Reagan wasn't evoking the quality of compassion, was he? No, but the same principles apply to the emotion he was creating: indignant anger. The identified victim effect can transform into the identified perpetrator effect under the correct conditions.

STRATEGY #3: USE SENTENTIA

As complexity goes up, ease of recall goes down. As ease of recall goes down, weight as evidence goes down. In short: As complexity goes up, weight as evidence goes down, because ease of recall goes down. And that's not what you want. You want your evidence to be weighed higher, not lower. You want it to be remembered, not tossed aside by the mind.

COMPLEXITY, EASE OF RECALL, AND INFLUENCE

HOW COMPLEXITY IMPACTS EASE OF RECALL

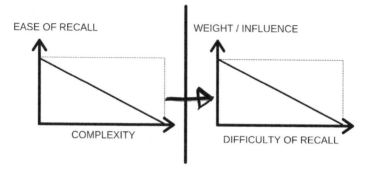

FIGURE 24: As complexity rises, ease of recall drops. As ease of recall drops (or as difficulty of recall rises), weight and influence drops.

But what if your message must be complex? What if you can't cull the complicated landscape of details? Enter stage left: Sententia. American Rhetoric defines sententia as such: "A figure of argument in which a wise, witty, or pithy maxim or aphorism is used to sum up the preceding material." They provide an example from Abraham Lincoln:

> We are now well into our fifth year since a policy was initiated with the avowed object and confident purpose of putting an end to slavery agitation. However, under the operation of that policy, that agitation has not only not ceased, but has constantly augmented. In my opinion, it will not cease until a crisis shall have been reached and passed. *A house divided against itself cannot stand.*

The italicized portion is sententia because it summarizes the preceding material in a memorable way. It anchors the entire message – something complex and convoluted – to a short and eloquent phrase, something easy to remember. Thus, it extends the memorability of the sententia to the message, because the two link.

The result of sententia? You weaken the inverse relationship between complexity and ease of recall. Without sententia, complex material is significantly less easy to recall. With sententia, it is still less easy to recall, but not as difficult as without. Applying sententia allows you to maintain more complexity without destroying memorability. This raises ease of recall. This raises the perceived importance of your message when the availability bias activates.

THE IMPACT OF SENTENTIA ON COMPLEXITY AND RECALL

HOW SENTENTIA WEAKENS THE UNFAVORABLE RELATIONSHIP

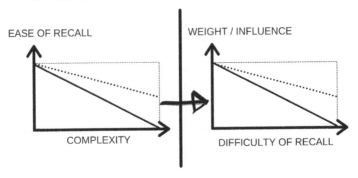

FIGURE 24: As complexity rises, ease of recall drops. As ease of recall drops (or as difficulty of recall rises), weight and influence drops. However, when you implement sententia, you weaken the relationship between complexity and ease of recall. Ease of recall drops as complexity rises, but not as much.

HOW SENTENTIA ACTS AS A "STEPPING-STONE" TO RECALL

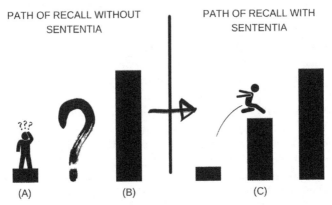

FIGURE 25: Without sententia, people are stuck at "no recall" (A) and have no way to make the leap to "full recall" (B). With sententia, people have an accessible "stepping-stone" to complete recall (C).

STRATEGY #4: PROJECT IMAGES

Scientific evidence proves we understand pictures better than words, both heard and read. Show people pictures. If you are using presentation software, it's as simple as projecting an image.

Just like sententia makes your message available because the two link, images make your message available because the memorable image links to the not-so-memorable message.

But what if you don't have presentation software? You don't need it to project images. Why not? Because people have a mental movie screen, and you can project images there with your words.

How? Describe visually stimulating scenes, use visual metaphors and analogies, and talk about your answer to this question: "If I were to make a movie of this sentence, what would I point the camera at?"

And let's zoom out for a moment. Why do any of this? Think about the four-step availability-bias process:

First, we consider a question: "How likely is a shark attack?" Second, we start an associative cascade, digging up anything related to the question: "What do I remember about shark attacks?" Third, we dig up a piece of information quickly: "That's right! I remember seeing the movie Jaws." Fourth, we overweigh the available information: "Yes, shark attacks are quite frequent. I remembered an example quickly." This is all a subconscious process.

By making your information visual, you make it easy to recall. The result? When they start the cascade search (step two), they quickly recall the information you buried in their minds with an image. And they'll overweigh it, which can tip their judgement in your favor.

STRATEGY #5: MAKE IT PERSONAL

People remember personal information. How do you make your message personal? I'm going to present two strategies.

First, use counterfactual simulation. What is it? Here's what best-selling author of *The Personal MBA*, Josh Kaufmann, has to say about counterfactual simulation:

Counterfactual Simulation is applied imagination: consciously asking a "what if" question, and letting your mind imagine the rest. Based on the stored Patterns, Associations and Interpretations, your brain will produce what it believes is the most likely scenario. Counterfactuals are very useful because of their flexibility: you can simulate anything you want. When you use Counterfactual Simulation, you assume the event or state you're simulating is already true. The mind then fills the gaps between A (where you are) and B (where you want to be). (Kaufmann, 2010)

How do you activate counterfactual simulation? It's simple: Ask them to think about how they would act in a given situation; ask them to think about what they would do if faced with a potential challenge, opportunity, or injury; ask them to put themselves in the shoes of those impacted.

Maybe you want to inspire donations for hurricane relief efforts. What do you do? How do you apply this strategy? Don't only tell them what's happening to others. Ask them to imagine it happening to them. Don't only say this: "Thousands of people lost their homes, livelihoods, and businesses." Say this: "Imagine if everything you held near and dear to your heart – your home, your livelihood, your business – was instantly wiped out by an event totally outside of your control." Why? This prompts counterfactual simulation, which makes the message personal. And this, in turn, makes the message memorable, and thus makes it available. And availability is weight, influence, and impact.

The second strategy? Positive reception affirmations. According to an *Influence at Work* article on the strategies of persuasion:

People like to be consistent with the things they have previously said or done. Consistency is activated by looking for, and asking for, small initial commitments that can be made. In one famous set of studies, researchers found rather unsurprisingly that very few people would be willing to erect an unsightly wooden board on their front lawn to support a Drive Safely campaign in their neighborhood. However in a similar neighborhood close by, four times as many homeowners indicated that they would be willing to erect this unsightly billboard. Why? Because ten days previously, they had agreed to place a small postcard in the front window of their homes that signaled their support for a Drive Safely campaign. That small card was the initial commitment that led to a 400% increase in a much bigger but still consistent change. So when seeking to influence using the consistency principle, the detective of influence looks for voluntary, active, and public commitments and ideally gets those commitments in writing. For example, one recent study reduced missed appointments at health centers by 18% simply by asking the patients rather than the staff to write down appointment details on the future appointment card. ("The Science of Persuasion," n.d.)

Positive reception affirmations call people to counterfactually simulate your message and reflect on how it helps them. If you are trying to sell a product, ask them "what if?" personal questions prompting counterfactual simulation of the benefits the product offers. Then ask them to reflect on those benefits, and when they repeat them to you, the consistency principle will activate. They become more likely to perceive your message positively in the future. Why? Because it would be consistent with what they just said.

For example: "What would it mean for you if you got [benefit one], [benefit two], and [benefit three]? How would it feel? How would it impact you and your business?"

So far, you activated counterfactual simulation. But when they say "it would be wonderful, honestly" you'll activate the consistency principle. In the future, they'll act in ways consistent with their past actions; they'll quickly recall what they said to you, and feel the need to behave in a manner consistent with it.

Counterfactual simulation is extremely persuasive. Positive reception affirmations are vastly influential. Combining them and sprinkling the availability bias on top is exceptionally powerful.

STRATEGY #6: KEEP IT SIMPLE

Omit anything unnecessary. Omit anything without persuasive value. Omit anything blurring the clarity of your message.

Here's what you have to understand: People have a finite attention budget. When they place 100% of their attention on something, it is imprinted in their mental landscape. It becomes easy to recall and activates the availability bias later down the road. But when you sprinkle unnecessary information into your communication, you're diluting the attention budget.

HOW SUPERFLUOUS INPUTS WASTE AUDIENCE ATTENTION

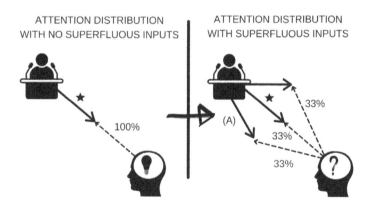

FIGURE 26: When you produce only the most important input, it receives 100% of the audience's attention (or more accurately of the attention you've obtained). When you produce, for example, two non-essential inputs (A), each input, all else equal, receives 33% of your obtained attention. Of course, the 33% of attention paid to each of the two competing and unimportant inputs is largely wasted. This is why simplicity and focus is essential.

Focused attention activates the availability bias by retaining the focal information in memory. Diluted attention lowers retention across the board.

What do you end up with? Poor recollection of a bunch of irrelevant details. And that can't activate the availability bias. Instead, achieve crystal clear recollection of the most important information, and nothing else. The more you add, the less likely they'll remember any of it. Direct their attention fully and completely to one idea at a time. Otherwise, they'll forget.

KEY INSIGHT:

If You Have Too Many Priorities, You Have None. Can You Have Two "Number One" Priorities?

Simple Speech is Successful Speech. Make Your Message the Focus of Your Communication.

STRATEGY #7: PROVIDE TANGIBLE TAKEAWAYS

What do you remember with greater ease? Something you heard five years ago? Or something you heard five minutes ago? Something you heard five minutes ago.

How does this principle translate into action? To make your message available, deliver it as close to the moment of decision as possible. If people remember recent events with greater ease, and events remembered with ease are overweighed in decision-making, you want to convey your message as close to the moment of decision as possible. This much is obvious.

But what if you can't? You don't always control when you convey the message. So how can you capitalize on this if you can't control when you communicate with the decision maker?

It's easy: Provide a tangible takeaway. A one-sheet that summarizes the big-picture on one page; a packet of related images and visuals; something quick and easy to jog their memory.

Now, it's no guarantee that giving them a tangible takeaway will result in them reading it. It might languish on the kitchen island for eternity, unread. But I know this: If you don't give them one, it's certain they won't read it. Even if it sits on their counter for months, unread, glancing at it every day will boost ease of recall tremendously.

Try your luck. Who knows? They might read it five minutes before decision-time, massively overweighing your message when it matters most by raising ease of recall. Or they might read it two minutes after receiving your message, but one month before decision-time. Even this offers an availability-based benefit: Repetition creates memory.

STRATEGY #8: ALWAYS SUMMARIZE

There's a dictum in public speaking: "If you can't say it in a sentence, you can't say it in a speech." Just like astronauts and high-stakes engineers have "one-sheets" summarizing critical systems, one page per system, you should have a one-sentence: a single sentence summarizing your entire message.

And not only should you have one; you should deliver it. Why? Summaries work in an interesting way, much like sententia. This is how summaries interact with the four-step availability-bias process: First, they see the question. Second, they start the associative cascade. Third, they get a quick piece of information (your summary), but they don't stop there. They continue to "cascade" off of the information they just retrieved. What does this mean? They remember your summary, and they continue to search for information related to it. This prompts recollection of a host of details. A summary raises recall of the entire message, not only itself. Fourth, they overweigh not only your summary, but the cascade of related information the summary prompted.

STRATEGY #9: INVOKE FEAR

Fear is incredibly compelling. Remember the principle of emotional arousal? Fear is one of the emotions producing the most emotional arousal. People can't ignore it, and will always remember it, even after it subsides. People live their lives accommodating for decade-old fears.

I'm not saying that you should use scare-tactics. Just raise the stakes, and tell them what they have to lose. Don't make it up. Just draw attention to the potential losses and risks that always existed.

Why do this? Because by invoking the risk of loss, you activate fear, and fear is memorable; thus, it is available, and overweighed in decision-making.

Loss-aversion is a pertinent part of the mechanism for this strategy. People suffer from a loss of $1,000 up to twice as much as they take pleasure in a gain of $1,000. We are incredibly risk-averse and loss-averse, to the point of mathematical irrationality. All these qualities of human cognition make fear-activating messages extremely memorable.

USING LOSS AVERSION TO CRAFT IMPACTFUL APPEALS

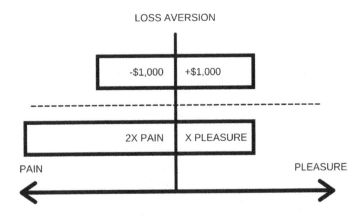

FIGURE 27: People have been shown to regularly fear loss more than they hope for an equivalent gain. While the extent of loss aversion differs between people, it can often be a factor of two.

HOW FEAR INTERACTS WITH THE PSYCHOLOGY OF STORIES

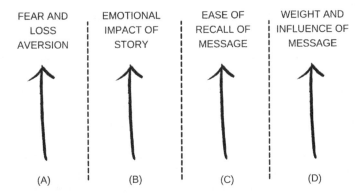

FIGURE 28: As fear and loss aversion rise (A), the impact of your persuasive narrative rises (B). As the impact of your persuasive narrative rises, so does its ease of recall (C), which raises its overall weight and influence (D).

STRATEGY #10: INVOKE DESIRE

There's a magic acronym in digital marketing and sales: "WIIFM?" It stands for the question people are subconsciously asking themselves every second, every minute, and every hour of every day: "What's in it for me?"

We are inherently self-interested creatures. It's how we evolved. And this doesn't mean we are completely selfish. Cooperative behavior is in our self-interest, and there are abundant accounts of truly altruistic behavior. It simply means that any information related to how we can help ourselves, further our ambitions, or reach our goals is memorable. How do you use this principle in your favor? Pour on the benefits.

According to Dr. Drew Eric Whitman, author of *Cashvertising*, the following "life-force" desires intrinsically motivate us. (I italicized those salient to modern life and easiest to invoke, in my view):

> Survival, enjoyment of life, life extension.
> Enjoyment of food and beverages.
> *Freedom from fear, pain, and danger.*
> Sexual companionship.
> Comfortable living conditions.
> *To be superior, winning, keeping up with the Joneses.*
> Care and protection of loved ones.
> *Social approval.* (Whitman, 2008)

Evolution embedded these in us. We can't shake them. And we can't help thinking about them, and thus remembering them, and thus overweighing messages tied to them.

STRATEGY #11: USE MNEMONICS

What's a mnemonic device? According to *PsychCentral*, the definition of a mnemonic device is as follows:

> Mnemonic devices are techniques a person can use to help them improve their ability to remember something. In other words, it's a memory technique to help your brain better encode and recall important information. ("Memory and Mnemonic Devices," n.d.)

See how these activate the availability bias? They have "availability heuristic" written all over them.

Roy G. Biv is a name we can use to remember the colors of the rainbow: Red, orange, yellow, green, blue, indigo, and violet. The most common mnemonic is a word in which each letter stands for another word. Create your own to activate the availability bias with ease.

What's the deal with sententia, summaries, and mnemonics? It's the same story: They all attach an easy-to-recall anchor to a hard-to-remember message. Why? Because doing so aides recall of the entire message. How? By providing a stepping-stone to complete recall. We remember the memory anchor, and the memory anchor yields the entire message.

AVAILABILITY BIAS CONCLUSION

Ronald Reagan tied an abstract message to a concrete story. In doing so, he appealed to the availability bias. The story is memorable; as a result, it is available; as a result, the human mind overweighs it. By embedding his message in the story and allowing the persuasive epiphany to emerge out of the story, Reagan made his message significantly more available.

......................Chapter Summary............................

- The availability bias is our human tendency to overweigh memorable or "available" information.
- The availability bias occurs in four steps: prompt, associative cascade, "quick find," overweighing of "quick find."
- The availability bias explains why we overweigh the likelihood of certain types of "available" crises.
- You use the availability bias in communication by applying strategies that make your message memorable.
- You overcome the availability bias in part by extending the associative cascade to retrieve more information.
- Ronald Reagan used the availability bias by embedding his core message in a memorable story.

KEY INSIGHT:

The Truth That Helps Us Most Is the Truth We Remember When We Need a Guiding Compass.

Making Truth and Wisdom Memorable Is a Service of the Highest Moral Significance.

HOW TO OVERCOME THE PSYCHOLOGY (PART ONE)

1	The Availability Bias
1.1	Gather All Available Statistics Instead of Relying on Ease of Recall
2	The Anchoring Effect
3	Munger's Biases
4	The Contrast Effect
5	Zero-Risk Bias
6	The Halo Effect
7	Agent Detection Bias
8	Attribute Substitution
9	Base Rate Neglect

KEY INSIGHT:

Stories Provide Meaning. Statistics Contextualize Meaning. Clear Thinking Demands Both.

The Best Place to Grasp Truth is at the Intersection of the Qualitative and the Quantitative.

Claim These Free Resources that Will Help You Unleash the Power of Your Words and Speak with Confidence. Visit www.speakforsuccesshub.com/toolkit for Access.

18 Free PDF Resources

12 Iron Rules for Captivating Story, 21 Speeches that Changed the World, 341-Point Influence Checklist, 143 Persuasive Cognitive Biases, 17 Ways to Think On Your Feet, 18 Lies About Speaking Well, 137 Deadly Logical Fallacies, 12 Iron Rules For Captivating Slides, 371 Words that Persuade, 63 Truths of Speaking Well, 27 Laws of Empathy, 21 Secrets of Legendary Speeches, 19 Scripts that Persuade, 12 Iron Rules For Captivating Speech, 33 Laws of Charisma, 11 Influence Formulas, 219-Point Speech-Writing Checklist, 21 Eloquence Formulas

Claim These Free Resources that Will Help You Unleash the Power of Your Words and Speak with Confidence. Visit www.speakforsuccesshub.com/toolkit for Access.

30 Free Video Lessons

We'll send you one free video lesson every day for 30 days, written and recorded by Peter D. Andrei. Days 1-10 cover authenticity, the prerequisite to confidence and persuasive power. Days 11-20 cover building self-belief and defeating communication anxiety. Days 21-30 cover how to speak with impact and influence, ensuring your words change minds instead of falling flat. Authenticity, self-belief, and impact – this course helps you master three components of confidence, turning even the most high-stakes presentations from obstacles into opportunities.

SPEAK FOR SUCCESS COLLECTION BOOK

I

HOW HIGHLY EFFECTIVE PEOPLE SPEAK CHAPTER

III

THE ANCHORING EFFECT:
Why First Impressions
Influence Final Decisions

"I HAVE DIRECTED ALL HEADS OF GOVERNMENT DEPARTMENTS..."

J OHN F. KENNEDY MET THE ECONOMIC CLUB OF NEW YORK at the Waldorf Astoria hotel in New York on December 14, 1962, to discuss taxation. He sought to lower the tax rates in order to spur the economy of the United States. He only needed to build the political momentum necessary to pass his vision for economic reform through Congress. In his speech to the Economic Club, he achieved subtle influence by using the anchoring heuristic in his favor.

In addition, I have directed all heads of government departments and agencies to hold federal employment under the levels authorized by congressional appropriations, to absorb through greater efficiency a substantial part of this year's federal pay increase, to achieve an increase in productivity which will enable the same amount of work to be done by less people, and to refrain from spending any unnecessary funds that were appropriated by the Congress. It should also be noted that the federal debt, as a proportion of our gross national product, has been steadily reduced in the last years. Last year the total increase in the federal debt was two percent – compared to an eight percent increase in the gross debt of state and local governments. Taking a longer view, the federal debt today is 13 percent higher than it was in 1946, while state and local debt is 360 percent higher than it was in 1946 – and private debt by over 300 percent. In fact, if it were not for federal financial assistance to state and local governments, the federal cash budget would show a surplus. Federal civilian employment, for example, is actually lower today than it was in 1952, while state and local government employment over the same period has increased 67 percent. It is this setting which makes federal tax reduction both possible and appropriate next year. I do not underestimate the obstacles which the Congress will face in enacting such legislation. No one will be satisfied. Everyone will have his own approach, his own bill, his own reductions. A high order of restraint and determination will be required if the "possible" is not to wait on the "perfect." But a nation capable of marshaling these qualities in any dramatic threat to our security, is surely capable, as a great free society, of meeting a slower and more complex threat to our economic vitality. This nation can afford to reduce taxes, we can afford a temporary deficit – but we cannot afford to do nothing. For on the strength of our free economy rests the hope of all free nations. We shall not fail that hope – for free men and free nations must prosper and they must prevail. Thank you.

Believe it or not, but there is a subtle science behind how JFK used those numbers; their sequence, their relationship to one another, and their proportionality. There is a subtle psychological effect emerging from the manner in which he presented his quantitative evidence. In this section, we explore the strategy behind the numbers JFK cites. He used it to argue for a high-stakes policy proposal in a contentious political moment. You can use it to charge more, pay less, and influence more.

WHAT IS THE ANCHORING EFFECT?

The anchoring effect is our tendency for the first number we hear (the anchor) to irrationally influence us. We reach an inaccurate judgement by starting at the anchor and insufficiently adjusting either downward or upward.

THE ANCHORING EFFECT VISUALIZED

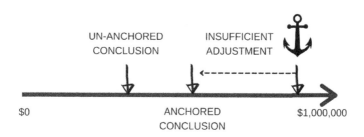

FIGURE 29: An anchor set at a high value becomes the starting point of your evaluation. You begin at the anchor and adjust from it in the appropriate direction, but do so insufficiently. In this example, this leaders to a higher anchored conclusion. Your un-anchored conclusion would have been lower. This is in favor of the "anchorer."

The anchoring effect functions through the following characteristics of human psychology: perceptual relativity, comparative perception, directional judgement, insufficient adjustment, and primacy.

What is perceptual relativity? All our judgements form relative to other perceptions we have. Is it good or bad that we have a 10% global extreme poverty rate? Most will have a difficult time answering with certainty. Why? Perception is relative, and this statistic lacks a point of reference. What about this? 20 years ago, we had a global extreme poverty rate of 40%. Now, it's 10%. In this case, the perception is typically positive: "Yes, that's fairly good." Why? 10% is low relative to the rest of the information, namely that it was once 40%. (Fun fact: It was once 99.9999% prior to the industrial revolution).

PERCEPTUAL RELATIVITY VISUALIZED

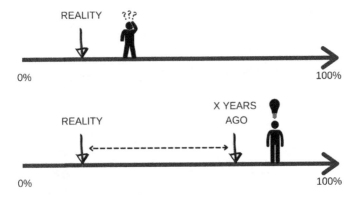

FIGURE 30: Humans struggle to judge reality in a perceptual vacuum. We need points of comparison. If we are judging "how good reality is now," we often find ourselves confused. We lack relativity. The statement of "how bad reality was X years ago" provides it.

KEY INSIGHT:

This Does Not Mean "Everything Is Relative." It Merely Means Comparative Judgment is Easier.

Good is Good is Good, Not Just Because It's Better Than Bad. But Knowing Bad Helps Us Know Good. Consider the Yin-Yang.

What is comparative perception? Our judgements are based on comparison between alternatives. People are happy to earn $60,000 a year if their closest co-worker earns $55,000, but unhappy if their closest co-worker earns $65,000. Isn't $60,000 equal to $60,000, no matter what someone else earns? Of course, but that's not how human perception and judgement work. We can't judge a single item unless we have a point of comparison. And once we find a point of comparison, it becomes our anchor, against which we measure subsequent items.

COMPARATIVE PERCEPTION VISUALIZED

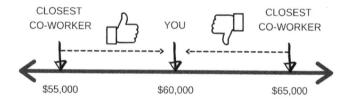

FIGURE 30: Humans struggle to judge reality in a perceptual vacuum. We need points of comparison. If we are judging "how good my salary is," we often find ourselves confused. We lack relativity. The statement of "how it stacks up against the salary of my closest co-worker" provides it.

What is directional judgment? We are more concerned with the direction of trends rather than their magnitude. We are more concerned with the direction of the jump from our salary to that of our closest co-worker, and if it is a jump up or a jump down. We don't care so much about the size of the jump. This is part of why we overweigh the initial anchor: We care if subsequent numbers are higher or lower, but not how much so. We know that we want to negotiate downward (direction) from an excessively high price in a negotiation, but by how much (magnitude)? We decide magnitude by adjustment from an anchor.

DIRECTIONAL JUDGMENT VISUALIZED

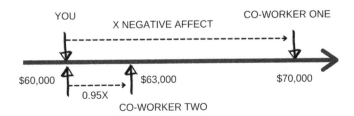

FIGURE 31: We overweigh direction compared to magnitude. If we earn $60,000 a year and a close co-worker earns $70,000 a year, this produces "X" negative affect; "X" negative emotion. If a second close co-worker earns $63,000 a year, this is 10% less than the first co-worker, but produces 95% of the negative emotional impact; that is, only 5% less emotional impact. This is a hypothetical example with hypothetical numbers, but it mirrors experimental evidence. It shows us that direction influences our emotions more than magnitude. If our closest co-worker makes more than us, that "directional" fact alone influences us more than facts related to magnitude; than facts related to the size of the disparity.

What is insufficient adjustment? Insufficient adjustment impacts number-related estimations. This is how anchors influence us. It follows this process: The first number we encounter roots itself in our memory, and it becomes an anchor. Next, based on our interests, we begin to negotiate in the direction we seek, but determine the extent of our renegotiation by starting at the anchor and adjusting downward, often by an insufficient amount.

Consider this example. "This car, our newest model, is worth $200,000," says the agent. This prompts you to make a judgement: "How much do I think this lower-end SUV is worth?" Instead of starting over, we begin our valuation at the anchor, and adjust accordingly. In this case, we adjust downward from $200,000. "$100,000? Too much. $80,000? Still too much. $60,000? Getting there. $40,000? Seems about right."

What's the problem? We often adjust insufficiently, resulting in a higher valuation than if we didn't see the anchor at all. If we first encountered a lower anchor, $20,000, we would have insufficiently adjusted upward, perhaps landing at $30,000.

What is the primacy effect? The primacy effect is our tendency to overweigh the first information we encounter. Why does the primacy effect occur? Because of two features of psychology. The first? We take new evidence as confirmation of old conclusions (or primary conclusions – the first ones we make). This is confirmation bias. The second? We evaluate new information by comparing it to what we first learned. We can't judge a 10% extreme poverty rate on its own as easily as when we compare it to what we heard first: 40%.

THE PRIMACY EFFECT VISUALIZED

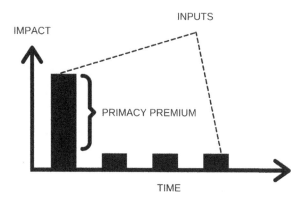

FIGURE 32: All else equal, the first item we perceive impacts us more than subsequent items. We may refer to this increased impact as the primacy premium.

WHAT IS AN EXAMPLE OF THE ANCHORING EFFECT?

When you are shopping online and see a high price crossed out next to a lower price, they are trying to anchor you to the high price. If the "retail price" is $1,000, but they are offering you the product for $500, you insufficiently adjust downward from $1,000 when evaluating the true worth. Perhaps you insufficiently adjust downward to $750, a higher number than $500, which makes the $500 price seem more attractive.

If you are reading the eBook version of this book, you probably noticed the price of the print book, $22.99, crossed out above the price of the eBook. When we ask ourselves "should I buy this thing?" we answer the question by comparing what we pay to how much we value the product. If we value the product more than we value the money we exchange for it, we buy. If not, we don't. Anchoring makes us think we value the product more, because we insufficiently adjust from the higher number (in this case, the $22.99). We might value the eBook at $12 on its own, and say "sure, I'll buy it, as it's $9.99." But when we insufficiently adjust from the $22.99 price of the print copy, we might think we value the product at $15. And we'll want to buy it even more. This is why Amazon posts prices in this manner for nearly all of the books published on the platform.

In *Win Bigly*, Scott Adams presents an example of unrelated anchoring. What does he suggest? If you are negotiating a price, at the beginning of the meeting, talk about some random person spending an exorbitant amount of money on a yacht (like

$2,000,000). This will anchor your prospect to $2,000,000, and they will insufficiently adjust downward and probably offer more for your product (Adams, 2017). Anchors need only to be somewhere in the same neighborhood as the range of appropriate values. The $2,000,000 anchor will exert more influence if the range of appropriate values is somewhere between $1,000,000 and $1,500,000. You can't use a $2,000,000 anchor to raise the price paid for a $10 product. The $2,000,000 anchor is so absurdly far out of the appropriate range of evaluation that the prospect readily discards it.

Does anchoring in this manner work even if your product isn't a yacht? Yes, and this is the reason why this model of anchoring is called unrelated anchoring. Anchors work even if the first number describes a completely different item. Anchors work even if the high anchor you set describes the price of a yacht and you're selling a house. This is how desperately our minds scramble for information we can use to form comparisons. It's a shortcut we use to save mental resources. Since comparison-based decision-making is easy, we irrationally select a point of comparison subconsciously and unknowingly.

Let's talk about the science before getting into proven anchoring strategies you can use to pay less, earn more money, and drive stronger results in your professional career by "winning" every negotiation.

HOW DO YOU OVERCOME THE ANCHORING EFFECT?

You can overcome the anchoring effect by educating yourself on the subject of your evaluation, striving to ignore the first number you hear outright, realizing unrelated numbers you might hear can have an outsized impact, seeking historical evidence related to your valuation instead of relying on an anchor, and countering a high anchor with concentrated attention on a lower number (or vice-versa).

THE IMPACT OF KNOWLEDGE ON THE EFFECT OF ANCHORING

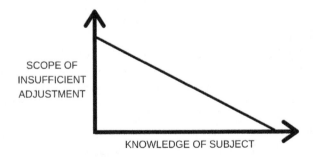

FIGURE 33: As your knowledge of the subject rises, the extent of the insufficient adjustment to which you are prone drops.

VISUALIZING COUNTER-ANCHORING

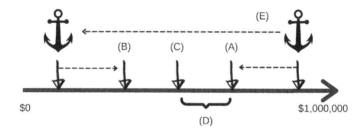

FIGURE 34: An anchor will cause a degree of insufficient adjustment (A). Your counter-anchor will do the same (B). From this point, assuming the negotiation is occurring on roughly equal grounds, you will likely take the average of these two positions (C). Thus, this strategy produces a cost reduction of the difference between the first position and the average between the first position and the second position (D). Of course, this strategy is not a silver-bullet, as the first anchor may anchor your counter-anchor (E).

HOW DO YOU USE THE ANCHORING EFFECT IN COMMUNICATION?

Need to convey value? You can use the anchoring effect in your favor. Need to negotiate a price? Need to negotiate any number? You can use the anchoring effect in your favor. Need to sell a product? You can use the anchoring effect in you favor. Need to pay less? You can use the anchoring effect in your favor. Need to charge more? You can use the anchoring effect in your favor.

What are the different anchors in your toolbox? High anchors cause insufficient downward adjustment. Low anchors cause insufficient upward adjustment. Positive anchors make a number seem appropriate, accurate, and attractive. Negative anchors make a number seem inappropriate, inaccurate, and unattractive. Unrelated anchors are not relevant to the subject at hand. Related anchors are.

STRATEGY #1: RAISE THE PERCEIVED VALUE OF A PRODUCT YOU OFFER (HIGHER RELATED ANCHOR)

You must remember one key aspect of successful anchoring: While the anchor need not necessarily relate to the current evaluation, it must be on the same scale of measurement. You can anchor a monetary transaction to an amount of money someone exchanged in an unrelated transaction for a completely different good or service. Does the scale of measurement match? Yes, and as a result, you successful anchor an amount of money to another amount of money.

HOW TO AVOID THE MOST COMMON ANCHORING MISTAKE

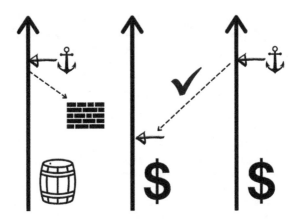

FIGURE 35: You cannot anchor a number of barrels to a number of dollars. No insufficient adjustment will occur here. You can anchor a number of dollars to another number of dollars. In this case, insufficient adjustment will occur.

You can't anchor a monetary transaction to the weight of all bananas that exist on Earth. (Fun fact: It's 50 billion tons). Why not? Because the numbers represent entirely different scales of measurement. With that, I introduce you to our first anchoring strategy: raising the expected value of a product you offer by presenting a related anchor.

Remember the key algorithm governing human transactions: "If I value this thing more than I have to pay for it, I'll buy it." And all you have to do to effortlessly execute this strategy is present a high related anchor. How? Like this: "[insert competitor] charges [insert high related anchor] for this same service [pause]. We charge [insert lower price]." The prospect anchors his valuation of your product to the high related anchor you set – let's say it's $10,000 – and then insufficiently adjusts downward.

"How much should this product cost? $10,000? $9,000? $8,000? $7,000? That seems about right (insufficient adjustment). How much is this person selling it for? Woah! $5,000? That's a great price. It's $2,000 less than $7,000 (the prospect's valuation, pulled higher by the anchor)."

And here's the best part: You don't have to artificially lower your price. Manipulate the anchor, not your price. Find a competitor with an exorbitantly-priced product, for example.

Your higher related anchor doesn't have to be a competitor's product. You have many options: suggested retail price, previous price versus discounted price, cost of similar results (for example, if you're selling a $20 book you can apply a higher related anchor of a $2,000 course on the same subject), and even the price of a higher-end model with similar features (like a $200,000 car in the dealership next to $20,000 cars with similar functionalities).

STRATEGY #2: RAISE THE PERCEIVED VALUE OF A PRODUCT YOU OFFER (HIGHER UNRELATED ANCHOR)

Here's the key: You can use this strategy in tandem with the first one. An unrelated anchor is a completely irrelevant number on the same scale of measurement, as per the example of the yacht. If you want to get an offer of $1,000,000 in a negotiation, you can set an unrelated high anchor by mentioning how someone spent $2,000,000 on an unrelated product. Does this work? Yes, and the science is conclusive. But I recommend combining it with the previous strategy. Who says you can't throw out multiple anchors?

In any case, this underscores the sheer irrationality of human psychology. Even though the number has nothing to do with the current transaction, not only does it influence the value estimation, but it becomes the starting point of the value estimation.

STRATEGY #3: RAISE THE LIKELY OFFER BY STARTING A NEGOTIATION (HIGHER RELATED ANCHOR)

Let's say you don't want to randomly throw in an anecdote about someone buying a $2,000,000 yacht. In this case, you can apply a directly related anchor by speaking first and offering an exorbitantly high price. Your negotiation partner will probably reject it. But it will inevitably influence their subsequent offer, pushing it higher. There are two reasons. Anchoring is the first. Social pressure – their aversion toward straying too far from your expectation – is the second.

Here's what would happen without anchoring. Remember, you want at least $1,000,000. You open like so: "I'll sell you this for $1,000,000." Their desire for the lowest possible price sets the direction of their counteroffer, but insufficient adjustment from the anchor price of $1,000,000 sets the magnitude of their counteroffer. And if that's the case, why not start their insufficient adjustment at a higher anchor?

"No thanks, that's a little much for me…"

Insufficient downward adjustment ensues in their subconscious mind: "$1,000,000… $900,000… $800,000… that seems about right." They speak: "How about $800,000?" You haggle a little over that price, and end up at $900,000. Not what you wanted, is it?

But what happens with anchoring? You still want $1,000,000. But this time, you don't start there. Instead, you start like this: "$1,500,000 is my asking price."

"Woah – that's a little out there, isn't it?"

"I don't think so, but do you have a counteroffer?" Insufficient downward adjustment ensues: "$1,500,000, $1,400,000, $1,300,000, $1,200,000... that seems about right."

"1,200,000?"

"Deal."

And remember the fascinating flexibility of anchoring. You don't have to set a high related anchor in the form of your starting offer. You can also set a high related anchor in the form of what someone similar to your negotiation partner recently paid for a similar product. This likely has lower influence, but you can use multiple anchors.

KEY INSIGHT:

Your Immediate Responsibility May Be Getting the Best Deal. But Your Transcendent Responsibility is Justice and Fairness. Don't Use Anchoring to Obfuscate, But to Illuminate.

STRATEGY #4: RAISE THE PERCEIVED BENEFIT OF A PRODUCT YOU OFFER (LOWER RELATED ANCHOR)

Value is not based on price alone, but how price compares to net benefit. And all numbers can anchor as long as they share a scale of measurement with the evaluation. The mind easily rejects anchoring across scales of measurement, and won't use a cross-scale anchor as a starting point, which is the basis of anchoring.

How does this strategy change that dynamic? It shifts the scale of measurement from monetary cost to benefit quantification. For example, let's say you're selling Search Engine Optimization (SEO) services to get companies web traffic through Google. The most salient benefit is "website views."

How do you set a related lower anchor? Like so: "Most SEO firms charging $5,000 a month get an average of 10,000 monthly website views according to [insert reliable source], but we typically get 30,000 for the same price." In this case, it's in your best interest to find the lowest possible related anchor without dishonestly fabricating one.

Why should you apply this strategy? Because the number "30,000 web views a month" means nothing to most people. They can't judge it as good or bad. Why not? Because of how human judgement works. We need contrasts and relativity. "30,000 web views a month" offers neither. When you introduce the "10,000" lower related anchor, you give human judgement a point of comparison. People insufficiently adjust expectations upward, and identify "30,000" as superior to their evaluation.

A brief point: Anchoring happens only when someone is evaluating what a number ought to be or is likely to be. In situations along the lines of this previous example, the prospect to which you are speaking will always try to estimate the value of your product, as well as its benefits and how it can help them.

What is the result of this model of anchoring? When you say "Most SEO firms charging $5,000 a month get an average of 10,000 monthly website views according to [insert reliable source]," your prospects think the following: "I would want above average. 11,000? 12,000? 13,000? 14,000? 15,000? I would be satisfied with that (insufficient upward adjustment)."

But when you finish the sentence, and say "...but we typically get 30,000 for the same price," they are taken aback in pleasant surprise. Why? Because you shattered their expectations. And the positive breaking of expectations gives this kind of anchoring tremendous persuasive force. You set expectations you were certain you could break by introducing a low anchor and allowing the audience to insufficiently adjust upward.

Before we move on, remember this: You can use this model of anchoring with many measurements, like number of features, number of benefits, number of happy customers, number of positive reviews, etc.

STRATEGY #5: LOWER THE PERCEIVED RISKS AND HARMS OF YOUR OFFER (HIGHER RELATED ANCHOR)

"Most [insert description of supplier] create [insert higher quantification of risks or harms per unit of time]. In the past [insert same unit of time], we created 0." "Most SEO providers create 20 potential Google terms of use violations per year of service. In the past year, we created 0." This is incredibly compelling because of human loss-aversion. We fear loss more than we hope for gain. Why? Because loss hurts us more than gain pleases us, up to twice as much for some particularly loss-averse people. This is a scientifically proven function of human psychology. Remember the importance of contrast in communication. "0 violations in the past year" means nothing. "We had 0, most had 20," means so much.

STRATEGY #6: LOWER THE PERCEIVED VALUE OF A PRODUCT (LOWER RELATED ANCHOR)

This time, you're not selling a product. You're buying one. You want to cause insufficient upward adjustment from a lower anchor, like so: "I'll offer you [insert 60% of the price you really want]." And make sure you speak first. Recall the primacy effect. People overweigh what they hear first. The first number anchors, not the second.

STRATEGY #7: LOWER THE PERCEIVED VALUE OF A PRODUCT YOU WANT (LOWER UNRELATED ANCHOR)

This time, you're not selling a product. You're buying one. This time, you set an unrelated low anchor, like so: "Someone bought [insert different product] for [insert 30% of price you want]." Why anchor it to 30% in this case, but 60% when it's a related anchor? Because this circumvents the possible offense caused by such a cheap offer, as you're not offering anything, just an "unrelated" anecdote.

ANCHORING EFFECT CONCLUSION

John F. Kennedy presented smaller numbers first. He did not always do this, but he did do it. The smaller numbers acted as anchors. As a result, the audience insufficiently adjusted upward, so the second number JFK presented – the number he wanted them to perceive as outsized – really did appear as outsized. He made the second number seem inappropriately large by first anchoring the audience to a smaller number.

..........................Chapter Summary...............................

- The anchoring effect is our tendency to overweigh the first number we hear in an evaluation.
- The anchoring effect functions in part through "insufficient adjustment" from an anchor, using it as the starting point.
- The anchoring effect explains why many products have a "marked-down" price, which acts as the value anchor.
- You use the anchoring effect in communication by setting various anchors to change perceived value in your favor.
- You overcome the anchoring in part by speaking first, to use the effect, or by self-imposing a "counter-anchor" in mind.
- John F. Kennedy used the anchoring effect with a low anchor to raise the perceived exorbitance of following numbers.

HOW TO OVERCOME THE PSYCHOLOGY (PART TWO)

1	The Availability Bias
1.1	Gather All Available Statistics Instead of Relying on Ease of Recall
2	The Anchoring Effect
2.1	Educate Yourself on the Subject of Evaluation
2.2	Strive to Ignore the First Number You Hear
2.3	Be Cognizant of the Impact of Unrelated Anchors
2.4	Seek Historical Evidence Related to Your Evaluation
2.5	Concentrate Attention on a Self-Supplied Counter-Anchor
3	Munger's Biases
4	The Contrast Effect
5	Zero-Risk Bias
6	The Halo Effect
7	Agent Detection Bias
8	Attribute Substitution
9	Base Rate Neglect

Email Peter D. Andrei, the author of the Speak for Success collection and the President of Speak Truth Well LLC directly.

pandreibusiness@gmail.com

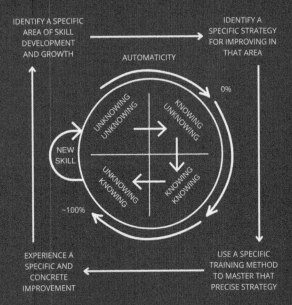

How do anxious speakers turn into articulate masters of the craft? Here's how: With the bulletproof, scientifically-proven, 2,500-year-old (but mostly forgotten) process pictured above.

First, we identify a specific area of improvement. Perhaps your body language weakens your connection with the audience. At this point, you experience "unknowing unknowing." You don't know you don't know the strategy you will soon learn for improving in this area.

Second, we choose a specific strategy for improving in this area. Perhaps we choose "open gestures," a type of gesturing that draws the audience in and holds attention.

At this point, you experience "knowing unknowing." You know you don't know the strategy. Your automaticity, or how automatically you perform the strategy when speaking, is 0%.

Third, we choose a specific drill or training method to help you practice open gestures. Perhaps you give practice speeches and perform the gestures. At this point, you experience "knowing knowing." You know you know the strategy.

And through practice, you formed a weak habit, so your automaticity is somewhere between 0% and 100%.

Fourth, you continue practicing the technique. You shift into "unknowing knowing." You forgot you use this type of gesture, because it became a matter of automatic habit. Your automaticity is 100%.

And just like that, you've experienced a significant and concrete improvement. You've left behind a weakness in communication and gained a strength. Forever. Every time you speak, you use this type of gesture, and you do it without even thinking about it. This alone can make the difference between a successful and unsuccessful speech.

Now repeat. Master a new skill. Create a new habit. Improve in a new area. How else could we improve your body language? What about the structure of your communication? Your persuasive strategy? Your debate skill? Your vocal modulation? With this process, people gain measurable and significant improvements in as little as one hour. Imagine if you stuck with it over time. This is the path to mastery. This is the path to unleashing the power of your words.

Access your 18 free PDF resources, 30 free video lessons, and 2 free workbooks from this link: www.speakforsuccesshub.com/toolkit

SPEAK FOR SUCCESS COLLECTION BOOK

I

HOW HIGHLY EFFECTIVE PEOPLE SPEAK CHAPTER

IV

MUNGER'S BIASES:

How to Reverse-Engineer the Psychology of Misjudgment

"THE CHALLENGE OF THE NEXT HALF-CENTURY..."

L YNDON B. JOHNSON TOOK THE STAGE ON May 22, 1964 to deliver the University of Michigan commencement address. He sought to inspire a new generation to pursue what he called "The Great Society." It was a progressive vision for a new America; a vision for greater equality, greater opportunity, and greater civic virtue. He sought to use the levers of government to drive broad-based improvement in the lives of all Americans, and to do so quickly. But first, he had to build the public awareness and the public support to push forward this agenda; to take big leaps toward The Great Society.

President Hatcher, Governor Romney, Senators McNamara and Hart, Congressmen Meader and Staebler, and other members of the fine Michigan delegation, members of the graduating class, my fellow Americans: It is a great pleasure to be here today. This university has been coeducational since 1870, but I do not believe it was on the basis of your accomplishments that a Detroit high school girl said, "In choosing a college, you first have to decide whether you want a coeducational school or an educational school." Well, we can find both here at Michigan, although perhaps at different hours. I came out here today very anxious to meet the Michigan student whose father told a friend of mine that his son's education had been a real value. It stopped his mother from bragging about him. I have come today from the turmoil of your Capital to the tranquility of your campus to speak about the future of your country. The purpose of protecting the life of our Nation and preserving the liberty of our citizens is to pursue the happiness of our people. Our success in that pursuit is the test of our success as a Nation. For a century we labored to settle and to subdue a continent. For half a century we called upon unbounded invention and untiring industry to create an order of plenty for all of our people. The challenge of the next half century is whether we have the wisdom to use that wealth to enrich and elevate our national life, and to advance the quality of our American civilization. Your imagination, your initiative, and your indignation will determine whether we build a society where progress is the servant of our needs, or a society where old values and new visions are buried under unbridled growth. For in your time we have the opportunity to move not only toward the rich society and the powerful society, but upward to the Great Society. The Great Society rests on abundance and liberty for all. It demands an end to poverty and racial injustice, to which we are totally committed in our time. But that is just the beginning. The Great Society is a place where every child can find knowledge to enrich his mind and to enlarge his talents. It is a place where leisure is a welcome chance to build and reflect, not a feared cause of boredom and restlessness. It is a place where the city of man serves not only the needs of the body and the demands of commerce but the desire for beauty and the hunger for community. It is a place where man can renew contact with nature. It is a place which honors creation for its own sake and for what it adds to the understanding of the race. It is a place where men are more concerned with the quality of their goals than the quantity of their goods. But most of all, the Great Society is not a safe harbor, a resting place, a final objective, a finished work. It is a challenge constantly renewed, beckoning us toward a destiny where the meaning of our lives matches the marvelous products of our labor. So I want to talk to you today about three places where we begin to build the Great Society – in our cities, our countryside, and in our classrooms.

Lyndon B. Johnson presented his proposal as the intersection between pain and progress; harms and benefits. This activated the reward and punishment tendency. He opened his speech with casual, lighthearted, complimentary, conversational pleasantries. This activated the liking and loving tendency. At the end of the quoted portion of the speech, he presented a preview of his solution by revealing three places where it would manifest itself. This activated the curiosity tendency. Throughout, he spoke of justice and injustice; right and wrong. This activated the Kantian fairness tendency. The lighthearted manner of his opening, as well as the promises of benefits throughout the speech, activated the reciprocation tendency. The term "The Great Society" itself activated the excessive self-regard tendency. The bold promises for a better future activated the over-optimism tendency. The pain-based language of injustice, as well as the implications of loss and missed opportunity, activated the deprival superreaction tendency. Phrases like "a society where progress is the servant of our needs, or a society where old values and new visions are buried under unbridled growth" activated the contrast misreaction tendency. The alliterative list of three places at the end of the quoted segment delivered in parallel form, "in our cities, in our countryside, and in our classrooms," with the repetition of the words "in" and "our" and the words arranged by increasing length, activated the availability mis-weighing tendency. Lyndon B. Johnson speaking these words – the President – activated the authority-misinfluence tendency. The appeals to reason sprinkled throughout activated the reason respecting tendency. And lastly, all of these biases working together, which form part of the bundle of biases referred to as "the psychology of human (mis)judgment," activates the Lollapalooza effect. In this section, we discover the 25 biases identified as part of the psychology of human misjudgment, where they come from, and how to use them. Lyndon B. Johnson used 13 of them, just at the beginning of his message.

WHAT IS THE PSYCHOLOGY OF HUMAN MISJUDGEMENT?

A cognitive bias is a systematic thinking process that typically acts as a shortcut to conserve mental resources. Cognitive biases, also called mental heuristics, can help us. Why? They keep our brains focused on important questions by taking resource-saving shortcuts around unimportant questions. But this is a double-edged sword: They can also lead to systematic, repetitive, predictable judgement errors as a result.

Charlie Munger is one of the world's most respected financial professionals, completely removed from the 2008 financial scandals. He is an investor, businessman, former real estate attorney, accomplished philanthropist, and the vice chairman of Berkshire Hathaway, Warren Buffett's firm. He lives an incredibly accomplished life. He surrounds himself with the world's most intelligent people. He is one of the world's most intelligent people. He observes countless memorable events teaching him life-long lessons, and he is quick to share them.

What is one of the most important life-long lessons he learned? This: Human beings have cognitive biases, and these can negatively impact us in dramatic ways by systematically causing us to make false judgements and reach erroneous conclusions.

Moreover, he learned this: People who succeed in life do so because they are aware of their biases and actively fight them. Want to succeed? Fight your biases so you can experience crystal-clear judgement in every single situation.

When did he identify these biases? Charlie Munger first identified these biases in his famed, renowned, and legendary Harvard Law School commencement address titled *The Psychology of Human Misjudgement*. He expanded on them over the multiple iterations of *Poor Charlie's Almanack:* a fantastic, practical, and informative chronicle of his extensive wisdom.

So, our working definition of the psychology of human misjudgment is the clump of psychological processes, cognitive heuristics, and systematic biases revealed in Munger's famous speech. Further in this section, we will cover one strategy with which to activate each bias.

WHAT IS AN EXAMPLE OF THE PSYCHOLOGY OF MISJUDGEMENT?

In the speech, Munger offers several examples of one component of the psychology of human misjudgment: the reward and punishment super-response tendency. He writes the following about Federal Express:

> One of my favorite cases about the power of incentives is the Federal Express case. The integrity of the Federal Express system requires that all packages be shifted rapidly among airplanes in one central airport each night. And the system has no integrity for the customers if the night work shift can't accomplish its assignment fast. And Federal Express had one hell of a time getting the night shift to do the right thing. They tried moral suasion. They tried everything in the world without luck. And, finally, somebody got the happy thought that it was foolish to pay the night shift by the hour when what the employer wanted was not maximized billable hours of employee service but fault-free, rapid performance of a particular task. Maybe, this person thought, if they paid the employees per shift and let all night shift employees go home when all the planes were loaded, the system would work better. And, lo and behold, that solution worked. (Munger, 1995)

HOW DO YOU OVERCOME THE PSYCHOLOGY OF MISJUDGEMENT?

Mindfulness defeats misjudgment. In the cult classic *Designing the Mind*, Ryan Bush reveals two powerful mechanisms for reducing the power our emotions have over us:

> One of the most highly touted benefits of mindfulness is its ability to pull a person out of undesirable emotions. [...] Though useful, mindfulness is not the most thorough solution to unwanted emotions. When you circumvent an emotion through mindfulness, the original emotional algorithm remains unchanged, and similar situations will continue to trigger it. [...] Immediately after an emotional response, our rational mind has the opportunity to reflect and reinterpret the information before it feeds back into our emotions. Reappraisal, also called reframing, is the act of reinterpreting the meaning of an emotional stimulus, altering the resulting emotional trajectory. (Bush, 2021)

These tools work against misjudgment as well. First, understand the biases. Second, apply mindfulness. Direct careful attention inward, and place a "gap of attention," or what Eckart Tolle calls a "gap of no-mind" (Tolle, 1997) in his bestseller *The Power of Now*, before the automatic bias-driven judgment. This awareness often dissolves the bias, turning what would have been an automatic thinking pattern into an intentional pause. Third, apply cognitive reappraisal, using system two thinking.

KEY INSIGHT:

The Most Powerful Force in a Speaker's Arsenal is the Vigilant and Attentive "Gap of No-Mind."

It Empowers the Speaker-Audience Connection, And Nothing is More Important.

HIJACKING MINDFULNESS AND COGNITIVE REAPPRAISAL

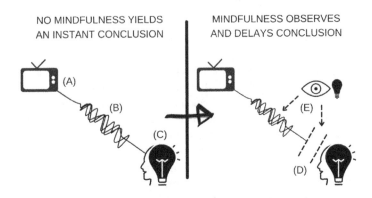

NO MINDFULNESS YIELDS
AN INSTANT CONCLUSION

MINDFULNESS OBSERVES
AND DELAYS CONCLUSION

FIGURE 36: Without mindfulness, an input (A) produces biased cognition (B) that leads to an instant conclusion (C). With mindfulness, you implement a "gap of attention" or a "gap of no mind" to delay the conclusion (D). Then, with metacognition, you can fill this gap with awareness of the biased thinking process (E). The next diagram details this more closely.

KEY INSIGHT:

Be Wary of Quick Answers to Difficult Questions. Interrogate Your Instincts. Reason Against Your Reflexes. It's Rarely Obvious.

TEASING APART THE PSYCHOLOGY OF MISJUDGMENT

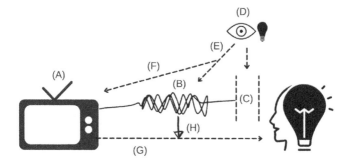

FIGURE 37: This will reveal more closely a strategy for defeating almost all cognitive biases. First, an input appears in your field of perception (A). You instinctively evaluate this input in a biased way (B). A gap of mindfulness, attention, or "no mind" (C) – whatever you seek to call it – prevents the biased cognition from yielding an instantaneous and likely incorrect conclusion. Metacognition (D) allows you to observe the biased thinking (E) (which demands knowledge of the biases). Then, you can perform cognitive reappraisal (F), reinterpreting the input and forming a correct, accurate, careful judgement based on system two cognition (G). As a result, you turn biased thinking into correct thinking (H).

REVISITING METACOGNITION

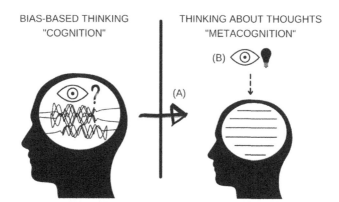

FIGURE 38: The shift labeled (A) in this diagram is the result of the process revealed in the previous diagram.

HOW DO YOU USE THE PSYCHOLOGY OF HUMAN MISJUDGEMENT IN YOUR COMMUNICATION?

Let's turn to the critical question: How can you use these biases in communication? How can you drastically, dramatically, and instantly improve your professional emails, proposals, pitches, presentations, meetings, and conversations? How can you easily influence nearly anyone and quickly persuade people to adopt your point of view? How can you supercharge your professional success by pulling back the curtain of human psychology and discovering the little-known secrets of human cognition that make people tick? Let's get into it.

A bias is bad if it creates misjudgment. Are you trying to persuade a boardroom to adopt your offering? Obviously, you don't perceive a purchase as a misjudgment. (Or maybe you do – in which case, pick a new line of work, or at least push a better product).

Would listening to you be good for them? Then it's not unethical to get one (or 25) of their biases to activate, and not just activate, but specifically turn on in your favor, subconsciously pushing them to listen to you.

In summary: You can use a bias in communication by activating it in people's minds to make them see things your way. You are using bad thinking to help people reach the right conclusions. In this way, you use the momentum of the psychology of misjudgment against itself, turning it into the psychology of accurate judgment, at least in that particular instance. Perhaps the seemingly oxymoronic phrase "the psychology of accurate misjudgment" describes this better; believing the right things for the wrong reasons, which is surely better than believing the wrong things for the wrong reasons.

In seeking to explain the origins of the biases, I adopted an evolutionary framework, as this is the framework Charlie Munger himself worked from in *The Psychology of Human Misjudgment*.

BIAS #1: REWARD AND PUNISHMENT TENDENCY

What is it? We adopt behaviors that benefit us, protect us from harm, or both.

Where does it come from? Human life is choosing between behaviors and experiencing a benefit or punishment as a result of the choice. Due to the inherent, inalienable, intrinsic nature of our existence in this universe, we evolved to seek benefits in all situations, and avoid losses in all situations. Of the two, the threat of a loss is more motivating. Loss-aversion strikes again.

How do you use it in communication? This strategy alone will make you a better communicator than the vast majority of your professional competitors. Understanding this one simple concept sets you apart from the majority of people who can't communicate effectively because they don't. Tell people doing what you want them to do will benefit them and protect them from loss. Tell them not doing it will waive a benefit and compel a loss. And remember this: The more benefit or loss at stake, the higher your persuasive punch.

UNDERSTANDING WHY PEOPLE DO WHAT THEY DO

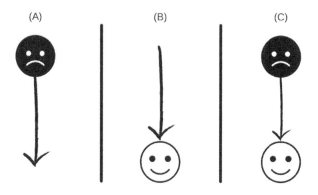

FIGURE 39: People move away from pain (A), toward pleasure (B), or both (C).

KEY INSIGHT:

Freud Thought Pleasure Motivated Most. Adler Thought Power. Frankl Thought Meaning.

In the Image Above, Replace "Pain" with "Meaninglessness" and "Pleasure" with "Meaning." Our "Will to Meaning" May Be Our Most Fundamental Motive.

BIAS #2: LIKING AND LOVING TENDENCY

What is it? We find people we like or love more persuasive, and we ignore their flaws and faults.

Where does it come from? We are social creatures who evolved in the presence of our fellow humans. This psychological tendency emerged because it conferred an evolutionary advantage (which helps us survive and thus pass on our genes containing the tendency). What's the advantage? Stronger human relationships protecting us in urgent moments.

How do you use it in communication? By applying the "two mosts" strategy. Candidly communicate to people about what they like most, and what they hate most; what they want most, and what they most seek to avoid, within the realm of what is relevant to the situation and appropriate. This invokes the previous bias. See how these strategies stack for greater persuasive power?

Blair Warren reveals another compelling framework for achieving likeability in his book *The One Sentence Persuasion Course:*

Justify their failures.
Encourage their dreams.
Allay their fears.
Throw stones at their enemies.
Confirm their suspicions. (Warren, 2013)

THE FIVE LITTLE-KNOWN KEYS TO IRRESISTIBLE INFLUENCE

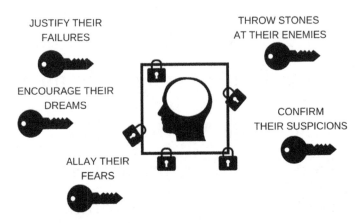

FIGURE 40: People "will do anything" (according to Blair Warren) for those who justify their failures, encourage their dreams, allay their fears, throw stones at their enemies, and confirm their suspicions. These are the five keys that will unlock cognitive defenses.

BIAS #3: DISLIKING AND HATING TENDENCY

What is it? We find people we hate less persuasive, while amplifying their faults and ignoring their positive qualities.

Where does it come from? This is a possible explanation, and one not scientifically validated. It's just my hypothesis. The disliking and hating tendency evolved because it activates the liking and loving tendency, which helps us survive by forming stronger human bonds.

The disliking and hating tendency offers no advantage on its own. But it activates something that does. How can hating someone make us love someone? The explanation is this: You hate person X, you hear person Y hates person X too, and now you and person Y are best buddies.

In other words, the disliking and hating tendency strengthens group bonds unified around hatred, which can help members of the in-group survive. Why? Because they have stronger bonds through the liking and loving tendency with other members of the in-group. We've seen historical disasters stemming from this time and time again. The short-term beneficiaries? Members of the in-group.

How do you use it in communication? People will immediately reject ideas from a source they despise. So, tell them an attack on your position came from a source they dislike. It's a form of inoculation, the art of inspiring people to strongly defend a position by expressing a weak attack. Dr. Drew Eric Whitman summarized it as follows in *Cashvertising:* "Warn of an impending attack. Make a weak attack. Encourage a strong defense." (Whitman, 2008)

"Now, [insert disliked person] will tell you that my position is [insert attack]. But..."

"[Insert politician of opposing party] wants you to believe that [insert thing you don't want them to believe]..."

Why does this work? Because telling people someone they disliked attacked your stance causes them to reject the attack, thus removing a potential objection against your position. Sneaky, isn't it?

BIAS #4: DOUBT AVOIDANCE TENDENCY

What is it? We tend to avoid doubt. We tune-out opposing information, gravitate toward unambiguous "truths," arbitrarily select sources of "truth," and prematurely leap to a conclusion to escape doubt, where we remain entrenched no matter what we hear.

Where does it come from? This stems from our tendency to conserve cognitive resources. Why did we evolve to conserve cognitive resources? In the dire straits of a life-threatening situation, we need our minds to be agile and active, not sluggish from the strain of unimportant decisions. In fact, all biases stem, in part, from our tendency to conserve cognitive resources. Why? They are all resource-saving shortcuts.

How do you use it in communication? People gravitate to doubtless communicators. Why do people who have little going for them but overconfidence rise to positions of leadership? Why do people take the suave, loud-talking, clear-speaking idiot seriously, just because he's confident, as if he's not still an idiot? Why do we accept a confident-sounding statement, but reject an identical statement when we sense even an ounce of doubt in the speaker's voice? Because we tend to avoid doubt.

Portray confidence in your message. Speak with no reservation. Speak loudly, strongly, and confidently, with your words, your voice, and your body language all conveying extreme self-belief. People will gravitate to you. They won't be able to help it. Your confidence will draw them to you like moths to a flame, because they sense your doubtlessness.

The follow section outlining the process of belief-transfer, by which your self-confidence earns the trust of others, as well as a step-by-step plan for conveying that confidence, is reprinted from my book *Trust is Power.*

"You have three languages: your word language, your body language, and your vocal language. And if you want to be a little edgy, you have visual aids, like PowerPoints. That makes four. Most of the credibility-boosting techniques we discussed fall in the domain of your word language: earning trust with the words you say. But not this one. This one directs the proper use of your body language and vocal language to the end of earning the trust and confidence of everyone in the room.

So, what's the strategy? How do you instantly get everyone's trust and confidence? How do you exude credibility not only with your words but with your body language and vocal tonalities?

You earn everyone's trust and confidence by using body language and vocal language that says you have your own trust and your own confidence, both in your abilities and in your ideas.

Before we get into the how, let's discuss the why. Why do certain patterns of body language and vocal tonalities exude immense trustworthiness?

We can manipulate our words with great ease. It's easy to speak confident words. We can read them right off of a paper. We can easily lie with our words. It's much more difficult to lie with our body language and vocal tonalities. As a result, people look to these nonverbal cues to decide whether or not to trust you. And certain use-patterns of these languages are associated with confidence – with self-trust.

Why does that self-trust transmute itself to the minds of your audience members as trust in you? Why is the trust you portray in yourself replicated in the minds of your audience? Why is there a belief-transfer? Three reasons.

First, mirroring: People mirror the sentiments they see in those around them. It's the story every time a grumpy person makes a happy person grumpy, or a happy person makes a grumpy person happy, simply through interacting; it's why waiters and waitresses nod when they say "would you like some dessert?" The table physically mirrors the nodding and then subconsciously thinks, "I am nodding! That must mean I want dessert." So, your audience has another bias, if it can be called a bias. In their psychology lies a sleeping giant, a massive lever you can pull for immense credibility: sentiment mirroring. This lever isn't just "up" or "neutral." It goes all the way from "up" to "down," which means it can work against you too. If you are not deliberately pushing the lever up, chances are you are accidentally pushing it down. It's why belief-transfer through paralanguage, "the nonlexical component of communication by speech, for example, intonation, pitch and speed of speaking hesitation noises, gesture, and facial expression," is so important. If your paralanguage is working against your lexical language, it ruins you. The same words spoken by different speakers, one with confident paralanguage and body language, and one without, receives drastically different reactions. The same words receive dramatically different judgements simply because of how each speaker delivered them. Mirroring is why paralanguage communicating hesitation on your part transmutes itself into your audience as hesitation. A study once reported that 55 percent of communication is visual (body language), 38 percent is vocal, and only 7 percent is verbal. If this study is even half-right (which I believe it is), you would be remiss to leave this credibility-lever untouched. And one final note: Emotional facial expressions and emotional vocal inflections are particularly effective at facilitating mirroring.

VISUALIZING THE MIRRORING PRINCIPLE

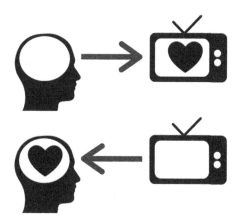

FIGURE 41: People mirror the emotions they see in others. This is part of the persuasive power of stories: People mirror the emotional tenor of the characters.

Second, snap categorization: As we discussed previously, people have preexisting categories in their heads, and when they see a new item (like a new speaker), they snap-categorize it to one of their preexisting categories. People will see quality X in you, remember that people in category Y have quality X (in addition to a bundle of qualities Z), and snap categorize you to category Y, thereby inferring that you also have the bundle of qualities Z. This probably explains why the halo effect is so powerful. The halo effect is when one strongly displayed positive quality leads an observer to assign a halo of unobserved positive qualities to the observed item. Perhaps snap categorization is the mechanism of the halo effect: perhaps people snap-categorize someone portraying the good quality of confidence to the category of "capable people," producing the halo of "smart, driven, and trustworthy," even though they never portrayed those qualities.

Capable people is a category. So is incapable people. So is smart people. So is credible people. There are multiple levels of categories and categories within categories. Items can belong to multiple categories. Snap-categorization contributes to belief-transfer because your body language and vocal language convey some of the first impressions upon which the snap categorization will be based. Therefore, confident body language and vocal language will snap categorize you to a category like "credible people," thereby transferring your trust in yourself and your ideas to the observer.

VISUALIZING THE SNAP CATEGORIZATION PRINCIPLE

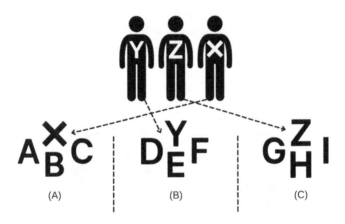

FIGURE 42: The audience perceives three people. The first person portrays quality Y. The audience has a mental category that includes items with the quality Y (B). Items in this category also have qualities D, E, and F. The audience lumps the first person into this category, transmuting the qualities D, E, and F to them. The second portrays quality Z, and he gets lumped into a category that transmutes the qualities G, H, and I to him (C) – qualities he never portrayed. Person X portrays quality X. You know the story: Now, he is not only a person who portrayed X, but a member of a mental category that includes the un-portrayed qualities A, B, and C (A), which the audience now transmutes onto him. This is a form of influence by mere association.

Confidence is self-fulfilling. This is the third major reason for belief-transfer. The person who speaks with calm and controlled confidence likely believes in themselves, and thus will get the damn thing done. Not only that, but people know that your confidence will help you win other people over because it helped win them over. They know your confident communication will create belief-transfer with other people as you progress toward your goal, and thus yet more belief-transfer occurs in their minds. They believe you'll get something done because you portray confidence, and they know that your confidence will get more people to believe you'll get something done, which will make you more likely to get it done, which makes them believe you'll get something done even more. This is closely tied to the credibility-cascade.

The following strategies verbally and nonverbally portray immense self-belief, transferring that belief to your audience and achieving immense credibility.

You must understand the perception-pathways; you must understand nonverbal input and output. You must have the ability to say to yourself, "If I do X with my body language or vocal language, it will have Y impact my audience." And not only must you understand cause and effect; you must also perform the input correctly. I'll teach you what to do and how to do it, and I'll show you easy ways to do it correctly, but the only guarantee is practice.

Use gentle modulation. Confident people who believe in themselves modulate their voices in gentle, smooth flows, not jagged, rapid, and jarring undulations. Vocal variation is always a necessity, but when you want to portray self-confidence, smooth out your vocal variation so that each variation happens slowly and smoothly. Don't let your vocal variations leap up and down in pitch, pace, and projection jarringly, like a roller-coaster.

HOW CONFIDENT PEOPLE SOUND: GENTLE MODULATION

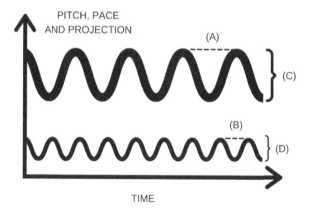

FIGURE 43: "Gentle" modulation, represented by the upper line, sounds confident. This is due to the longer – but not too long – gaps in time between peaks and valleys (A). "Shaky" modulation, represented by the lower line, sounds nervous. This is due to the short gaps in time between the peaks and valleys of the modulation (in pitch, pace, and projection) (B). It is possible that the extent of the difference between peaks and valleys in the gentle (C) and shaky (D) modulations is also a factor. Note that modulation need not be, and probably shouldn't be, a perfect "up and down" wave, with equal times between peaks and valleys. This is merely a symbolic representation for the purpose of contrasting the time disparities between peaks and valleys in the two styles. Treat both lines as starting from the same X value.

Use contained excitement. Confident people who believe in themselves feel like whatever they are currently working on might be their big breakthrough. And they know it's going to work as intended; they know they have it in themselves to seize the moment and achieve their objectives. This manifests itself in a voice as contained excitement. Confident people think their current project is their big opportunity. They think it is their shot at making it big. As a result, talking about it excites them. However, it must be excitement bubbling just under the surface. It must be excitement under the reigns of an objective, logical, and controlled mind; a mind that is patient and poised.

Use hypophora. Asking a rhetorical question and answering it immediately thereafter is hypophora. Questions are open loops. They create curiosity and suspense. Questions are scientifically proven to be memorable. Questions grab attention. The human mind likes questions. The human mind interacts effortlessly with questions. And asking a question mirrors the uncertainty some people might be feeling, while answering the question expresses your confidence cutting through the confusion with a clear answer. "Why does this happen? Because..." "But what can we do about it? The first step is..." "So, what does this mean for us? It means that..."

Use a slower pace. Nine times out of ten, a nervous speaker will speak quickly, unleashing a rapid-fire barrage of poorly enunciated, wavering words onto the perplexed audience. Why do they do that? Why do they speak quickly? Because they want to sit down. They want to leave the limelight. They don't want to be the center of attention anymore. They want to escape the stage, which is the source of their nervousness. Signal confidence by doing the opposite. Get up there, and speak slowly. Slowly walk to the podium. Stand silently for a few seconds. Then calmly begin to speak. Speak with precision; with enunciation; with controlled pace and deliberate articulation. Signal to everyone that you are both methodical in your ways and willing to command the limelight for as long as needed. An additional advantage is that speaking slower makes it easier for others to hear you, and easier for you to apply deliberate modulation.

Use the precise-analysis tonality. I call this the precise-analysis tonality because coupled with hypophora (a word-language technique), it is extremely compelling and produces the undeniable perception of confidence. You achieve open rapport tonality by raising your pitch at the end of a sentence. It signals a question; it is associated with uncertainty, impromptu and questioning rumination, and with imprecise confusion. But it grabs attention and signals the start of rapport, the start of two-way communication. And breaking rapport tonality signals the breaking off of rapport, conclusion, confidence, clarity, and the perception that your message needs no validation. You achieve breaking rapport tonality by dropping your pitch at the end of a sentence. Achieve precise-analysis tonality by applying open rapport to the question portion of a hypophora paradigm and breaking rapport to the answer. This vocal modulation patterns appears sharp, well-researched, perceptive, insightful, and analytical.

THE THREE PRINCIPAL VOCAL TONALITIES

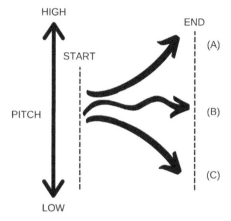

FIGURE 44: Open rapport tonality ends your sentence at a higher pitch than its starting pitch (A). Even tonality ends your sentence at roughly the same pitch as its starting pitch (B). Breaking rapport tonality ends your sentence at a lower pitch than its starting pitch (C).

THE PRECISE-ANALYSIS TONALITY VISUALIZED

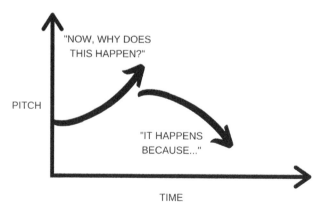

FIGURE 45: This tonality uses open rapport when asking a rhetorical question and breaking rapport when transitioning to the answer.

Use emphasized absolutes. Which of the following two sentences sounds more confident? "This might possibly be the best opportunity given the right circumstances." "This is the best possible opportunity." Definitely the second one. It uses absolutes: Not "this could be," but "this is." Not "I think this might be," but "this is." Not "it appears to me that..." but "the truth is that..." Assert yourself. Assert your ideas. Assert your analysis. And do it with absolutes. This is the payoff of staying in your circle of competency. Like hypophora, this calls upon a particular vocal technique for added impact: emphasis. Emphasis is using your vocal modulation to lend extra importance to a word, a sequence of words, or a unit of meaning. "This is the solution" becomes "THIS IS *THE* solution." Step one: Rephrase unclear, unassertive, weak sentences into absolute assertions (only if you are in your circle of competency, of course). Step two: Emphasize the absolutes. Say the first syllable slightly louder than the other words in the sentence, make the pitch of the word either higher or lower than the other words in the sentence (I recommend lower but higher has its place), say it slower than you normally would, stretch the vowel sound, and make a brief pause after you say it. And, as always, use your body to express the same sentiment as your voice; if you want to emphasize a word, do so with accompanying gestures as well.

Use upward facial positioning. What seems more confident to you, someone who is looking down, or someone who tilts their head ever-so-slightly up? Someone who tilts their head ever-so-slightly up. This indicates that you are not afraid to be seen, which evokes confidence. Don't over-tilt it; just a gentle upward nudge.

Use precise gestures. Confidence and control are so closely associated that one almost always indicates the presence of the other. Precise gestures are controlled; they are closely tied to your words; they are smooth, and they do not include anything unintentional. They are tied to your words because they mirror the flow of your modulation. Are you emphasizing the three big ideas in a proposal? Are you are providing verbal emphasis on the "first... second... third..." signposts? Do it with your gestures too. Take your right hand and touch your right shoulder. Twist your hand 90 degrees to the left (the tips of your fingers should point to your left). Extend your arm at the elbow until the angle between your upper arm and your forearm is about 45 degrees. Extend your fingers and moderately tense up your hand. Don't have T-Rex arms: If your elbow at this point is taped up against your side, unglue it. Then when you say "first," from this position, jut out your hand decisively and rapidly, but ever-so-slightly. Do the same for "second" and "third." Every new number, move the gesturing-point of the hand an inch lower. This is a precise, punchy gesture that delineates the items in the list.

Use deep breaking-rapport. The greater the breaking rapport (the lower the pitch drops at the end of a sentence), the greater the sense of conclusion. And breaking rapport is not limited to pitch, but projection and pace too. Your PPP qualities (projection, pace, and pitch) can all follow the breaking-rapport pattern.

KEY INSIGHT:

Miniscule Non-Verbal Cues May Kill A Good and Truthful Message.

THE THREE COMPONENTS OF VOCAL MODULATION

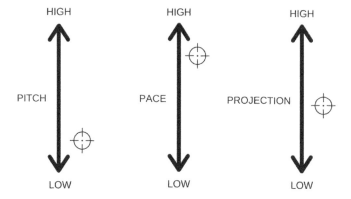

FIGURE 46: Vocal modulation occurs along three main spectrums: pitch, pace, and projection. We may conceive of vocal "texture" as a fourth dimension of modulation.

USING YOUR PPP QUALITIES FOR BREAKING-RAPPORT

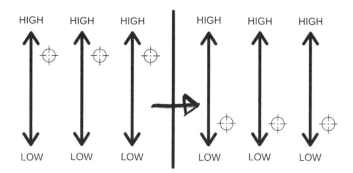

FIGURE 47: This reveals breaking-rapport along the three dimensions of vocal modulation.

Use **conviction-transitions**. Conviction transitions couple emphatic vocal modulation with a clump of words that delivers the impression of massive confidence and intellectual clarity. For example, after providing some evidence, a conviction-transition sounds like this: "What this unequivocally proves, beyond the shadow of a single doubt, is [claim]." Transitions connect what you just said to what you are about to say, and conviction-transitions embed in that connection a sense of the undeniable truth, the unequivocal reality, of what you are about to say. Other examples are as follow:

"What we know for sure is that..." "What is abundantly clear to us based on the massive mountain of evidence is that..." "What we can't deny is the obvious fact that..." The basic pattern is this: "What is [insert list of qualities portraying complete confidence] is that [insert claim]." The vocal component accompanying this is a sort of a power-voice; it's a rasp, a forceful inflection; it has force, potency, but sounds almost like a loud whisper, like you are employing the energy of your entire body to say what you are going to say, but you also want to restrain it at the same time. It emanates from deep inside of you and engages your entire speaking apparatus. I've heard it called a power-whisper before. Apply this tonality to your conviction-transitions and the subsequent claim. And sprinkle some magic conviction words in the transition (and elsewhere too), like so: "What this undeniably, unequivocally, and unambiguously proves." This is a personal favorite of mine because of the tricolon, the micro-repetition, the scesis onomaton, the alliteration, the "ly" rhyming, the flow, the assonance, and the assertive, confident meaning it imparts. Combined with confident delivery, few strategies can emulate its rhetorical force.

Use lower depth. It's simple, and it's silly, but it's true, and you should take advantage of it if you can: Speaking with a lower depth gives you gravitas, grandeur, and the perception of complete confidence. It hijacks the ancient perception pathways in our minds, as do many of these other strategies. We associate a lower depth with more confidence. Take two versions of the same exact statement. Have a deep-voiced speaker deliver it. Have a high-voiced speaker deliver it. The depth gives it more strength. It portrays more confidence, and for no rational reason whatsoever. Listen to former Mayor Pete Buttigieg speak, and you will observe how his baritone voice makes everything he says appear more confident. The same is true of Bernie Sanders and Barack Obama.

HOW VOICE DEPTH IMPACTS YOUR INFLUENCE

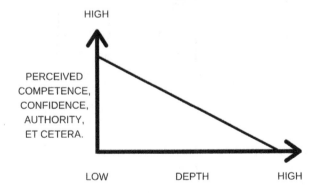

FIGURE 48: Scientific evidence shows us that for men, a low depth produces many positive perceptions.

Use stumble-free flow. Stumbles are not the problem. Reacting poorly to them is the problem. Accept stumbles if they come, do not panic, recollect yourself with the understanding that nobody cares if you stumble, and continue with confidence. That said, to prevent them, do the following: Know your content, have it firmly embedded in your mind instead of on paper (fumbling while looking back-and-forth at the paper is a source of countless stumbles), speak slowly, think one sentence ahead, lift your inhibitions and focus on the meaning you want to impart.

Use sentence-remapping. Phrases like "uh, um, like," and "you know" are known as conversation fillers. Why do they constantly pop into our speech? Because our brains tell themselves something like this: "Right now I am speaking, when I am speaking I must be making sound, if I am not making sound that means something I will compensate by making sound that doesn't mean anything but is still sound, because then I will at least be making sound, which is what I'm supposed to do when I'm speaking, and right now, I am speaking." And this is a difficult process to override, but it becomes easier over time if you watch yourself. Be like an attentive guard watching out for conversation fillers. Accept them if they come, but be aware of how often and when you use them. Simply take your awareness of your conversation fillers, and move it from your subconscious mind to your conscious mind. Once you pay conversation fillers notice, they slowly slide back out of your speech just as easily as they first slid in, simply because you mentally preempt them, planting an actual word or a pause where a conversation filler would have occurred. Eventually, this process because automatic. A pause is infinitely, dramatically, drastically better than a conversation filler. Just pause. And slow down so you can feel the conversation fillers coming, reacting with more ease and fluency. Sentence-remapping works when all else fails. When you are speaking, you often plan your next sentence. You have your next sentence booted up and ready to launch in your mind. So, you start speaking it. Let's say it was this: "And that's why we should vote for a Republican in 2020." You say, "And that's why…" which is great so far, but then "they" instead of "we." You accidentally deviated from your plan. Nine times out of ten, this is where a stumble or conversation filler will occur, and a mistake that blurs your clarity. Maybe you say this: "And that's why they- uh, um, we- should vote for a Republican in 2020." But sentence-remapping circumvents this common pitfall. It alters the plan to flow with the mistake, thereby removing the conversation filler and stumble. It alters the plan to render the mistake invisible. For example, like this: "And that's why they, …*(ditch the original plan and reform the planned sentence to flow with the mistake)…* the Republican party, should get the support of our votes and voices in 2020." See how remapping the sentence to flow with the mistake instead of sticking to a plan you already deviated from circumvents the error? It all comes down to this: Don't go back to satisfy the plan you had, go forward with a new plan. Some people do this automatically and naturally. Some people need specific practice in this technique. But it is a powerful one nonetheless.

Use sentence-chains. One of the most common confidence-precluding fears is your mind going blank when you're in front of everyone. Think about it. It's pretty scary, right? You have a brilliant set of ideas to share, but then they get vacuumed out of your mind, leaving it empty right as you claim the floor. 20 seconds pass. You've said nothing.

30. 40. A minute. Two minutes. Embarrassed, you excuse yourself. Scary, right? No, not at all. Don't listen to this part of your brain. And realize that all you have to do to instantly generate valuable content to share with your audience is to apply the sentence-chain principle. Pick the single most important thing you want to say, summarize it in one or a few sentences, say it, and then simply chain the rest of your communication off of that. Simply say something, and build your next something off of the first something. This forms a continuous chain of fluent, natural sentences, simply because one leads to the other. By having a sentence behind you to build your next one on, you give your mind the necessary stimulus to quickly and fluently produce the content you want to share.

HOW TO MASTER EASY EXTEMPORANEOUS SPEAKING

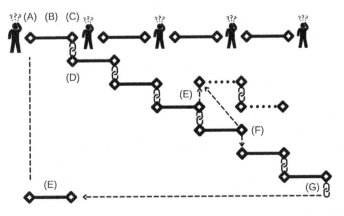

FIGURE 49: When you must speak extemporaneously, you may experience some difficulty fluently finding your content; your sentences (A). When you find your first sentence after some effortful thinking (B), you have two choices. You can either proceed in this manner (C), effortfully thinking of your content and appearing unsure, nervous, and inhibited as you need to brainstorm every sentence all-over again, or you can apply the sentence-chaining principle (D). Your first sentence was the most important piece of content you needed to get across. The sentence-chaining principle then uses this as a launching pad into the second sentence, chaining the start of the second sentence to the end of the first one. Perhaps three sentences later, you receive another two sentences to incorporate (E), but you have a more important sentence to deliver. After you deliver it, you may find that you don't have an easy, natural chain from your previous sentence. So, you recall and use the deferred two sentences (F). When you conclude, you chain the final sentence (G) back to the first (E).

Use confidence-words and confidence-phrases. Some words communicate uncompromising confidence in your abilities, your analysis, and your ideas. "Self-evident, doubtlessly, completely, dramatically, drastically," are some examples. Sprinkle these words throughout your communication to appear more confident. It's the difference between "This is a good idea" and "This is doubtlessly and self-evidently the best idea for us now."

Use planted feet. When people lack confidence, they typically resort to one of two unconscious gestures: rapidly shifting their body weight from foot to foot, or walking forward and backward over and over again. None of that madness. None of it. Plant your two feet, and do not move unless you do so for a deliberate, intentional purpose, such as moving to another side of the room to engage people closer to that side. People may say they do it because planting their feet in a position and not moving around would make them seem stiff. That's not true at all, and it's also not the real reason they do it. They do it because they are incredibly nervous, which is okay. But minimize the impacts of it if you can by planting your two feet, which communicates that complete control and confidence instead of nervous energy is the state of your mind.

Use mid-ground projection. This is projection approaches the highest volume at which you can use your talking voice. Speak like you would to a professional contact in a loud restaurant. You'd talk much louder, but you wouldn't yell. Find the line where you go from speaking to shouting and tread near it. Projection signals confidence."

KEY INSIGHT:

Communication is Not Merely a Dance of Words. It Demands the Participation of the Entire Being.

Words, Voice, Body, Mind, Heart, Psyche, Soul... All Engaged, All Aligned, And All Aimed at the Truth.

BIAS #5: INCONSISTENCY AVOIDANCE TENDENCY

What is it? People tend to avoid acting inconsistently with past actions.

Where does it come from? Our innate human desire to limit confusion and conserve cognitive resources by organizing the world in artificially neat ways, in which we always acted correctly (meaning there is no need to be inconsistent with our past selves). We also conserve mental resources by thinking the following: "I probably thought this action through the first time, so this time, I'll trust my past self."

How do you use it in communication? Use consistency indicators. What are consistency indicators? Statements tying previous audience actions to your proposed action. Make it seem like doing what you want would be consistent with their history of related actions: "You've probably always done [insert related action – the basis for consistency]. The truth is that [insert your proposal] is essentially continuing this history of positive action, of [insert type of action], because [insert reasons]. This is just the next step of the journey you have been on for a long time."

USING THE PRINCIPLE OF CONSISTENCY TO INSPIRE ACTION

FIGURE 50: When evaluating a new option, people will be much more likely to accept it if it is consistent with their history of related actions.

BIAS #6: CURIOSITY TENDENCY

What is it? We want to know, particularly if we know there's something we don't know. For example, you're more curious if I say "there are ___ tons of bananas on Earth," than if I never said anything about Earth's aggregate banana tonnage.

Where does it come from? Evolution. Noticing a pattern here? If you are, that's because we also evolved to notice patterns. Why? Once again, to conserve mental resources. But how is it evolutionary? Knowing more, a function of a curious mind, helps us survive and pass on our genetic material. Thus, the genes creating curiosity survive.

How do you use it in communication? Open-loop rhetorical questions. What is an open-loop rhetorical question? I just used one. Want to get undivided attention when you speak? Want to command respect and own the room? Use these. They work because they expose a knowledge-gap, which makes the curiosity tendency more powerful and attention-grabbing.

Here's a specific formula that also activates the reward and punishment tendency: "How do other [insert description of audience] get [insert benefit] and prevent [insert loss]?" For example, "How do other small business owners get five times more customers and prevent breaking down their supply chains?"

"What is the best way to [insert goal] without suffering [insert specific difficulty]?"

"Why is it that [insert surprising event] happens the way it does?"

"What is the little-known truth about [insert subject] that the 'experts' won't tell you?"

NOT KNOWING WE DON'T KNOW VERSUS A KNOWLEDGE GAP

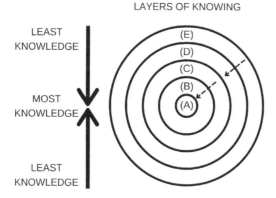

LAYERS OF KNOWING

FIGURE 51: (A) represents what you understand. (B) represents what you know. (C) represents what you think you know but don't know – the most dangerous layer of knowing. (D) represents what you know you don't know. (E) represents what you don't know you don't know. You have the most credibility in the center circle. Credibility tends to fall as you move outward. The goal of education, particularly continuing self-education once your professional career is under way, is to expand (A). (A) and (B) collectively represent your circle of competency. (C) is no-man's land. Moving what people don't know they don't know into the set of things they know they don't know creates tremendous curiosity. Expressing that you will move something they think they now but don't into the set of things they know and understand also creates tremendous curiosity.

BIAS #7: KANTIAN FAIRNESS TENDENCY

What is it? We tend to believe the world ought to be fair, we try to treat others how we want to be treated, and we get extremely, irrationally offended when someone breaches fairness.

Where does it come from? Anything that fosters positive relationships between humans helps us survive. The genes containing survival-boosting traits or tendencies, because we survive and reproduce when we have these tendencies, get passed on.

How do you use it in communication? Emotional arousal grabs attention. And negative emotions tend to produce the most emotional force. This is an emotional force that you, by now an expert communicator, can channel as a motivating drive to action. People don't act without an emotional impetus to do so.

If you can't create emotional arousal, you can't get (or hold) attention, command respect, influence, persuade, communicate effectively, and motivate people to act. And if our Kantian Fairness Tendency causes extreme offense when fairness is breached, if extreme offense is a highly arousing emotion, and if high emotional arousal is necessary for effective persuasion, convince people that fairness has been breached against them, and that you can fix it. This doesn't mean you should fabricate a breach in the fabric of fairness. To quote Curtis "50 Cent" Jackson III, "life is just unfair." He is correct: The world is sufficiently saturated with injustice that you don't need to fabricate any more to use this strategy.

But how do you properly expose a breach in the fabric of justice? With a simple, proven, step-by-step model. I call it the Victim-Perpetrator-Benevolence triad. Present a perpetrator who breached justice against victims and what you offer as a benevolent force for good that can heal the victims and protect them from the perpetrator, beat back and punish the perpetrator, and restore justice. Remember: This structure is subtle. Do not flatly state its constituent parts. Show, don't tell.

Step one: Tell people why someone treated them unfairly; explain why they are victims of a breach in the bond of fairness. You can tell them someone somewhere acted unfairly against someone else, inspiring the audience to join you as the "benevolent benefactors," or you can tell them they are the victims, in which case they need only to put their trust in you as the benevolent force for good who can repair the situation.

Step two: Who did this to them? Who, specifically, victimized them? This triad gains more force with a clear, vivid perpetrator, plus a vivid explanation of how they broke justice.

Step three: Paint yourself (and if you are selling something, your product or company) as a healing force for the victim, punishing the perpetrator and restoring justice. Explain how you can help. Don't just say "I can help," but elaborate on exactly how you can fix the broken justice and the victim's problem.

THE FIRST "VPB" VARIANT: "LET ME HELP YOU"

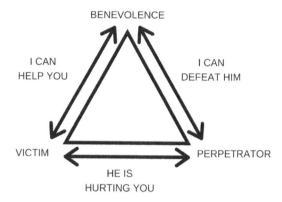

FIGURE 52: This reveals the first victim, perpetrator, benevolence variant. The audience is comprised wholly of people who are being victimized by the perpetrator.

THE SECOND "VPB" VARIANT: "JOIN ME TO HELP THEM"

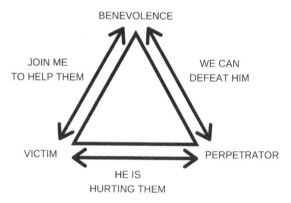

FIGURE 53: This reveals the second victim, perpetrator, benevolence variant. The audience is comprised wholly of people who you are calling to help you help the victims, who are not themselves necessarily victimized.

THE TWO "VPB" VARIANTS CAN OVERLAP

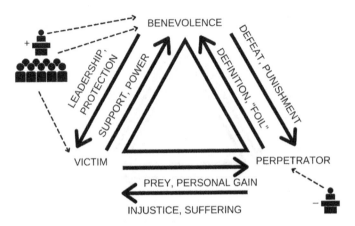

FIGURE 54: This reveals how the model connects its three ingredients; how each part connects to the others, and the relationships between them as well as what they offer one another. The audience can be both the victims, called to offer support to the benevolent force who can heal them, and also candidates for joining the benevolent force, called to help in healing the victims. The speaker's opposition is typically the perpetrator.

See how you can activate extremely complicated psychological machinery with relative ease, and thus experience dramatically more success as a communicator? The 2020 Democratic primary candidates used this strategy extensively. Andrew Yang said:

I believe everyone on this stage [benevolent force for good] would do the right thing by DREAMers [victims] in the first hundred days. I would make it a top priority [benevolent force for good]. I'm the son of immigrants myself. The fact is almost half of fortune 500 companies were started by an immigrant or children of immigrants [benevolent force for good]. Immigrants make our country stronger and more dynamic [benevolent force for good]. And immigrants are being scapegoated for issues they have absolutely nothing to do with [victims]. If you go to the factory in Michigan, it's not wall to wall immigrants [victims]. It's wall to wall robot arms and machines [perpetrators]. We have to send the opposite message of this administration [perpetrators] and, as your president, I think I could send a very clear message, where if you're considering immigrating to this country and I'm the president, you would realize my son or daughter can become president of the United States [benevolent force for good]. That's the opposite of the current administration [perpetrators] and that's the message I would love to send to the world [benevolent force for good].

Joe Biden said the following:

Well, I don't think they really do like the economy. Go back and talk to the old neighbors in the middle-class neighborhoods you grew up in [victims]. The middle class is getting killed [victims]. The middle class is getting crushed and the working class has no way up as a consequence of that [victims]. You have, for example, farmers in the Midwest, 40 percent of them could pay, couldn't pay their bills last year [victims]. You have most Americans, if they've received the bill for 400 dollars or more, they'd have to sell something or borrow the money [victims]. The middle class is not, is behind the eight ball [victims]. We have to make sure that they have an even shot [benevolent force for good]. We have to eliminate [benevolent force for good] significant number of these god-awful tax cuts [perpetrator] that were given to the very wealthy [perpetrator]. We have to invest in education [benevolent force for good]. We have to invest in healthcare [benevolent force for good]. We have to invest in those things that make a difference in the lives of middle-class people [victims] so they can maintain their standard of living [benevolent force for good]. That's not being done, and the idea that we're growing, we're not growing. The wealthy, very wealthy are growing [perpetrators]. Ordinary people are not growing [victims]. They are not happy with where they are [victims], and that's why we [benevolent force for good] must change this presidency [perpetrator] now.

BIAS #8: ENVY AND JEALOUSY TENDENCY

What is it? We dislike seeing possessions or achievements we want for ourselves in the clutches of others.

Where does it come from? Our inherent need to compete for limited resources, and our attempts to satisfy our unlimited demands with a finite pool of resources.

How do you use it in communication? You can use the envy and jealousy tendency to immediately add yet another emotional pull to your offer, making it more compelling and captivating.

How? How can you make anyone vigorously want anything by activating their envy and jealousy tendency? How can you immediately make your offer seem much more attractive, possibly raking in more money for the same product? (And you are a product, as are your ideas).

Here's how: Apply the formula "[insert rival] has [insert what you are offering] and they have protected themselves from [insert harm] while enjoying [insert benefit]."

Let's draw an example from the critically acclaimed show *Mad Men.* (It's my favorite show. I've watched all 7 seasons, with 15 hour-long episodes per season, probably 10 times by now. You do the math if you want).

The protagonist's advertising agency, Sterling Cooper Draper Pryce (SCDP), is locked in a competitive grapple with an agency called Cutler Gleason and Chaough (CGC). Anyone trying to sell something to CGC, let's say a professional branding service, could activate the envy and jealousy tendency like this: "SCDP recently picked up a professional branding service, protecting themselves from the rat race of obscurity while benefiting from a mountain of new business with high billings and a national presence."

Now not only does CGC want the service for its inherent benefits, they also want it because SCDP has it and they don't. The more reasons you create to want your offer, and the more emotionally compelling those reasons, the more persuasive you become. And nobody said you have to use their honorable emotions. Jealousy works just fine. But the "golden-rule" emotion, the reciprocation tendency, is available too. Let's turn to it now.

BIAS #9: RECIPROCATION TENDENCY

What is it? We seek to reciprocate behaviors, positive or negative.

Where does it come from? Evolution. Much like the loving and liking tendency, it fosters stronger human bonds. And it yields punishment in the form of negative reciprocation when those bonds are betrayed, disincentivizing betrayal.

How do you use it in communication? This one is easy. And it's incredibly powerful. Great ease and massive efficacy wrapped up in one strategy – a good combination if I ever heard one.

How do you activate the reciprocation tendency, until people scramble to do you favors? How do you get undivided attention, complete respect, and higher rates of compliance with your professional communication? How do you make professional prospects gravitate to you, channeling opportunities in your direction?

Give them something. A free bite to eat. A discount. A free white-paper or industry report. A free consultation. A free referral.

There's no such thing as a free lunch. None of these are really free. There's a price: A strong psychological need to repay the favor in the future. Make it a "no-catch" gift. Make it a genuine kindness. Even if you don't expect anything return, and even if you don't seek any direct benefit, you will still get something powerful back: the need to reciprocate.

If you are speaking to them, they will pay significantly more genuine consideration to your persuasive appeals, and pay you significantly more attention and respect.

BIAS #10: INFLUENCE FROM MERE ASSOCIATION

What is it? When we see a new item clumped in a group of good items, we believe it is also good. When we see a new item clumped in a group of bad items, we assume it is also bad. We identify the traits of a new item by extrapolating from its surroundings.

Where does it come from? Our need to conserve cognitive resources.

How do you use it in communication? When you're persuading, you deal with two elements. The first? An alternative to your proposal, including inaction. The second? Your proposal.

Not only do you want to nudge them toward the second, you want to keep them from leaping towards the first. How? Attach words with negative sentiment to the alternative. Describe painful associated anecdotes. Use words like "abysmal, painful, difficult, tiresome, self-defeating, and unnecessary."

The core of your message – that the alternative is abysmal –influences them consciously. But they also subconsciously perceive a compelling association between the alternative, the negative emotional states, and the words with negative connotations. And mere association influences us. The alternative is inundated by a clump of negative items, so it must be negative too.

And reverse it: Attach positive words and anecdotes to your proposal. Influence by mere association empowers your proposal just as it disempowers any alternatives.

HOW TO INFLUENCE WITH ASSOCIATION PSYCHOLOGY

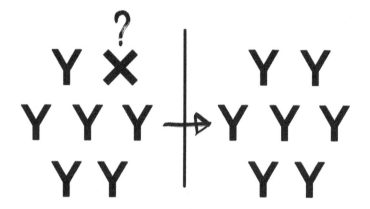

FIGURE 55: When we see a new item clumped with items of a particular kind, we tend to assume that it too is one of those items. This is influence by mere association. Present the proximity between what you argue against and patently bad items, and association psychology will blend the two together. Present the proximity between what you argue for and patently good items, and association psychology will blend the two together.

BIAS #11: SIMPLE, PAIN-AVOIDING PSYCHOLOGICAL DENIAL

What is it? We habitually ignore or deny psychologically painful information until it is bearable.

Where does it come from? Our evolutionary need to maintain an active and agile mind, unbridled by draining concerns.

How do you use it in communication? When you are persuading, you are pushing a solution to a problem. And the key of effective persuasion is that the bigger the harms of the problem, the bigger the pull of the solution. This is true unless one obstacle derails you: their denial tendency blinding them to the problem altogether.

This is a big obstacle for you. Until you defeat denial tendency and validate the problem, you can't create the emotional pull necessary for motivation and, ultimately, action.

How can you overcome denial tendency? How can you guarantee your persuasive appeals don't die on arrival? How can you protect yourself from the biggest persuasive obstacle? Two strategies working as one: prospect-driven hypothetical admissions matched with the presentation of incontrovertible proof. Ask questions prompting them to hypothetically consider the consequences of a problem. They sound like this: "If [insert problem] were true, how would that impact you?" They sound like this: "If [insert proof] were the case, would you see that [insert problem] is in fact a serious threat?" And they sound like this: "If [insert proof] were true, would that convince you to reconsider your position on [insert claim]?" These are prospect-driven hypothetical admissions. And depending on the question, they may feel compelled to offer their assent to avoid sounding unreasonable. Normally they would resist this temptation, as in a debate, but they are more likely to give in if it is hypothetical.

HYPOTHETICALS CIRCUMVENT REACTANCE AND DENIAL

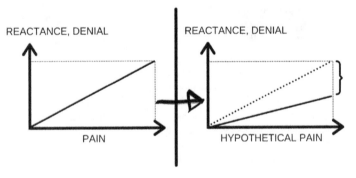

FIGURE 56: As psychological pain rises, so do reactance and denial. As hypothetical pain rises, so do reactance and denial, thought to a significantly lesser degree. The difference in the extent of denial between pain and hypothetical pain is the benefit of this strategy.

Then apply declarations like this one: "Well, I agree with you. And sadly, this is the case. [Insert proof] is true according to [insert source]. But so is [insert further proof] and [insert further proof]. Sadly, [insert problem] is very real and very harmful, and that impacts you by, like you said, [insert their exact words they used when answering the first question hypothesizing on the impact]."

Why does this work? It asks them to hypothesize on the negative harms of a problem that could happen; something that could be true, but probably isn't – until you prove it is. You circumvent psychological denial by painting pictures of the problem in a hypothetical world. There's much less psychological denial in a hypothetical world.

In a debate, they won't zealously avoid answering these questions to your favor. Why not? because it's all hypothetical – until you show them, and the audience, that it isn't.

"If X, would you Y?"

"X."

This beats flatly stating "X," because in this situation, they will often say this: "if Z, not X."

"Z."

BIAS #12: EXCESSIVE SELF-REGARD TENDENCY

What is it? We all think we are above average.

Where does it come from? Humans have a biological tendency to fight, physically and otherwise, only if we perceive our opponent as unwilling or unable to fight back successfully. Excessive self-regard tendency makes us willing to fight. So, we avoid a fight in the first place, survive, and pass down excessive self-regard tendency.

How do you use it in communication? People trust those with symmetrical worldviews. How do you present world-view symmetry? How do you show them you see the world how they do? Match their excessive tendency to over-regard themselves. How? Not by over-regarding yourself, but by over-regarding them.

Describe their organization as "cutting-edge, innovative, ahead of the curve." Describe their personnel as "ambitious, capable, better than most." Describe their institution as "impactful, prestigious, well-known."

BIAS #13: OVER-OPTIMISM TENDENCY

What is it? Excess optimism is the normal human condition.

Where does it come from? It helps us conserve mental resources. It ties to many cognitive biases and mental heuristics. It lightens the burden of life on a difficult planet.

How do you use it in communication? People follow visionaries. You can't persuade if you don't sell your vision. You must "screen-share" your mental movie, so they see what you see, so they see all the unfulfilled potential your proposal can help them actualize.

How does over-optimism tie into this? How can you become a compelling communicator and come off as an astute visionary by activating this bias? How can you use it to achieve extreme influence and easy persuasion?

Don't hold back in describing your vision. Be straightforward about the bounty of benefits. Provide some perfunctory proof, some quantitative evidence from reliable sources, and then use the authority this offers you to launch into vision-sharing; optimistic and overwhelmingly positive vision-sharing. You'll match their optimism. Or, rather, you'll reignite their latent optimism after a layer of pessimism calcified over it. And this excites people. Optimism is, by definition, the anticipation of a future benefit.

And you want people to anticipate the accrual of future benefit as the consequence of adopting your proposal.

BIAS #14: DEPRIVAL SUPERREACTION TENDENCY

What is it? Loss aversion, but something more, too: Once we lose something, we react with overwhelming intensity – irrational intensity – in trying to restore the loss. You know loss aversion can overweigh the pain of a loss, rendering it up to twice as painful as an equivalent gain. Thus, if someone loses $1,000, gaining $1,000 "back" is not only a gain in the form of an additional $1,000; it also eases the pain of the initial loss, which can offer more psychological benefit than the gain, simply because the pain of the loss was twice that of a gain.

We also tend to place an irrational amount of effort in pursuing a goal we just barely missed. This is why slot machines are rigged to produce "near-misses" in relatively higher, non-random frequencies. In *Atomic Habits*, author James Clear writes the following about the neurotransmitter dopamine:

> Habits are a dopamine-driven feedback loop. When dopamine rises, so does our motivation to act. [...] It is the anticipation of a reward – not the fulfillment of it – that gets us to take action. The greater the anticipation, the greater the dopamine spike. (Clear, 2018)

This may explain our proclivity to intensify our chase of goals we just barely missed. Anticipation creates dopamine. Dopamine creates action. Near-misses temporarily raise anticipation, which raises dopamine, which creates action.

MAPPING THE DOPAMINE TRAJECTORY OF "NEAR-MISSES"

HOW NEAR-MISSES TRIGGER ENTHUSIASTIC ACTION

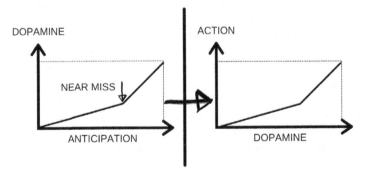

FIGURE 57: As dopamine rises, so does anticipation. Or, as anticipation rises, so does dopamine. It is difficult to isolate the explanatory factor in this case. In any case, a "near miss" of the

desired goal temporarily produces higher anticipation and higher dopamine. As dopamine rises, so does action. And you are speaking to persuade action.

Where does it come from? 1,000,000 years ago, behaviors tied to protecting what we had – territory, resources, food, members of our tribe – probably helped us survive more than striving to get more. Thus, we are evolutionarily and genetically coded to avoid loss and play the game of life conservatively.

How do you use it in communication? Raise the stakes and explain what they can lose. You can also apply the "you just missed it!" strategy. Tell them they were so close to achieving a goal. A deeply desired goal was in their reach, and they barely missed it. Paint your proposal as placing the "almost there!" goal in their reach once and for all.

KEY INSIGHT:

Those Who Seek to Understand the Psychological Motives of Mankind Must Study Both Evolution and Theology.

Learn Everything. For Soon, You Will Find Nothing is Superfluous.

BIAS #15: SOCIAL-PROOF TENDENCY

What is it? We follow the crowd and look to others for direction.

Where does it come from? We have two salient evolutionary needs genetically coding this tendency. We need to conserve mental resources and we need the protection offered by a tribe. Social proof conserves mental resources because instead of using mental calories to make our own decisions, we outsource our judgement to the crowd. Second, it helps us maintain "group-member status," because aligning our actions with the crowd offers us membership into it.

How do you use it in communication? Make statements evidencing a crowd acting how you want your prospects to act, or thinking how you want them to think. "87% of [insert audience identifier, like 'small business owners'] state that [insert the problem you solve] is a massive drain of funds." "97% of our customers left us a five-star review on Amazon." "So far, 30,000 happy customers have used our product." These are examples of quantitative social proof. Qualitative social proof would be, for example, what a small number of specific reviewers said in detail. The number of positive reviews is quantitative; what one of the reviews says, in detail, is qualitative. Which one should you use? False dilemma. Use both.

THE SOCIAL PROOF HEURISTIC VISUALIZED

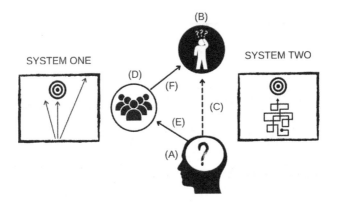

FIGURE 58: Prompted by a question (A), we seek to evaluate the target question of "what we should do" (B). However, this evaluation (C) is difficult. So, we substitute the heuristic question "what other people are doing" (D), evaluate this (E), and transfer the answer to the target question (F).

BIAS #16: CONTRAST-MISREACTION TENDENCY

What is it? We judge items not on their inherent qualities, but on how they compare to points of reference. This is covered more fully in a later section, but is also part of *The Psychology of Human Misjudgment.*

Where does it come from? This is a side-effect of our cognitive machinery. It can cause silly and frequent misjudgments. We can't judge anything on its own, unless we have a point of comparison. We're happy with our $60,000 salary until we find out our coworker makes $62,000. But $60,000 equals $60,000, no matter what anyone else makes. Sadly, that's not how our judgement works. We always use points of comparison to reach conclusions.

How do you use it in communication? This bias is ubiquitous in communication. Countless strategies activate it. How can you use the contrast-misreaction tendency to inspire vigorous and enthusiastic action in your favor? How can you influence people to see things your way, do what you want, and help you advance in your professional career? With the path-contrast structure, activating this powerful psychological heuristic in a compelling way.

Persuading is trying to get someone to take one path instead of another. And path one is meaningless and unpersuasive on its own. Path one versus path two is where real persuasion happens.

The simple, straightforward, step-by-step path-contrast process is as follows. Step one: Identify path one; what you want them to do. Explain it. Step two: Identify path two; the alternative. Explain it. Step three: Explain the benefits of path one. Step four: Explain the harms of path two. Step five: Repeat steps three and four until you heighten the contrast as needed.

BIAS #17: STRESS-MISINFLUENCE TENDENCY

What is it? We make premature, extreme, and irrationally quick decisions under high stress.

Where does it come from? When a saber-tooth tiger jumped in front of us, creating high cognitive stress, we needed to make a quick decision: run, or fight?

In this situation, a part of the brain called the amygdala turns on. It shuts down the prefrontal cortex, which performs slow, methodical, deliberate logical operations.

The problem with this? The amygdala turns on and suppresses logic even if we need logic to solve the source of the stress; even if it's a sales pitch or an interview (primarily logic-demanding), not a saber-tooth tiger (primarily agility-demanding).

How do you use it in communication? Create stress, then ease it. Raise the stakes, then offer an escape. Paint a painful problem, then present a solution. Apply pressure, then offer relaxation.

This is an act of Kairos, an Ancient Greek term with many meanings. In archery, Kairos denotes the moment in which an arrow may be fired with sufficient force to penetrate a target. In weaving, Kairos denotes the moment in which the shuttle could be passed through threads on the loom. Similarly, in his *Kaironomia*, E.C. White defines Kairos as the "long, tunnel-like aperture through which the archer's arrow has to pass" and as the moment "when the weaver must draw the yarn through a gap that momentarily opens in the warp of the cloth being woven." Both are examples of a decisive act predicated on precision. (Onians, 1951).

THE STRESS-MISINFLUENCE TENDENCY AND "KAIROS"

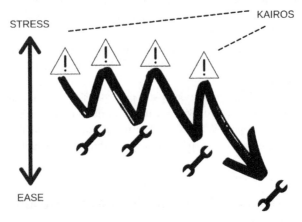

FIGURE 59: The ancient Greek masters of rhetoric – known as "rhetors" – found the concept of Kairos to be absolutely fundamental to persuasion. It is also a metaphysical concept, woven into the fabric of our reality: conflict and resolution. Describe a stressful problem; ease the stress by promising a way out. Repeat this process, creating stressful conflict and following it with easeful resolution. How does this definition link with the "opportune moment" definitions? The "opportune moment" is the one when the world provides conflict for your proposed solution to resolve; when reality validates the need for your idea.

THE PROBLEM, AGITATE, SOLUTION, AGITATE STRUCTURE

STRUCTURE	"PASA" Structure			
BEHAVIORAL DUALITY	Escape		Approach	
SEMANTIC DUALITY	Problem		Solution	
EMOTIONAL DUALITY	Pain		Pleasure	
TEMPORAL DUALITY	Now		Later	
EXISTENTIAL DUALITY	Here		There	
DESIRE DUALITY	Aversion		Desire	
MODAL DUALITY	Chaos		Order	
STATE DUALITY	Actual		Potential	
KAIROS DUALITY	Conflict		Resolution	
THE SEQUENCE	**Problem**	**Agitate**	**Solution**	**Agitate**

"You have a problem. Here's why this is a problem: [stress-induce]. But I can help you. Here's how I can prevent these harms: [stress-ease]."

Stress puts them in a mental state of rapid-response, making it easier to persuade through emotion, and to elicit an "impulse buy." People impulsively jump to your solution if and only if they have something to escape; if and only if they have something to jump away from: stress. They won't make the leap in the absence of some stress-inducing information triggering the need for escape. And if there is no stress-inducing reality your proposal solves, why should they adopt it?

BIAS #18: AVAILABILITY MIS-WEIGHING TENDENCY

What is it? We overweigh evidence that comes quickly to mind.

Where does it come from? Conservation of mental resources. It's a mental short-cut that is a rough, approximate, "good enough" judgement in most cases. In other cases? It produces serious misjudgments.

How do you use it in communication? We covered this in the section on availability:

Strategy #1: Tell Stories
Strategy #2: Use Pathos
Strategy #3: Use Sententia
Strategy #4: Project Images
Strategy #5: Make it Personal
Strategy #6: Keep it Simple
Strategy #7: Provide Tangible Takeaways
Strategy #8: Always Summarize
Strategy #9 Invoke Fear
Strategy #10: Invoke Desire
Strategy #11: Use Mnemonics
Strategy #12: Make it Eloquent
Strategy #13: Visualize Data

I included the bias here because it was part of Charlie Munger's initial list of 25 biases.

BIAS #19: USE IT OR LOSE IT TENDENCY

What is it? We lose stored information if we don't use it.

Where does it come from? To conserve our finite budget of mental resources, we gradually dump information we don't use.

How do you use it in communication? Make your message practical. Make it educational. Provide information people can use to improve their lives. Inspire them to adopt thinking patterns they will use again and again. They won't forget it. They'll use it, not lose it.

BIAS #20: DRUG MISINFLUENCE TENDENCY

This is what Charlie has to say about this tendency:

This tendency's destructive power is so widely known to be intense, with frequent tragic consequences for cognition and the outcome of life, that it needs no discussion here to supplement that previously given under [the section] "Simple, Pain-Avoiding Psychological Denial." (Munger, 1995)

There is one exception: offering prospects coffee. Coffee makes your audience more attentive, and gives them a dopamine hit. The happier people are, the more open they are to persuasive appeals. It also activates reciprocity, likeability, and related biases.

BIAS #21: SENESCENCE-MISINFLUENCE TENDENCY

This is wholly irrelevant to communication, but is part of Charlie's 25. This is what he has to say about it: "Continuous thinking and learning, done with joy, can somewhat help delay what is inevitable."

BIAS #22: AUTHORITY-MISINFLUENCE TENDENCY

What is it? We find authority figures persuasive.

Where does it come from? This probably facilitated more fruitful and well-organized tribe- and group-relations, and as a result, helped us survive. It also conserves mental resources. It would strain our cognitive resources to learn the entire medical discipline when we have a sickness. It's more efficient to outsource to an expert.

How do you use it in communication? This one is tremendously powerful, and like almost all cognitive processes, acts as a double-edged sword. People will do nearly anything if an authority figure tells them to. It's part of the horror of warfare.

We listen to doctors, coaches, and experts because they are doctors, coaches, and experts. When a doctor or scientist says something, we take it at face value.

How can you use this proven and powerful psychological tendency for more compelling communication? How can you use it for easy persuasion? How can you portray your authority without bragging and achieve instant trust?

Answer these questions: What are your credentials? What is your experience? Why should they trust you? And you can also take advantage of the authority-transfer principle: You adopt some of the authority of the evidence you advance, the experts you cite, and the organization you represent. Keep that in mind, and activate authority-transfer in tandem with presenting direct authority.

KEY INSIGHT:

The Basis of Legitimate Authority is Ability. Of Immoral Authority, Power.

AUTHORITY-TRANSFER VISUALIZED

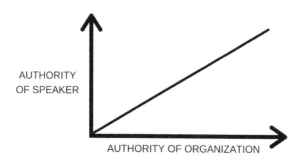

FIGURE 60: As the perceived authority of the organization you represent rises, so too does your perceived authority.

BIAS #23: TWADDLE TENDENCY

What is it? Our tendency to procrastinate.

Where does it come from? Our innate drive to keep cognitive load down. Why procrastinate? Because it is easy. Starting the next task, or taking the next action, taxes our discipline. Our discipline functions like a finite budget: it runs out eventually. After a long day, when we know the next task is mentally straining, we twaddle because it is so much easier.

How do you use it in communication? This one is deeply detrimental to effective persuasion if left unchecked. It can undermine everything you say. It can kill an otherwise perfect presentation or pitch. It can ruin your attempts to influence, no matter what else you say or do correctly. Even if you activate the other biases, even if you provide evidence, logic, and emotional appeals, and even if the people like you on a personal level, the twaddle tendency can derail everything.

How do you avoid this? By answering the question "why should I do this now?" What is the self-inflicted problem so many communicators face? They focus on the wrong question. They focus on answering the question "why?" This is a flawed approach. You can convince someone on the "why?" but they will not act until you definitively answer the question "why now?" Remember this mantra: not "why?" but "why now?"

BIAS #24: REASON RESPECTING TENDENCY

What is it? We respect requests and believe statements justified by reasons.

Where does it come from? One of the processes we use to conserve cognitive resources is called substitution. We substitute an easy question for a hard one. How does this create reason-respecting tendency? We substitute the easy question "is there a reason for this?" for the hard question "is this a good and valid reason?" Simply hearing a reason often does the trick, even if it is invalid.

How do you use it in communication? Provide justifiers and meta-justifiers. Meta-justifiers are incredibly compelling, captivating, and attention-grabbing. They justify the communication itself: "I'm calling today because I want to tell you about..." Regular justifiers justify a particular request or a statement: "[insert statement] because [insert reason]," or "could you [insert request] because [insert reason]?"

Let me paraphrase a study into the nature of human compliance, and how to get more of it. People in an office are waiting in a long line for a printer. The experimenter cuts the person in front, in one of three ways. One way is for no reason, with no justification. "Can I cut you?" This garners the lowest compliance of the three. Another way is with a justifying reason. "Can I cut you because I need to be in a big presentation in five minutes?" This garners the most compliance of the three. Another way is with a reason, but one that doesn't logically justify the request. "Can I cut you because I need to print these documents?" This "bad reason" only garnered moderately less compliance than the logically sound "good reason."

People respect reasons. They demand that actions are justified by a reason. They often need to hear that there is a reason, without paying regard to its validity. Human minds have a checkbox: "Does this action have a supposed reason for it?" The validity of the reason, and whether or not it logically justifies the action, takes a backseat. This is not to say the validity is irrelevant: Valid reasons command the highest compliance.

HOW REASONS AND JUSTIFICATIONS IMPACT COMPLIANCE

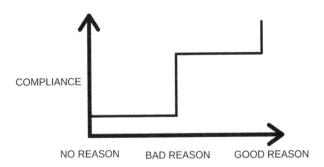

FIGURE 61: Compliance increases significantly when moving from no reason to a bad reason, and increases again by a smaller increment when moving from a bad reason to a good reason.

This seems rudimentary, but people frequently forget to put a "because" after their asks. No reason is the least effective. Any reason is much more effective. A valid reason is moderately more effective than an invalid one.

We often look at reasons without judging their quality, only seeking to assure their existence in binary fashion.

While fake reasons work, as per this study, I only revealed it to reveal the immense impact of a "because." That an invalid reason is significantly more persuasive than no reason is not an argument for producing fewer real justifiers, but more: lots more. After all, the valid reason garnered the most compliance.

BIAS #25: THE LOLLAPALOOZA TENDENCY

What is it? Any psychological tendency pushing a particular behavior persuades. Multiple pushing the same behavior persuade exponentially more, resulting in massive persuasive force. Munger calls it a "lollapalooza effect." It happens when multiple cognitive biases converge all at once, in the same direction.

Where does it come from? It comes from the individual influence of each bias. Combined, their persuasion is more than their sum. It is a case of one plus one equals three.

How do you use it in communication? You know how to activate the other 24 cognitive biases. So how do you activate the lollapalooza tendency? Activate multiple of the other biases, all at once, and in the same direction. You already know exactly how to activate them individually, and the results will shock you when you combine their persuasive power.

THE LOLLAPALOOZA TENDENCY

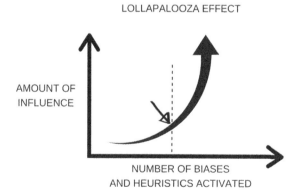

LOLLAPALOOZA EFFECT

AMOUNT OF INFLUENCE

NUMBER OF BIASES
AND HEURISTICS ACTIVATED

FIGURE 62: Activating multiple cognitive biases toward the same persuasive objective in the same people at the same time is often a case of 1 + 1 = 3 (or 100 + 100 = 1,000 – why not?). The biases and their persuasive influence complement each other and achieve synergy. At a certain point, the biases hit a "critical mass" that sets off a Lollapalooza effect which creates explosive and enthusiastic action – disproportionately more action than would be achieved by subtracting just one bias, according to the theory.

THE PSYCHOLOGY OF MISJUDGMENT CONCLUSION

Lyndon B. Johnson activated 13 of these cognitive biases in the same direction at the same time. In doing so, he created the perfect conditions for a Lollapalooza effect.

.............................Chapter Summary.............................

- The psychology of human misjudgment is a set of 25 interweaving cognitive biases identified by Charlie Munger.
- The 25 biases, acting together, produce a "Lollapalooza effect," or a massive persuasive push to instant action.
- The Lollapalooza effect explains historical moments of mass, collective, enthusiastic action toward one purpose.
- You use the psychology of human misjudgment in communication by activating the individual biases together.
- You overcome the psychology of human misjudgment by watching out for bias-triggering circumstances.
- Lyndon B. Johnson sought to produce a Lollapalooza effect by simultaneously activating 13 complementary biases.

KEY INSIGHT:

Our Nervous Systems Take in an Incalculable Number of Inputs, Consciously and Unconsciously.

Judgment is the Result of Reason Acting on These Inputs, As Well As Past (And Anticipated) Inputs.

HOW TO OVERCOME THE PSYCHOLOGY (PART THREE)

1	**The Availability Bias**
1.1	Gather All Available Statistics Instead of Relying on Ease of Recall
2	**The Anchoring Effect**
2.1	Educate Yourself on the Subject of Evaluation
2.2	Strive to Ignore the First Number You Hear
2.3	Be Cognizant of the Impact of Unrelated Anchors
2.4	Seek Historical Evidence Related to Your Evaluation
2.5	Concentrate Attention on a Self-Supplied Counter-Anchor
3	**Munger's Biases**
3.1	Watch Carefully for Bias-Activating Circumstances
4	**The Contrast Effect**
5	**Zero-Risk Bias**
6	**The Halo Effect**
7	**Agent Detection Bias**
8	**Attribute Substitution**
9	**Base Rate Neglect**

KEY INSIGHT:

The First Step to Defeating Misjudgment is Knowing What Triggers It.

Claim These Free Resources that Will Help You Unleash the Power of Your Words and Speak with Confidence. Visit www.speakforsuccesshub.com/toolkit for Access.

2 Free Workbooks

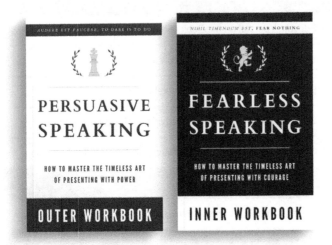

We'll send you two free workbooks, including long-lost excerpts by Dale Carnegie, the mega-bestselling author of *How to Win Friends and Influence People* (5,000,000 copies sold). *Fearless Speaking* guides you in the proven principles of mastering your inner game as a speaker. *Persuasive Speaking* guides you in the time-tested tactics of mastering your outer game by maximizing the power of your words. All of these resources complement the Speak for Success collection.

Claim These Free Resources that Will Help You Unleash the Power of Your Words and Speak with Confidence. Visit www.speakforsuccesshub.com/toolkit for Access.

18 Free PDF Resources

12 Iron Rules for Captivating Story, 21 Speeches that Changed the World, 341-Point Influence Checklist, 143 Persuasive Cognitive Biases, 17 Ways to Think On Your Feet, 18 Lies About Speaking Well, 137 Deadly Logical Fallacies, 12 Iron Rules For Captivating Slides, 371 Words that Persuade, 63 Truths of Speaking Well, 27 Laws of Empathy, 21 Secrets of Legendary Speeches, 19 Scripts that Persuade, 12 Iron Rules For Captivating Speech, 33 Laws of Charisma, 11 Influence Formulas, 219-Point Speech-Writing Checklist, 21 Eloquence Formulas

SPEAK FOR SUCCESS COLLECTION BOOK

I

HOW HIGHLY EFFECTIVE PEOPLE SPEAK CHAPTER

V

THE CONTRAST EFFECT:
Why Changing Context
Changes Perception

"YOU AND I ARE TOLD INCREASINGLY WE HAVE TO CHOOSE BETWEEN A LEFT OR RIGHT..."

R ONALD REAGAN'S PERSUASIVE *TOUR DE FORCE* in what he called "the speech" didn't end with the availability bias. There is a reason the speech was called "A Time for Choosing."

> You and I are told increasingly we have to choose between a left or right. Well I'd like to suggest there is no such thing as a left or right. There's only an up or down – [up] man's old-aged dream, the ultimate in individual freedom consistent with law and order, or down to the ant heap of totalitarianism. And regardless of their sincerity, their humanitarian motives, those who would trade our freedom for security have embarked on this downward course. In this vote-harvesting time, they use terms like the "Great Society," or as we were told a few days ago by the President, we must accept a greater government activity in the affairs of the people. But they've been a little more explicit in the past and among themselves; and all of the things I now will quote have appeared in print. These are not Republican accusations. For example, they have voices that say, "The cold war will end through our acceptance of a not undemocratic socialism." Another voice says, "The profit motive has become outmoded. It must be replaced by the incentives of the welfare state." Or, "Our traditional system of individual freedom is incapable of solving the complex problems of the 20th century." Senator Fullbright has said at Stanford University that the Constitution is outmoded. He referred to the President as "our moral teacher and our leader," and he says he is "hobbled in his task by the restrictions of power imposed on him by this antiquated document." He must "be freed," so that he "can do for us" what he knows "is best." And Senator Clark of Pennsylvania, another articulate spokesman, defines liberalism as "meeting the material needs of the masses through the full power of centralized government." Well, I, for one, resent it when a representative of the people refers to you and me, the free men and women of this country, as "the masses." This is a term we haven't applied to ourselves in America. But beyond that, "the full power of centralized government" this was the very thing the Founding Fathers sought to minimize. They knew that governments don't control things. A government can't control the economy without controlling people. And they know when a government sets out to do that, it must use force and coercion to achieve its purpose. They also knew, those Founding Fathers, that outside of its legitimate functions, government does nothing as well or as economically as the private sector of the economy. Now, we have no better example of this than government's involvement in the farm economy over the last 30 years. Since 1955, the cost of this program has nearly doubled. One-fourth of farming in America is responsible for 85 percent of the farm surplus. Three-fourths of farming is out on the free market and has known a 21 percent increase in the per capita consumption of all its produce. You see, that one-fourth of farming that's regulated and controlled by the federal government. In the last three years we've spent 43 dollars in the feed grain

program for every dollar bushel of corn we don't grow. Senator Humphrey last week charged that Barry Goldwater, as President, would seek to eliminate farmers. He should do his homework a little better, because he'll find out that we've had a decline of 5 million in the farm population under these government programs. He'll also find that the Democratic administration has sought to get from Congress [an] extension of the farm program to include that three-fourths that is now free. He'll find that they've also asked for the right to imprison farmers who wouldn't keep books as prescribed by the federal government. The Secretary of Agriculture asked for the right to seize farms through condemnation and resell them to other individuals. And contained in that same program was a provision that would have allowed the federal government to remove 2 million farmers from the soil. At the same time, there's been an increase in the Department of Agriculture employees. There's now one for every 30 farms in the United States, and still they can't tell us how 66 shiploads of grain headed for Austria disappeared without a trace and Billie Sol Estes never left shore. Every responsible farmer and farm organization has repeatedly asked the government to free the farm economy, but how – who are farmers to know what's best for them? The wheat farmers voted against a wheat program. The government passed it anyway. Now the price of bread goes up; the price of wheat to the farmer goes down.

In this section, we unpack the contrast effect. Reagan contrasted left with right, up with down, and man's old-aged dream with the ant heap of totalitarianism. He contrasted quotes from his political opponents with his resentment at their use of "the masses." He contrasted the performance of the government outside its legitimate functions with that of the private sector. He contrasted the agricultural performance of the past with that of his day, contrasting his worldview with that of his opponents. He contrasted Humphrey's charge against Goldwater with cited facts. He contrasted the decrease of two million farmers with the increase Department of Agriculture employees. He contrasted the wishes of farmers with the actions of government. And he contrasted the price of bread going up with the price of wheat to the farmer going down. All this contrast serves an unparalleled persuasive function: appealing to the contrast effect, one of the most powerful levers for influencing perception and motivating deeply positive responses to your proposal.

WHAT IS THE CONTRAST EFFECT?

Using the contrast effect is presenting differences between your subject and another item to enhance, diminish, emphasize, or deemphasize an aspect of your subject. The contrast effect appeals to comparative perception: forming beliefs based on differences between a subject of evaluation and a point of comparison.

WHAT IS AN EXAMPLE OF THE CONTRAST EFFECT?

The meanings of two opposite (or contrasting) words seem more extreme placed together. The sound of a trombone seems deeper followed by a high-pitched trumpet. White seems brighter next to black, and black darker next to white. When you perceive two contrasting items simultaneously, their contrasting qualities are emphasized.

HOW THE CONTRAST EFFECT PREVENTS CONFUSION

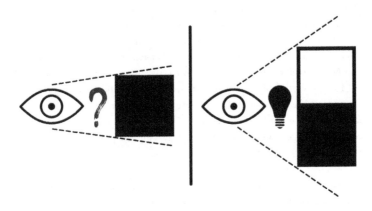

FIGURE 63: Humans perceive the world and make judgements by comparing things. In the absence of any available comparison, people miss the point and get confused. No comparison, no judgement. No judgement, no influence. The point of camouflage is to reduce contrast. Don't camouflage your point, rendering it invisible against its background. Do the opposite. Create contrast.

One particularly compelling example of the contrast effect in action? Real estate salesmen use it to get higher offers for the same homes. Watch out for this if you're buying a house soon. They'll show you three homes. Home one is run-down, ugly, and overpriced at $500,000. Home two is also run-down, ugly, and overpriced at around $500,000. Home three? Beautiful, perfect, completely sound, and competitively priced at the phenomenal, once-in-a-lifetime price of $400,000.

What's going on here? They artificially inflated the asking price of homes one and two, while maintaining or just slightly raising the asking price of home three. Home three is the only one priced at market value. Due to the contrast effect, buyers perceive home three as much nicer and significantly more well-priced than homes one and two. Why? Because they compare and contrast the three deals. They don't judge the third item in isolation, but stack it against the preceding two. The result? An instantaneous purchase of home three.

Why does this work? What is the hidden secret of human perception, decision-making, and judgement at work here, putting irresistible and instantaneous influence in your reach? Comparative perception: Humans cannot judge the value of an item in a vacuum; they need points of reference, relativity between two or more items, and ways to compare the salient item to points of reference.

In short: Because the prospects perceive two unattractive offers prior to the moderate offer, it suddenly appears outstanding. Why? Because the buyer contrasted it to the two unattractive offers. If the contrasts didn't influence them – if the agent just showed them home three – they probably would be less excited about it. Why? Because there would be no artificial points of comparison making it seem phenomenally well-built and well-priced.

HOW THE CONTRAST EFFECT SHAPES YOUR REALITY

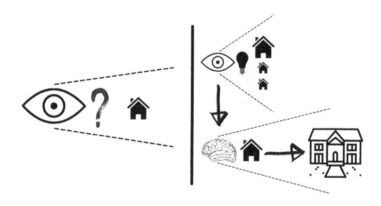

FIGURE 64: If real estate agents show a customer a house in isolation, the contrast effect is not in play. The customer does not instinctively leap to a particular conclusion as a result of interpreting contrasts. However, by pre-framing the same house with two worse offers, the real estate agents activate the contrast effect, altering the prospect's reality by giving him an outsized impression of the better house.

Let's quickly talk about the science behind the contrast effect before getting into the critical questions: How can you use it in communication? How can you use it to ethically persuade with ease? How can you make people reflexively gravitate towards you, your message, and your ideas?

KEY INSIGHT:

We Crave Contrasts. Contrasts Create Clarity. Clarity Compels Our Cognition.

HOW DO YOU OVERCOME THE CONTRAST EFFECT?

You overcome the contrast effect by supplanting an artificially inferior contrasting item presented to you with the best possible contrasting item you know of. Thus, you counter the effect of an inferior item positively contrasting with the item in question by also mentally contrasting the salient item with a positive item.

CREATING A COUNTER-CONTRAST

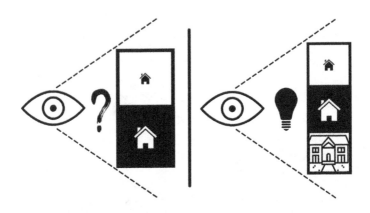

FIGURE 65: Activating multiple cognitive biases toward the same persuasive objective in the same people at the same time is often a case of 1 + 1 = 3 (or 100 + 100 = 1,000 – why not?). The biases and their persuasive influence complement each other and achieve synergy. At a certain point, the biases hit a "critical mass" that sets off a Lollapalooza effect which creates explosive and enthusiastic action – disproportionately more action than would be achieved by subtracting just one bias, according to the theory.

HOW DO YOU USE THE CONTRAST EFFECT IN COMMUNICATION?

You use the contrast effect in persuasion by applying the following strategies. All of them create contrasts between two items to add emphasis, provide persuasive value, and make the message more vivid and compelling. This is contrary to the significantly less persuasive strategy of presenting items, ideas or concepts in isolation, with no contrasts. Doing so constricts human judgement instead of productively influencing it in a direction of your choosing.

STRATEGY #1: USE ANTITHESIS

Antithesis, a little-known rhetorical device used by the world's most eloquent speakers, like JFK and MLK, creates tremendously persuasive contrast. It goes like this: "not X, but Y." Instead of only saying "Y," this strategy presents what your idea is not (X) before presenting what your idea is (Y). The result? Vivid and compelling contrast between X and Y, making Y much more attractive.

It's why JFK said "not because they are easy, but because they are hard," and in another speech, "ask not what your country can do for you – (implied 'but') ask what you can do for your country."

This contrasts "easy" with "hard," lends context to "hard," and compels audience perception while grabbing attention. And you can stack "not" statements for heightened contrast: "not X, not Y, not [...], but Z."

HOW THE ANCIENT STRATEGY OF ANTITHESIS CONTRASTS

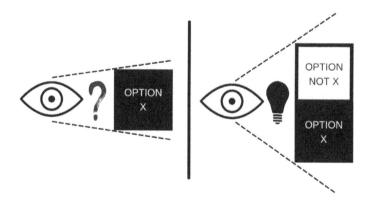

FIGURE 66: Antithesis is a short, punchy contrast, typically between "not what you want them to do" and "what you want them to do," although it can be used in other ways as well. This beats delivering what you want them to do in a vacuum, unsupported by persuasive contrasts.

STRATEGY #2: USE PARADOX

JFK, one of history's legendary communicators, used rhetorical paradox to great effect. What is a rhetorical paradox? Presenting two ideas that seemingly express a contradiction. This inherently creates contrast, making both ideas more vivid and captivating.

What is an example of rhetorical paradox in action? JFK said the following: "The greater our knowledge increases, the greater our ignorance unfolds." It's a paradox: It seemingly can't be true if you take it literally. But figuratively, it evokes a vivid sense of not knowing what we don't know. The more we find out, the more we learn how much we still don't know. And it paints tremendously captivating contrast between "our knowledge increases" and "our ignorance unfolds." Contrast equals persuasion and captivation, and paradox equals contrast, so paradox equals persuasion and captivation.

KEY INSIGHT:

Many of the Greatest Truths Are Paradoxical. The Weakness of the Power-Hungry, and the Power of the Humble. The Poverty of the Greedy, and the Wealth of the Generous. The Self-Defeating Accidental Self-Revelation of the Deceitful, and the Persuasive Purity of the Honest.

STRATEGY #3: USE DIRECT COMPARISON

Compare and contrast. Call out differences between two items. Are you advocating for one option over another? Don't just talk about benefits of the option you like. There's no contrast there. Choice is a game of alternatives. Even if your proposal benefits, what matters is whether or not it benefits more than alternatives. And until you compare it to the alternatives, you neglect the only important message you should be presenting.

"We produce a 14% revenue boost, on average, for our clients" means nothing.

"We get an average of 10,000 new prospects after a month of service" means nothing.

"We have 2,000 positive reviews" means nothing. Why? There's no contrast, thus humans cannot evaluate whether the numbers are good or bad.

"We produce a 14% revenue boost, on average, for our clients, while our closest competitor does 10%" means everything. Why? Contrast.

"We get an average of 10,000 new prospects after a month of service, our closest competitor gets 8,000" means everything. Why? Contrast.

"We have 2,000 positive reviews, our closest competitor has 1,000" means everything. Why? Contrast.

STRATEGY #4: USE ALTERNATIVE ENUMERATION

To reject alternatives, you must enumerate them. You can't contrast your ideas with inferior ones if people don't know the inferior ones exist. You can't contrast the $400,000 home with the inferior $500,000 ones if buyers never toured them. The process of touring the two inferior homes is alternative enumeration. How do you do it? Portray the inferior alternatives. Their mental machinery, their proclivity to contrast, will do the rest for you, making your proposal seem drastically and dramatically better.

STRATEGY #5: USE ALTERNATIVE REJECTION

Once you enumerate alternatives, you must reject them if their inferiority is not self-evident. How? By answering the following questions: Why is your proposal better than the alternatives? What are the problems associated with the alternatives? What are the benefits associated with yours? What is the biggest benefit your idea offers that the alternatives don't? What are the biggest problems alternatives cause that your option avoids? Why are the alternatives inherently self-defeating? What is the pro and con evaluation that suggests your proposal is better than the others?

STRATEGY #6: USE INFERIOR "SOFT" ANCHORING

The primacy effect overweighs information we hear first. Why does it happen? Partly through expectations. How? The first item we see sets our expectations for associated items, for items in the same category. When we first perceive a new item in a familiar category, we juxtapose what we perceive (a well-built and well-priced home) with what we expected to see (a third poorly-built and over-priced home, following the pattern of the first items we saw in the category). There's "hard" numerical anchoring. But that's another subject altogether, and one we already covered.

"Soft" anchoring follows this step-by-step process: Step one, present an inferior alternative first (the two bad homes), to anchor expectations for the category of available homes low. Step two, present the item you suggest, which now massively breaks the expectations you set with the inferior anchors, and thus seems significantly better through contrast.

How can you make your proposal or product seem significantly better, even after improving it to the max? For example, after you've improved the third house as much as possible, how can you make it seem even better? By selecting weaker inferior anchors; by providing the human mind artificially abysmal points of comparison.

STRATEGY #7: USE LOW PRIMARY EXPECTATIONS

This activates the primacy effect too. This time, you don't produce low primary expectations by presenting an inferior anchor (showing the two homes), but by telling them what to expect: "Chances are finding a well-made home for the price of $400,000 is unlikely; you can probably expect older, lower-quality homes for around $500,000."

This strategy makes the target home appear like a diamond in the rough. It works much like setting low inferior anchors. But it is easier. Why? Because it is easier to set low expectations by telling them what to expect than by touring the two inferior homes. That said, if I had to guess, low inferior anchoring is more compelling. Why? Because they see inferior alternatives with their own eyes. However, this is a false dilemma. You can do both.

First, set low primary expectations by telling them what to expect. Second, validate these low expectations with low inferior anchors. Third, shatter the expectations with your proposed item, achieving compelling and persuasive contrast with ease.

This is a versatile and flexible strategy. Why? It's easier to make your proposal seem better by making what precedes it (and thus sets expectations for items in its category) worse, than by actually making it better. This is not an argument for not making your proposal better; it's just a way to make it appear even better once you've made it the best it can be.

STRATEGY #8: USE PATTERN-INTERRUPTS

Anything breaking a pattern captivates us and creates contrast. Patterns "habituate" over time: They no longer captivate our attention. But new items do: Novelty grabs and holds attention like nothing else. Items that break away from patterns achieve novelty.

How do you apply pattern interrupts? Speak quietly and with strategic solemnity after speaking loudly and passionately; speak slowly and with a degree of emotion after speaking quickly and analytically; wear an expression of disdain when describing the problem and a satisfied smile when describing the solution ; talk about what's good after talking about what's bad; *ad infinitum.* Identify the communication patterns you're producing, particularly patterns of content (what you are saying), and break them for massive and easy contrast.

KEY INSIGHT:

Our Perception Clings to the Opportune, the Threatening, and the New. The Stagnant Slips By.

HOW TO USE PATTERNS TO CAPTIVATE FULL ATTENTION

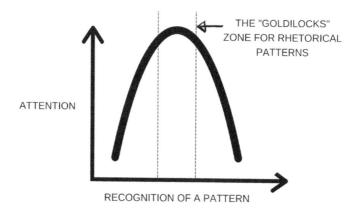

FIGURE 67: As your audience begins to perceive your pattern, attention rises. The pattern continues to captivate attention until it reaches the point of habituation. At this point – which can come quickly – the pattern becomes rote, routine, boring, and droning. As they see the pattern continuing, their attention dips. Bring your patterns to the goldilocks zone, but no further. Unfortunately, there is no silver-bullet rule for finding the point of habituation.

WHEN TO CREATE PATTERNS, WHEN TO BREAK THEM

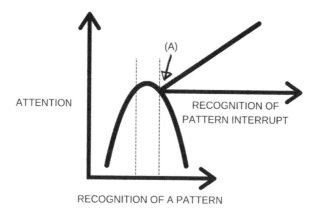

FIGURE 68: Up to the point of habituation (A), patterns grab attention. After the point of habituation, patterns lose attention. After the point of habituation, pattern-interrupts grab attention. The ideal sequence is this: produce rhetorical patterns until the point of habituation. Then, apply a pattern-interrupt. This guarantees attention rises (or at least doesn't fall) throughout.

STRATEGY #9: USE RHYTHMIC CADENCE AND BREAKAWAY PHRASES

This is a two-step strategy producing tremendous contrast. Step one: Build a rhythmic pattern. Step two: Introduce a breakaway phrase, breaking the rhythmic pattern.

An example from the show *West Wing* exemplifies this strategy well. A character, Toby Zeigler, was arguing for free trade. He said something along these lines: "Free trade raises wages, raises quality of life, raises rates of development, raises economic freedom and security, raises consumer surplus, and stops wars."

He set a pattern: "Free trade raises wages, raises quality of life, raises rates of development, raises economic freedom and security, raises consumer surplus," and then he broke away from it, "and stops wars." He also delivered the breakaway phrase with breakaway delivery, with vocal emphasis and emphatic body language.

This gives people plenty of contrast to munch on. The expectation is another "raises [insert good thing]," not a "stops [insert bad thing]." The contrast between expectation and reality grabs attention. Without it, we have a harder time evaluating meaning.

STRATEGY #10: USE FLOATING OPPOSITES

Bad sounds worse next to good. Knowledge sounds more erudite next to ignorance. And $400,000 sounds like a better price next to $500,000. JFK's inaugural address contains a compelling example of floating opposites. He said, "If a free society cannot help the many who are poor, it cannot save the few who are rich." There is a double contrast; almost a contrast within a contrast. There is contrast between many and few, and contrast between the poor and the rich.

HOW FLOATING OPPOSITES MAKE COMPELLING CONTRASTS

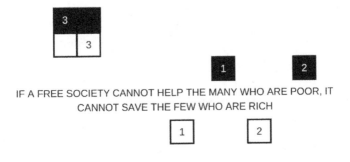

FIGURE 69: Floating opposites contrasted "many" with "few," "poor" with "rich," and "many poor" with "few rich," the third contrast and a sort of meta-contrast.

CONTRAST EFFECT CONCLUSION

Ronald Reagan presented several compelling contrasts. As a result, his audience perceived him as doubly good, and his opponents as doubly bad. Reagan's positions would have seemed moderately compelling on their own, but juxtaposed with the positions of his political opponents, Reagan's positions seemed immaculate to his audience.

...............................Chapter Summary................................

- The contrast effect is our tendency to be deeply influenced by observed contrasts between items.
- The contrast effect occurs because of the fundamental nature of human perception, which is relative.
- The contrast effect explains why items previously witnessed influence our current perceptions and judgments.
- You use the contrast effect in communication by applying strategies that send a message through contrasts.
- You overcome the contrast effect in part by supplying yourself with a "counter-contrasting" item.
- Ronald Reagan used the contrast effect by presenting not only "the right way," but "the wrong way" too.

KEY INSIGHT:

There Are Dark Shadows on the Earth, But Its Lights Are Stronger in the Contrast. - Charles Dickens

There Is No Quality in This World That Is Not What It Is Merely by Contrasts. - Melville

---

HOW TO OVERCOME THE PSYCHOLOGY (PART FOUR)

1	The Availability Bias
1.1	Gather All Available Statistics Instead of Relying on Ease of Recall
2	The Anchoring Effect
2.1	Educate Yourself on the Subject of Evaluation
2.2	Strive to Ignore the First Number You Hear
2.3	Be Cognizant of the Impact of Unrelated Anchors
2.4	Seek Historical Evidence Related to Your Evaluation
2.5	Concentrate Attention on a Self-Supplied Counter-Anchor
3	Munger's Biases
3.1	Watch Carefully for Bias-Activating Circumstances
4	The Contrast Effect
4.1	Generate Counteracting Contrasting Inputs
5	Zero-Risk Bias
6	The Halo Effect
7	Agent Detection Bias
8	Attribute Substitution
9	Base Rate Neglect

Claim These Free Resources that Will Help You Unleash the Power of Your Words and Speak with Confidence. Visit www.speakforsuccesshub.com/toolkit for Access.

30 Free Video Lessons

We'll send you one free video lesson every day for 30 days, written and recorded by Peter D. Andrei. Days 1-10 cover authenticity, the prerequisite to confidence and persuasive power. Days 11-20 cover building self-belief and defeating communication anxiety. Days 21-30 cover how to speak with impact and influence, ensuring your words change minds instead of falling flat. Authenticity, self-belief, and impact – this course helps you master three components of confidence, turning even the most high-stakes presentations from obstacles into opportunities.

SPEAK FOR SUCCESS COLLECTION BOOK

I

HOW HIGHLY EFFECTIVE PEOPLE SPEAK CHAPTER

VI

ZERO-RISK BIAS:
How to Use the Psychology of Certainty in Your Favor

"THAT IS THE RESOLVE OF HIS MAJESTY'S GOVERNMENT – EVERY MAN OF THEM..."

W INSTON CHURCHILL ADDRESSED HIS NATION in what he called its "darkest hour." Nazi Germany spread the grim grip of its evil regime around Europe. Britain stood alone. And if it continued to stand alone, it would soon find itself unable to stand at all. The might of the Nazi war machine would have buckled Britain. The British Expeditionary Force had just been miraculously evacuated from Europe at Dunkirk. They were spared disaster by the smallest possible margin. Over 300,000 British troops were stuck on a small stretch of beach, fully surrounded. German planes roared overhead, dropping bombs on the exposed men. They were fish in a barrel, and many were certain their demise was near. Under "Operation Dynamo," the naval rescue force sought to rescue 45,000 troops. And this was a hope, not a prediction. By an act of grace, they evacuated 338,000 Allied troops, including 26,000 French soldiers who valiantly held back the German line. On June 4, Churchill delivered an address from the House of Commons, which offered a direct appeal for action to the United States.

We have found it necessary to take measures of increasing stringency, not only against enemy aliens and suspicious characters of other nationalities, but also against British subjects who may become a danger or a nuisance should the war be transported to the United Kingdom. I know there are a great many people affected by the orders which we have made who are the passionate enemies of Nazi Germany. I am very sorry for them, but we cannot, at the present time and under the present stress, draw all the distinctions which we should like to do. If parachute landings were attempted and fierce fighting attendant upon them followed, these unfortunate people would be far better out of the way, for their own sakes as well as for ours. There is, however, another class, for which I feel not the slightest sympathy. Parliament has given us the powers to put down Fifth Column activities with a strong hand, and we shall use those powers subject to the supervision and correction of the House, without the slightest hesitation until we are satisfied, and more than satisfied, that this malignancy in our midst has been effectively stamped out. Turning once again, and this time more generally, to the question of invasion, I would observe that there has never been a period in all these long centuries of which we boast when an absolute guarantee against invasion, still less against serious raids, could have been given to our people. In the days of Napoleon the same wind which would have carried his transports across the Channel might have driven away the blockading fleet. There was always the chance, and it is that chance which has excited and befooled the imaginations of many Continental tyrants. Many are the tales that are told. We are assured that novel methods will be adopted, and when we see the originality of malice, the ingenuity of aggression, which our enemy displays, we may certainly prepare ourselves for every kind of novel stratagem and every kind of brutal and treacherous maneuver. I think that no idea is so outlandish that it should not be considered and viewed with a searching, but at the same time, I hope, with a steady eye. We must never forget the solid assurances of sea power and those which belong to air power if it can be locally exercised. I have, myself, full confidence that if all do their duty, if nothing is neglected, and if the best arrangements are made, as they are being made, we shall prove ourselves once again able to defend our Island home, to ride out the storm of war, and to outlive the menace of tyranny, if necessary for years, if necessary alone. At any rate, that is what we are going to try to do. That is the resolve of His Majesty's Government-every man of them. That is the will of Parliament and the nation. The British Empire and the French Republic, linked together in their cause and in their need, will defend to the death their native soil, aiding each other like good comrades to the utmost of their strength. Even though large tracts of Europe and many old and famous States have fallen or may fall into the grip of the Gestapo and all the odious apparatus of Nazi rule, we shall not flag or fail. We shall go on to the end, we shall fight in France, we shall fight on the seas and oceans, we shall fight with growing confidence and growing strength in the air, we shall defend our Island, whatever the cost may be, we shall fight on the beaches, we shall fight on the landing grounds, we shall fight in the fields and in the streets, we shall fight in the hills; we shall never surrender, and even if, which I do not for a moment believe, this Island or a large part of it were subjugated and starving, then our Empire beyond the seas, armed and guarded by the British Fleet, would carry on the struggle, until, in God's good time, the New World, with all its power and might, steps forth to the rescue and the liberation of the old.

In this section, we discuss the zero-risk bias, and why the human need for certainty offers an incredibly powerful persuasive hot-button. Churchill spoke of being "satisfied, and more than satisfied," of "an absolute guarantee against invasion" (albeit in the negative), of "a steady eye," of "the solid assurances of sea power," of "full confidence," of "the resolve of His Majesty's Government," of "defend[ing] to the death," of "the utmost of their strength." Famously, Churchill said "we shall not flag or fail." And he ended the address by stating that "we shall never surrender, and even if, which I do not for a moment believe, this island or a large part of it were subjugated and starving, then our empire beyond the seas, armed and guarded by the British fleet, would carry on the struggle, until, in God's good time, the New World, with all its power and might, steps forth to the rescue and the liberation of the old." He essentially ended by stating that "even if we fail, we can win." He suggested that "even if we fail here, which will not happen, then our empire will continue the fight, as will the United States." All of this certainty is tremendously influential. It produces a strong, motivating drive to action. We are predictably and irrationally risk-averse. You can use this tendency.

WHAT IS THE ZERO-RISK BIAS?

The zero-risk bias is systematically, repetitively and predictably overweighing the benefit of zero risk as opposed to an infinitesimally small risk. We often exchange a mathematically irrational number of resources to drop a minuscule risk to zero. This cognitive bias and mental heuristic particularly activates in high-stakes situations.

ZERO-RISK BIAS VISUALIZED

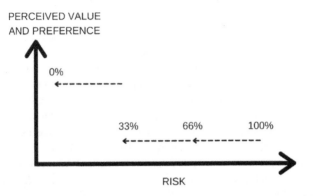

FIGURE 70: We seek a risk reduction from 100% risk to ~66% risk a given amount; we seek a risk reduction from 66% risk to 33% risk the same amount. However, we seek a risk reduction from 33% to 0% by a larger amount, although it is an identical risk reduction; a reduction of 33%.

WHAT IS AN EXAMPLE OF THE ZERO-RISK BIAS?

The expected monetary value (EMV) of an investment is its monetary return multiplied by likelihood of success (for example, 90%, or 0.9). Selecting investment opportunities based on EMV is the best practice because, over time, the success-rate statistically regresses to an average of, in this example, 90%.

How does the zero-risk bias activate, and to what effect? It pushes people to select an investment with lower return but zero risk (even after return was adjusted by risk with the EMV calculation), instead of one with a higher risk-adjusted return but slightly higher risk.

Consider a situation with two investment opportunities. Option one: 10 stocks with an expected return of $1,100 each with a 90% success-rate. Option two: 10 stocks with an expected return of $900 each with a 100% success rate. The EMV of option one is as follows: 10*$1,100*0.9 equals $9,900. The EMV of option two is as follows: 10*$900*1 equals $9,000.

Even though option one has a 10% higher EMV, zero-risk bias pushes people to irrationally select option two, even though it will probably result in $900 fewer dollars.

HOW DO YOU OVERCOME THE ZERO-RISK BIAS?

You overcome the zero-risk bias by conducting rational, mathematical risk-reward calculations when you feel an impulse to exchange resources for zero risk. These will tell you if it is a rational, empirically and statistically justifiable expense.

DEFEATING THE ZERO-RISK BIAS WITH SYSTEM TWO

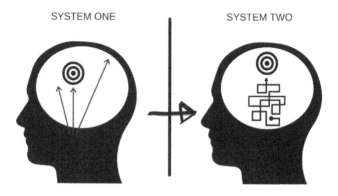

SYSTEM ONE   SYSTEM TWO

FIGURE 71: Defeating zero-risk bias necessitates switching from system one thinking to system two thinking.

HOW DO YOU USE THE ZERO-RISK BIAS IN COMMUNICATION?

In this section, you're going to learn exactly how to apply the zero-risk bias to your communication. These proven, step-by-step strategies are guaranteed to invoke one of the most compelling psychological biases in your favor. The result? Your communication will compel, your ideas will appear better, and you will propel your career forward by speaking with influence.

STRATEGY #1: PRESENT ZERO-RISK

This is the obvious one. Does your product, idea, or initiative offer zero risk? Does it guarantee a particular outcome with 100% certainty? Moreover, can you prove it? If so, present this and emphasize it.

Why? Because the zero-risk bias offers this information an outsized persuasive impact. But only in a perfect world do our plans, proposals, and products offer zero risk. What do we do to invoke the zero-risk bias when there is a risk? Apply the next five strategies. And it is possible to activate the zero-risk bias in the presence of risk and to do so ethically, without manipulating people or flat-out lying. In fact, not only is it not unethical, it actually represents value added.

STRATEGY #2: PROVIDE EXTERNAL GUARANTEES

External guarantees guarantee some result. External guarantees persuade for one key reason: They express zero risk. So, if there really is zero risk associated with your idea, offering, or proposal, make an external guarantee statement: "I guarantee [insert results]."

You can also make a justified or evidenced guarantee statement: "I guarantee [insert results] because [insert evidence one], [insert evidence two], and [insert evidence three]."

STRATEGY #3: PROVIDE "RESULTS, OR ELSE" STATEMENTS

Can you always guarantee external results? For example, can you always guarantee, beyond the shadow of a single doubt or risk, that your product produces the stated results in 100% of cases? No, you cannot, and even a 99% success rate doesn't activate zero-risk bias. It would be dishonest to pretend 99% equals 100%.

What are you left with? How can you activate the zero-risk bias in the absence of zero risk? You can activate zero-risk bias even if your product only works in 90%, 70%, or even 50% of cases. You just need the right strategy.

How? What strategy allows this? You can say something like this: "I guarantee you will either get exactly what we promised, or a 100%, instant, hassle-free refund."

Consider a situation in which your product succeeds in 90% of cases. That is a 10% failure rate. Why does this matter? Because it represents a 10% loss-rate for customers, and loss hurts humans like nothing else. But this strategy turns a 10% chance of loss into a 0% chance of loss. Thus, you activate the zero-risk bias. This will make you drastically more persuasive, influential, and successful as a communicator who needs to advocate for ideas, plans, or proposals.

STRATEGY #4: REFRAME THE "RISK FOCUS"

In every single evaluation, people subconsciously apply a risk-focus. What is the risk-focus in the example of EMV at the beginning of this chapter? The risk of a security failure, with the investment yielding $0. Decision-makers often judge the risk of one salient metric, neglecting others.

How do you shift the risk focus? Shift it from a metric without zero risk to one with zero risk. Building on the EMV example, shift the risk focus away from the risk of failing to earn a return and place it on the risk of failing to complete the necessary transactions, for example. How? "Even though this is a new type of security in a small market, there is already a fully operational clearinghouse, so there is a 0% risk of transaction failure: You'll be able to sell or buy whenever you want, instantly, with 0% risk of delays or transaction failure."

Shifting the risk focus is emphasizing the zero risk in a different dimension of your proposal; a dimension people didn't immediately and intuitively use as the risk focus, but one that is still salient to achieving the goals of the prospect.

REFRAMING THE RISK FOCUS ACTIVATES ZERO-RISK BIAS

FIGURE 72: Every proposal carries risks in different areas. For example, a marketing proposal carries risks in areas like costs running out of control, branding failing to click, and digital ad buys targeting the wrong audience. The art of reframing the risk focus is emphasizing the zero risk in the area of risk that truly does offer zero risk.

STRATEGY #5: PROVIDE INTERNAL GUARANTEES

We talked about external guarantees. In many situations, a cloud of uncertainty plagues even external guarantees. Can you always guarantee the market won't tank tomorrow? Can you guarantee some unknown disaster, like mass embezzlement, doesn't kill your company? Can you guarantee your customer doesn't have a peculiar situation rendering your product ineffective? Can you guarantee, in a production and supply chain involving thousands of people, that one of them doesn't make a critical mistake? You can't.

An external guarantee often makes the mistake of guaranteeing something outside of your direct control. And some people feel external guarantees are too good to be true. This doesn't mean you shouldn't use them at all. It means you should supplement them.

"How can you be sure?" "I'm skeptical..." "We'll just have to see about that now, won't we?" These common rejoinders typically respond to external guarantees.

What can you truly guarantee? Something internal; something in your direct control. And this allows you to activate the zero-risk bias. "I guarantee that every single person staffing your account is of the highest caliber our firm can offer." "I guarantee you can call anyone on this account at any time, and they will pick up." "I guarantee we will be conducting 24/7 monitoring on the status of your service to ensure any errors are caught instantly."

We can conceive of the dynamic behind this strategy as an equation: perceived risk equals skepticism * stated risk. Skepticism and stated risk are percentages: 0% to 100%

(0 to 1). Here's the issue: If you try to dramatically lower stated risk, skepticism drastically increases. In many situations, they are inversely proportional.

If you paint an exceedingly optimistic picture of risks (stated risks), skepticism goes up, thus the net result is an unchanged level of perceived risk. And if you are extremely optimistic, skepticism goes up so much that the level of perceived risk doesn't just stay unchanged, but goes up. Needless to say, you don't want to produce a higher perceived risk. You want a lower perceived risk. And you especially want zero perceived risk.

These strategies circumvent the dynamic of this equation. They allow you to lower stated risk without touching skepticism. And remember, this deals with perceived risk (a function of your communication), not real risk (a function of reality). With these strategies, we seek to optimize perceived risk, which informs decisions. Of course, we must also seek to eradicate real risk as well.

STRATEGY #6: PRESENT "100% SUCCESS RATE OR OUT-CLAUSE" STATEMENTS

This strategy evokes the "results or else" strategy. It explicitly enumerates the risk: 0%. It's not this: "If we don't get the promised results, we offer a full refund." It is this: "There's a 0% risk of loss for you because we either deliver results or deliver a refund. 100% of our customers in the past year got the stated results or a refund; 0% of them experienced any loss as a result of their relationship with us. And 95% got the results they wanted; only 5% opted for the refund."

THE PSYCHOLOGY OF AN OUT-CLAUSE

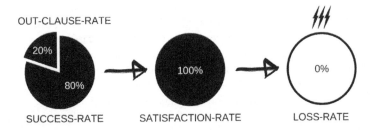

FIGURE 73: If 80% of your customers succeeded in using your product and the other 20% attained a full refund, this implies a 100% satisfaction rate: Every customer either gained or remained in the same place. This is a 0% loss-rate, which activates the zero-risk bias.

STRATEGY #7: PROVIDE A SUPERABUNDANCE OF PROOF

Remember the skepticism and stated risk equation, and recall those two critical elements you're dealing with, and how they interact. Remember that if you are not strategic, subtle, and artful in your manipulation of stated risk, people grow skeptical. Remember that you must apply these strategies to lower stated risk without raising skepticism. This strategy deals with skepticism, specifically with keeping it low no matter what. In the presence of this strategy (which is more common sense than anything else), you can lower stated risk while keeping skepticism low, thus lower overall perceived risk.

The strategy? Provide proof. Provide testimonials, commendations, industry reports, social proof statistics ("100% of customers reported extreme satisfaction with our service"), and expert endorsements of your solution. This strategy supports all other strategies activating the zero-risk bias, and renders the concept of zero risk significantly more believable by diffusing any lingering clouds of skepticism.

ZERO-RISK BIAS CONCLUSION

Winston Churchill spoke in the language of absolute certainty. Additionally, he revealed that failure was not exactly failure, but the chance to continue the fight in another way. First, the British Empire abroad would continue the fight, and then the United States. As a result, he evoked a sense of zero risk; he implied that Britain would not and could not lose. People are attracted to certainty. People are attracted to confidence. The zero-risk bias is part of the psychological machinery underlying this. And as you learned, you can evoke this bias even if there is some measure of risk associated with your proposal. If there is a 90% chance that your proposal will get results – or even a 99% chance – you can activate the zero-risk bias by telling them that if it fails, whether that represents a 10% or a 1% unlikelihood, you will provide a "refund," or activate some measure that guarantees they won't be worse-off than before they bought into your proposal. Another tactic is to reframe the focus of risk. If there is a 10% risk that a financial security won't provide a positive return, for example, but a 100% certainty that there won't be any transaction failure, then you can evoke the zero-risk bias by

..................Chapter Summary..................

- The zero-risk bias is our tendency to expend an irrational amount of resources to achieve zero risk.
- The zero-risk bias occurs because of loss aversion, our tendency to suffer from loss more than gain pleasures us.
- The zero-risk bias explains why many investors will essentially lose money overall to attain zero risk.
- You use the zero-risk bias in communication by applying strategies that imply a sense of certainty or zero risk.

- You overcome the zero-risk bias by applying rational, empirical, statistical "EMV" calculations.
- Winston Churchill used the zero-risk bias by speaking in the language of absolute certainty and providing "fail-safes."

KEY INSIGHT:

Faith is Self-Fulfilling. It Is, as Serial Entrepreneur Peter Thiel Would Say, An "Effective Truth."

The Faithful Have a Pillar Upon Which to Place Their Courage. They Have Vision and They Have Hope.

They Sacrifice More for Their Mission. They Try Harder, Rest Less, and Push Through More.

Why? Because They Do Not Believe Their Sacrifices Are in Vain.

Why? *Because They Believe.*

HOW TO OVERCOME THE PSYCHOLOGY (PART FIVE)

1	**The Availability Bias**
1.1	Gather All Available Statistics Instead of Relying on Ease of Recall
2	**The Anchoring Effect**
2.1	Educate Yourself on the Subject of Evaluation
2.2	Strive to Ignore the First Number You Hear
2.3	Be Cognizant of the Impact of Unrelated Anchors
2.4	Seek Historical Evidence Related to Your Evaluation
2.5	Concentrate Attention on a Self-Supplied Counter-Anchor
3	**Munger's Biases**
3.1	Watch Carefully for Bias-Activating Circumstances
4	**The Contrast Effect**
4.1	Generate Counteracting Contrasting Inputs
5	**Zero-Risk Bias**
5.1	Run Statistical, Empirical, Rational Risk-Reward Calculations
6	**The Halo Effect**
7	**Agent Detection Bias**
8	**Attribute Substitution**
9	**Base Rate Neglect**

Claim These Free Resources that Will Help You Unleash the Power of Your Words and Speak with Confidence. Visit www.speakforsuccesshub.com/toolkit for Access.

2 Free Workbooks

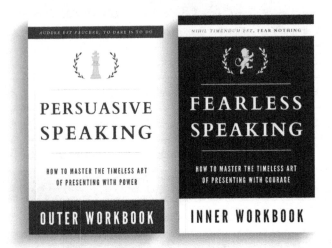

We'll send you two free workbooks, including long-lost excerpts by Dale Carnegie, the mega-bestselling author of *How to Win Friends and Influence People* (5,000,000 copies sold). *Fearless Speaking* guides you in the proven principles of mastering your inner game as a speaker. *Persuasive Speaking* guides you in the time-tested tactics of mastering your outer game by maximizing the power of your words. All of these resources complement the Speak for Success collection.

Claim These Free Resources that Will Help You Unleash the Power of Your Words and Speak with Confidence. Visit www.speakforsuccesshub.com/toolkit for Access.

18 Free PDF Resources

12 Iron Rules for Captivating Story, 21 Speeches that Changed the World, 341-Point Influence Checklist, 143 Persuasive Cognitive Biases, 17 Ways to Think On Your Feet, 18 Lies About Speaking Well, 137 Deadly Logical Fallacies, 12 Iron Rules For Captivating Slides, 371 Words that Persuade, 63 Truths of Speaking Well, 27 Laws of Empathy, 21 Secrets of Legendary Speeches, 19 Scripts that Persuade, 12 Iron Rules For Captivating Speech, 33 Laws of Charisma, 11 Influence Formulas, 219-Point Speech-Writing Checklist, 21 Eloquence Formulas

SPEAK FOR SUCCESS COLLECTION BOOK

I

HOW HIGHLY EFFECTIVE PEOPLE SPEAK CHAPTER

VII

THE HALO EFFECT:

Why First Impressions Make
or Break You

"MR. WEBB, MR. BELL, SCIENTISTS, DISTINGUISHED GUESTS, AND LADIES AND GENTLEMEN..."

J OHN F. KENNEDY WANTED TO PUT a man on the moon. He wanted to channel the best of America to broadcast American exceptionalism around the world and to defeat the Soviet Union in the "space race." On September 12, 1962, he took the stage at Rice University. The speech launched unparalleled technological initiatives in the United States. It is referred to as "the speech that put a man on the moon."

> President Pitzer, Mr. Vice President, Governor, Congressman Thomas, Senator Wiley, and Congressman Miller, Mr. Webb, Mr. Bell, scientists, distinguished guests, and ladies and gentlemen: I appreciate your president having made me an honorary visiting professor, and I will assure you that my first lecture will be very brief. I am delighted to be here, and I'm particularly delighted to be here on this occasion. We meet at a college noted for knowledge, in a city noted for progress, in a State noted for strength, and we stand in need of all three, for we meet in an hour of change and challenge, in a decade of hope and fear, in an age of both knowledge and ignorance. The greater our knowledge increases, the greater our ignorance unfolds.

John F. Kennedy introduced himself by acknowledging important members of the audience; by paying his respects to people who facilitated his visit to Rice University. He also acknowledged various roles: "scientists, distinguished guests, and ladies and gentlemen." He directly addressed everyone. He opened with gratitude, with the phrase "I appreciate." He described himself in humble terms, not as President but as "an honorary visiting professor." He paid respect to the audience members, stating his first lecture will be brief. He expressed his delight to be there, and particularly to be there on this occasion. He complimented the college – that it is "noted for knowledge" – and the city: that it is "noted for progress." He complimented the state, noting its reputation for strength. And he expressed how the virtues of his audience members are the virtues the country needs. Why all the respectful ingratiation? Why all the pleasantries? Why all the humility? Why all the compliments? Because of the halo effect; because your first impression determines your final impression. Using the halo effect allows you to instantly appear capable, confident, and captivating.

WHAT IS THE HALO EFFECT?

The halo effect is our tendency to observe a positive quality in someone or something, and then extrapolate from that positive quality, concluding the person or object has a clump (a halo) of unobserved positive qualities. The halo effect activates multiple related cognitive biases and mental heuristics.

THE HALO EFFECT VISUALIZED

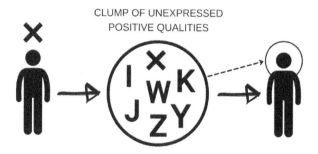

FIGURE 74: When people perceive positive quality "X" in you, the halo effect causes them to also judge you as possessing a clump of unexpressed positive qualities.

· WHAT IS AN EXAMPLE OF THE HALO EFFECT?

You meet someone new. They make an excellent first impression. You're not sure why you like them, but you know you do. They just have a confident, compelling presence, drawing you and others in with ease. What's really going on here? It could be the halo effect at work. Maybe they demonstrated they are empathetic right out of the gate. Suddenly, subconsciously, and largely out of your control, something interesting occurs in your psyche: They aren't just empathetic (what they demonstrated), they are also smart, capable, confident, driven, funny, etc. (the extrapolated halo of unobserved qualities).

What is the goal of these strategies? To become this person. To apply simple behaviors immediately activating the halo effect. To instantly appear as the best of your qualities, instead of the worst.

The halo effect is a mental shortcut; a cognitive "rule of thumb" designed, by evolution, to conserve mental resources. What causes it? Several other cognitive heuristics functioning in the same direction (what Charlie Munger called the Lollapalooza effect).

The halo effect functions through the primacy effect, confirmation bias, the undue-extrapolation tendency, the availability bias, the entanglement problem, the abstract-estimation problem, the low-stakes system-one problem, snap categorization, the crowding problem, learned correlations, and evolutionary beneficence.

We will pull back the curtain on each individual cognitive effect contributing to the halo effect. Know this: The causation is not always clear-cut. Someone can experience the halo effect because of some, all, or just one of these effects. Or perhaps it's one we don't even know of. These are just the most plausible players.

What's the primacy effect? We overweigh information we discern first. It's proven: If we feel good about someone because they presented the quality of empathy when we first met, we overweigh this positive first impression and stick to it even after discerning disconfirming information later on.

What's the undue-extrapolation tendency? This is a much bigger feature of human psychology with broader impacts, and it likely comes from the necessity to make snap judgements. We almost always take insufficient evidence and extrapolate from it prematurely, leaping to big judgements from inconclusive evidence that stands for very little in reality.

UNDUE EXTRAPOLATION VISUALIZED

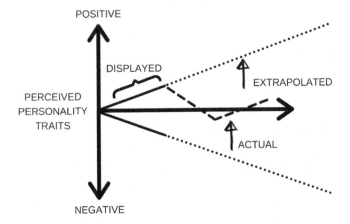

FIGURE 75: If you display a relatively small degree of positive qualities, people will extrapolate in that direction, inferring a halo of unexpressed positive qualities. This occurs in like fashion with negative positive qualities. The extrapolation flows from the display; the more positive the display, the more positive the extrapolation, and the more negative the display, the more negative the extrapolation. The truth likely lies somewhere in the middle.

What's confirmation bias? Not only do we overweigh the first impression, we see future events, even ambiguous or disconfirming ones, as confirming it. "This person showed empathy. I feel good about this person. See? I was right! They just did [insert ambiguous action], which proves the accuracy of my earlier beliefs."

CONFIRMATION BIAS VISUALIZED

FIGURE 76: This is the simplest symbolic representation of confirmation bias possible: our tendency to re-confirm our previous answer to a question.

THE OVERCONFIDENCE CYCLE

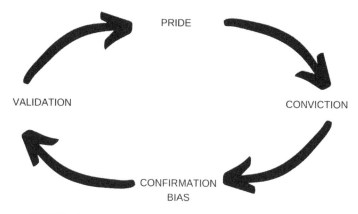

FIGURE 77: The overconfidence cycle reveals the cyclical relationship between pride, conviction, confirmation bias, and validation (Grant, 2021).

What's the availability bias? We overweigh evidence coming quickly to mind. The halo effect is, in part, overweighing first impressions. How does this tie into the availability bias? First impressions – our first interaction with a new "item" in the world – are more memorable, and thus the availability bias causes us to overweigh them.

What's the entanglement problem? Human characteristics are incredibly complex features of incredibly complex beings: insanely hard to tease apart, extremely close-knit, and entangled together like a rubber-band ball, they confound us. For example, take empathy, or understanding the emotions of another person. Think about the immense difficulty of isolating empathy. Think about the near-impossibility of saying "this is empathy, not something else, and not empathy plus something else either." Empathy is understanding; is understanding not also intelligence? Understanding someone else's emotions means making an accurate judgement about hidden feelings; does this not also demonstrate clairvoyance and strong judgement, as well as accurate perception? Doesn't it also demonstrate people-skills? Listening skills? Communication skills? And as a result, sales skills? The entanglement goes on, *ad infinitum.* The halo effect (extrapolating many positive characteristics from one demonstrated positive characteristic) happens because the many positive characteristics are near-indistinguishable from the one.

What's the abstract-estimation problem? Humans experience exceptional difficulty making judgements about abstract values. How do you measure empathy? On a one to ten scale? What is a one, and what is a ten? And what did you perceive? What even is empathy (the entanglement problem)? Dealing with abstract subjects of estimation, we end up judging based on intuition, and intuition more frequently falls prey to biases than our analytical skills.

What's the low-stakes system-one problem? Summarizing decades of groundbreaking cognitive-behavioral research by the two gifted researchers Daniel Kahneman and Amos Tversky, humans have a "system one" and a "system two." System one refers to fast, intuitive, and instinctual mental process; the mental processes relying on rough short-cuts like biases to subconsciously get fast results with little effort. System two? System two refers to our analytical mind, dealing with complicated situations system one can't manage, and doing so slowly, deliberately, and carefully. Math and complex analysis of any kind are system two work. System two expends calories, and when we are physically tired, we often bounce back to system one when we shouldn't. System one is our default. What triggers a switch to system two? High-stakes and unintuitive subject matter; new and uncomfortable situations demanding slow and deliberative thought. Evaluating someone's positive qualities probably isn't high-stakes, unintuitive, new, deliberation-demanding, and uncomfortable. Thus, we stay in system one; we use the system falling prey to cognitive heuristics like the halo effect.

KEY INSIGHT:

We Are Too Comfortable Judging The People Around Us; Too Comfortable Snap-Categorizing.

THE LOW-STAKES SYSTEM-ONE PROBLEM VISUALIZED

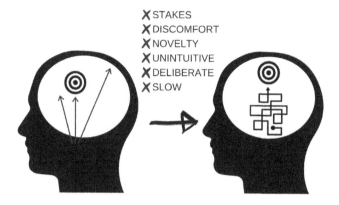

X STAKES
X DISCOMFORT
X NOVELTY
X UNINTUITIVE
X DELIBERATE
X SLOW

FIGURE 78: None of the situational factors that trigger a switch from system one to system two apply in the situation of forming first impressions.

What's snap categorization? We have mental categories in our heads. "Trustworthy person" is an example. When we see a new item, we often snap-categorize it to one of our preexisting categories based only on the first major observable quality. Did someone greet us respectfully? Trustworthy people (the category) share respect (the demonstrated quality), thus we assume this person shares the other undemonstrated qualities of the trustworthy people category, like punctuality, good temper, and intelligence.

What's the crowding problem? Humans have a finite mental budget. We can only focus on one item and think one thought at a time. A seemingly disconfirming experience is the sensation of having a lot on our frenzied minds. But in this case, we still only deal with one thought at a time; we just switch rapidly back and forth between different thoughts. Likewise, when we multitask, we deal with one thought at once; we just switch between different thoughts and activities frantically. Furthermore, we morph the world into artificially neat and organized patterns of existence. We tell ourselves non-existent stories about the nature of reality. We personify inanimate objects. Why? Why are we so incredibly irrational? Because our minds are amazing machines doing amazing things 24/7/365; they need to keep cognitive load down so they don't overheat. They have their limitations. And how does this relate to the halo effect? Like so: We have a hard time keeping multiple thoughts about one person in our mind at the same time. In fact, it's impossible. We need to rapidly switch between different thoughts, which is overwhelming. It grows more overwhelming the more contradictory, numerous, and complex the thoughts become. We can only think of one at a time, and switching takes effort. Thus, positive qualities demonstrated early can crowd out negative qualities demonstrated later.

What are learned correlations? Sometimes (in fact, quite often) the halo effect is spot on. The pretty person is smart. The aesthetically pleasing product is robust. The empathetic person is well-spoken. We learned certain qualities correlate with other qualities, and maybe this web of learned correlations informs some instances of the halo effect.

What's evolutionary beneficence? The halo effect works. It can give us better judgements faster. Thus, it helped and still helps us survive and pass down our genes, containing instructions for the mental machinery producing the halo effect.

Unfortunately, it's hard to tease apart the complex web of cognitive heuristics, especially when they are this closely related and acting in the same direction at the same time.

THE PERSUASIVE VORTEX OF THE HALO EFFECT

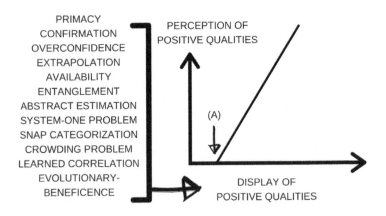

FIGURE 79: The biases and heuristics forming the halo effect form a potent, intertwined psychological admixture. They may be conceived as a Lollapalooza effect. When you display your first positive quality (A), people rapidly begin to perceive you as possessing many more.

HOW DO YOU OVERCOME THE HALO EFFECT?

Almost all strategies overcoming the halo effect hinge on one key: rigorous recording of behaviors to displace intuition. We can easily overcome the halo effect if we compile thorough and reliable records of behavior. Instead of saying "person X (who first demonstrated punctuality) should be promoted because they are punctual, capable, intelligent, and well-spoken," and saying "person Y (who was late the first time, but never again) should not be promoted because they are sloppy, error-prone, and bad at dealing with clients," you can defer to the actual records. Maybe your intuition is right. That's certainly possible. The halo effect is a "good-enough" heuristic, and it only exists because it produces correct judgements a "good-enough" portion of the time. But now you can know for sure.

There is also a "reverse halo effect." I don't use this terminology. When an observer perceives one quality in a new item and extrapolates a halo of related qualities, it is the halo effect at work. Some split the terminology into "halo effect" for positive qualities and "reverse halo effect" for negative qualities. Again, I'm not a proponent of this; I just didn't want you to hear "reverse halo effect" and think I omitted something.

HOW DO YOU USE THE HALO EFFECT IN COMMUNICATION?

All of these proven strategies immediately activate the halo effect in your favor. They present the best possible initial qualities. The result? You'll pick up a host of positive qualities without demonstrating them (though I'm sure you do, in fact, possess them): "Capable. Confident. Trustworthy. Going places. Sharp. Enthusiastic. Funny. Intelligent."

Moreover, these strategies guarantee you don't demonstrate a negative quality, thereby undermining your professional image by producing a halo of negative qualities.

KEY INSIGHT:

The First Step of Impression Management is Building a Good One. That's the Easy Part.

The Second Step of Impression Management is Living Up to It. That's the Hard Part.

STRATEGY #1: COMMANDEER AN IMPRESSIVE SPACE

I separate communication inputs into two categories: contextual and direct. Contextual communication refers to inputs you don't directly produce with your voice, words, and body language. Direct communication refers to inputs you do produce with your voice, words, and body language.

Most communicators overemphasize direct inputs, while neglecting contextuals altogether. But contextual inputs can make or break your communication, immediately turning weak words into a memorable message without even changing them.

People pay more attention to the same words spoken from an impressive podium in an impressive venue than a bland meeting room. Context matters. Context sets expectations, and we all-too-often perceive reality as lining up with our expectations.

How do you maximize the contribution of contextual inputs to the halo-effect cascade? By commandeering the most impressive, important-looking place you can. Are you holding a meeting? Don't do it in your office. Find the nicest conference room available to you, with the best view, the biggest table, and the most amenities. They will observe the quality "can commandeer important space," take the fairly small and reasonable leap to "is important," and then make the big leap to "capable, confident, trustworthy, etc."

MASTERING BOTH DIRECT INPUTS AND CONTEXTUAL INPUTS

DIRECT COMMUNICATION

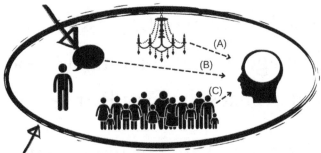

CONTEXTUAL COMMUNICATION

FIGURE 80: Direct communication comes directly from the speaker. Contextual communication comes from the surroundings. The glass chandelier in the venue is contextual, communicating a message of wealth, opulence, and prestige (A). The direct communication (B) is partly interpreted through the lens of the contextual communication. Another powerful piece of contextual communication is the large crowd (C), which sends a message of social proof, high value, and public approval. Switching contextual inputs can virtually switch the interpretation of the direct input.

STRATEGY #2: IRON OUT THE DETAILS EARLY

I've witnessed too many embarrassing and avoidable moments. Check the microphone. Check the presentation software. Check the slides. Check the projector. Confirm you have the room. Ensure with complete confidence everything you need is where it should be, functioning as intended.

It will be a big "reverse halo effect" (even though I don't like the term) if your first impression tells people you weren't thorough in checking the room, lacking attention to details.

STRATEGY #3: PROJECT YOUR VOICE

People respect a powerful voice. Project your voice. Extend it over the room. Stay exactly on the thin line between shouting and talking. You're not yet shouting, but you're talking loud enough for everyone to hear you with crystal clarity. There's a positive halo effect emerging from this. From "loud voice," they take a reasonable and small step to "confident," and then a big leap to "smart, capable, well-versed, skilled, expert, etc."

STRATEGY #4: APPLY THE "APP" OPENING

The first words you say define how people perceive you. You can overcome bad first impressions later on, but it is easier, much easier, to get it right the first time.

How you use your voice matters; how you use your body language does too. But this proven, step-by-step formula, the "APP" formula, perfects your words. How does it work? Consider this scenario: You are giving a big presentation to a sales force, and as you wait for the (ideally impressive) room to fill, you make some small-talk with new faces in the room.

"What's your presentation going to be about?" they ask. Apply this method. Agree with a pain point: "Well, as a salesman, you probably relate to struggling with keeping busy prospects on the line, right? I know that's been a struggle for me in the past." Promise a fix: "Right, exactly. This presentation uncovers some proven methods that keep prospects on the line and interested." Preview the fix: "For example, my favorite is the benefit-tagging technique, which I will teach in-depth."

You can (and should) also use this formula for opening the presentation itself. The result? An instantly positive first impression producing a wonderful halo of positive qualities.

STRATEGY #5: SET THE STAKES EARLY

How does this tie to demonstrating one positive quality early, and thus experiencing a massive halo of undemonstrated positive qualities? All communication compels people if it has high stakes; if people understand the impacts of your message are significant to their lives and ambitions. Someone communicating about a high-stakes subject carries a gravitas, commanding complete respect and full attention. Someone who is communicating about a low-stakes subject can barely hold a modicum of attention. "Can't keep me engaged" precedes a small step to "boring and undynamic," and then a big leap to the halo of "unimportant, disengaged, dim, etc."

What do you do? Raise the stakes. Tell people why it matters. "If we nail this strategy, we can each walk away with 20% more in commissions at the end of the year. If we don't? People will keep hanging up on us before we can say 'hello sir.' And keep in mind, a 20% bump is the average from a recent study of these strategies, which means some of you will make even more."

The PNP formula is a proven step-by-step process for quickly setting high stakes. Positive if: "If we do [insert what you want them to do], we will experience [insert high-stake benefits]." Negative if: "If we don't do [insert, or leave implied, what you want them to do], we will experience [insert high-stake losses]." Proof: "For example, in a recent study conducted by [insert source], they found that [insert supporting evidence]."

Painting your subject as the intersection between massive benefits and massive losses makes it seem tremendously consequential, creating a powerful positive halo effect.

SETTING HIGH STAKES GRABS ATTENTION FROM THE START

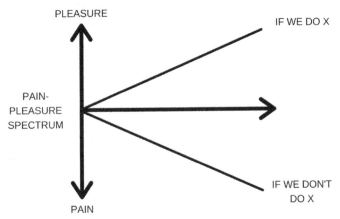

FIGURE 81: Present your message as the fork in the road between massive pain and massive pleasure; pain if they don't do what you propose, and pleasure if they do.

STRATEGY #6: DRESS SLIGHTLY ABOVE AVERAGE

If you dress less professionally than everyone else, you'll experience a halo effect of negative qualities. If you dress drastically nicer than everyone else, you'll experience another halo effect of negative qualities. But if you dress slightly above average, you are in the sweet spot that offers you a positive halo effect. This ensures you are better dressed than most, if not all, but not to the point of excess. You receive a positive halo effect: "This guy looks sharp, he's probably smart, capable, and trustworthy."

Too fancy? "This guy looks out of place. He probably isn't too aware, cognizant, or capable." Below average? "This guy looks off. He doesn't care about his appearance. He probably lacks attention to detail, an effective work ethic, and expertise."

The salience effect is another reason why the "slightly above average" approach works. Salience is defined as follows:

Distinctiveness, prominence, obviousness. The term is widely used in the study of perception and cognition to refer to any aspect of a stimulus that, for any of many reasons, stands out from the rest. ("Salience," n.d.)

The salience effect is our tendency to perceive salient inputs as more important. You want to be salient, and dressing slightly above average achieves just the right amount of salience, no more, no less.

STRATEGY #7: ELIMINATE CONVERSATION FILLERS

Opening one: "This new, uh, er, customer relationship, um, management system is designed to, uhh, manage outgoing communications, mm, more easily."

Opening two: "This new customer relationship management system is designed to manage outgoing communications more easily."

Which one creates a positive halo? Which one creates a negative halo? The answer is clear.

Conversation fillers like "uh, like, um," pop into our speech because we don't know the very next word, and our brains think the following: "Right now I am in a state of speaking and in this state I must be making constant sound so I will make a sound, any sound!"

How do you avoid conversation fillers? First, know your content. As your comprehension of your subject rises, the amount of conversation fillers popping into your speech drops. Why? Because they pop up when you are unsure of what to say next, and strong subject knowledge makes you certain of what to say next. Second, pause instead. A pause is infinitely better than a conversation filler. Are you unsure what to say next? Does it feel like your mind can't seem to retrieve your very next word? Take this opportunity to work in a pause. According to Mark Twain, words may be eloquent, but no word has ever been as eloquent as a rightly timed pause. Third, sentence-chain. Pick the single most important thing you want to say, summarize it in one or a few sentences, say it, and then simply chain the rest of your communication off of that. Simply say something, and build your next something off of the first something. This forms a continuous chain of fluent, natural sentences, simply because one leads to the other. By having a sentence behind you to build your next one on, you give your mind the necessary stimulus to quickly and fluently produce the content you want to share.

STRATEGY #8: REACT WELL TO STUMBLES

Conversation fillers are little sounds like "uh" and "um" that pop into your speech now and then. Stumbles are more severe: "This new customer relationship m-m-manager-management systems-system is designed to manage outgoing communications more easily. The same strategies helping you fight conversation fillers help you fight stumbles. But to some extent, stumbles are inevitable. You need a tremendous amount of practice to stop stumbles or hide them when they happen. When I was a competitive public speaker, going to around 15 tournaments a year for three consecutive years, each tournament consisting of about five hours of speaking, I was only ever able to reduce the frequency of my stumbles. I never removed them altogether.

The best way I can serve you is not by teaching you to avoid a stumble (apply the conversation-filler eliminating strategies to lower their frequency), but by teaching you how to react to one. Whether the halo effect will be positive or negative hinges not on whether you stumble – people don't care about that – but on how you react to it.

The best way to react is to ignore it. Everyone else probably did too. Get back on track and continue like it never happened. This creates a positive halo effect. No embarrassed smile – there's nothing to be embarrassed about. No washing the rest of the sentence out of your brain – there's no reason to do that, just get back on track. No negative emotions at all – there's no need for them, and they will seep into your facial expression, where everyone will see them.

STRATEGY #9: PRESENT FLUENCY OF COMPREHENSION

When people try to answer a question (like "how many of the president's policies do you know?"), they judge the strength of their knowledge of the president's policies on fluency and magnitude. They judge their comprehension by the fluency with which they remember the president's policies, and the magnitude, or the number, of the president's policies that they remember.

Fluency holds more weight than magnitude. If they quickly and thoroughly – or fluently – remember two policies, they have checked the fluency box, and they judge their knowledge to be reasonably robust. Not very strong, because they still lack a magnitude of examples, but moderately complete. If they do not quickly remember any policies, but sit down and manage to brainstorm twenty policies – or a magnitude – over five hours, then they judge themselves as less competent on this subject than they did when they portrayed fluency but not magnitude.

And fluency is not always easy. This is why it is such a potent litmus test of subject-area competency. Why do people say "name three examples" when accused of bad behavior? Because fluency is difficult, and there is a fairly high chance that the accuser will not be able to fluently riff off three examples of the bad behavior, even if they could think of thirty over a more extended timespan.

People judge their own subject-area competency based on the fluency and magnitude with which they respond to a related query. They will also judge your subject-area competency – a key component of credibility – based on fluency and magnitude.

And that's the secret.

Prepare yourself to portray immense fluency and magnitude in support of your claims and positions. Do it with examples. Examples are, in and of themselves, credibility boosters. The basic principle of this strategy is to make a claim and then fluently rattle off a large magnitude of examples. The "what" of this strategy may be simple, but the "how" can be difficult.

How do you deliver fluency? By speaking in a fast, unlabored, easy, and effortless way. By streaming out, without error or complication, a quick barrage of supporting examples. The speed and ease with which you rattle off the examples express your fluency, which bolsters your credibility. When you want to apply this strategy, don't make the mistake of taking a deep-dive into one example. There's time for that later. When you want to express fluency, just skim across the surface, like a jet-ski; don't go for a deep-dive just yet. Skim across ten examples, don't dig deep into one.

How do you deliver magnitude? By continuing until ten or so examples. Ten examples as a sufficient magnitude serves as a general guideline. It depends on your circumstances. Keep going until you have achieved what is considered a high magnitude of content for your particular circumstances: your subject, your audience, your position, your claim, etc.

This strategy works when the units in the list of examples (the number of units in the list being its magnitude) are short phrases.

For example, I gave a speech in college about why the world was getting much better. I said, "virtually every measure of human prosperity has drastically improved over time." And then I rattled off a magnitude of ten examples fluently. This is the critical part: The examples were just prosperity-measures that improved in recent decades. As such, the examples were one- or two-word phrases, like "democratic values," or "consumer surplus."

It is easier to fluently deliver single-word examples, and magnitude is not length, but number. If you have one example, and fluently describe that one example for a long duration, that is not a magnitude. It is still just one example. You must not emphasize your fluency and magnitude in your knowledge of one specific example, but your knowledge of many examples. One example is an example. Ten is a psychological magnitude. This is how the weight of your fluency and magnitude will lend you immense credibility.

You can also use this to create mic-drop moments. Let's say you anticipate a pointed question or a predictable objection. For example, let's say you are a conservative political pundit, speaking on liberal college campuses, and a politically left-leaning student extolls the virtues of socialism.

Anticipate this. Have at the ready a response that goes something like this: "Nearly every single Socialist country failed, costing lives, resources, and causing dramatic destruction and destitution (claim, which you will support with a fluently delivered magnitude of examples, where the examples are short phrases and thus easiest to work into this strategy). The Soviet Union failed. Serbia failed. Croatia failed. Slovenia failed. Romania failed. Poland failed. Hungary failed. Angola failed. Ethiopia failed. East Germany failed. Mozambique failed. Bulgaria failed. Yugoslavia failed. Czechoslovakia failed."

Remember: There are two elements of the fluency-magnitude matrix. First, a claim where the examples are short phrases (which are easiest to deliver fluently). Second, the ensuing magnitude of those examples, fluently delivered.

Another example of a pointed question or objection to the conservative pundit is "Capitalist countries produce terrible consequences." The counterclaim from the pundit using this strategy would be something like this: "Capitalist countries produce tremendous benefits. Higher consumer surplus. Higher protection of human rights. Higher protection of fundamental liberties. Nearly 80% of all corporate profit going to labor. Self-interest directed to the betterment of the public. Innovation. Longer life expectancy. Greater measures of self-reported happiness. More emancipative values. Lower poverty and extreme poverty. Lower rates of starvation. Lower levels of sickness and malnourishment."

See how there are two parts to this? The claim which lends itself to short examples? The magnitude of examples fluently delivered? Remember: This strategy is easiest with short examples. But, if you have a sufficiently fluent and extensive memory, you can use longer examples. Try to make the examples as specific as possible. Humans have a precision bias, which we discuss shortly.

I use the example of a conservative pundit because conservative college-campus speakers ubiquitously use this strategy. Virtually every single instance of the fluency-magnitude matrix in action created a chorus of applause. Virtually every single instance of the fluency-magnitude matrix in action went viral on social media. Virtually every single instance of the fluency-magnitude matrix in action crumbled the opposition under the massive weight of perceived credibility the speaker gained. It acts as a verbal kill shot that nearly instantly boosts your credibility to massive levels.

STRATEGY #10: USE OPEN BODY LANGUAGE

Closed body language portrays detachment. It feels like facing an unfriendly wall. Open body language presents a personable, influential, and affable nature. You now understand the halo effect, so you understand why using open body language is imperative.

Open body language does exactly what it sounds like. It opens you up. Smile. Hold your head high. Don't block your torso. Gesture outwardly, and keep your arms by your sides, not in front of you. Keep your feet pointed toward the audience. Make eye contact.

STRATEGY #11: APPLY THE TWO PRINCIPLES OF FLOW

Flow sounds satisfying. Sentences without flow sound stilted and off. Sentences with flow sound eloquent, creating a halo effect of positive qualities.

There are two elements of flow. The first element is that the rate of information exchange remains constant within a sentence (though it can and should change between sentences). If you are presenting information with abundant flourishment, extensive detail, and vivid language, do so throughout a sentence. Don't do so until a comma and change the rate of information exchange (and the depth of the information) after the comma. Do so in another sentence. The second element of flow is that the lengths of phrases in a sentence are balanced. Don't have twenty words, a comma, and one word in a sentence. Keep the parts relatively balanced.

Additionally, you must avoid tangents and parentheticals at the sentence level. When you are writing, go ahead and write longer sentences that wind about and include little folds, ideas in parenthesis, ideas delineated by dashes – like this – and semicolons; whatever suits your fancy. It's okay when you're writing. Your audience members – in this case, readers – can easily slow down the flow of communication to make it more manageable. They control the rate of information exchange: they can slow down, they can reread, they can break it up into parts, they can read it five times if they want. Now, this is not ideal, but it's not going to kill your writing. However, it will kill your spoken communication like nothing else.

When you are speaking, short of raising their hands and interrupting you to ask a question or to prompt a repetition, your audience members have no control over the rate of information exchange. They either match it or don't, and the moment your rate of information exchange exceeds their rate of interpretation, you risk losing them, *ceteris paribus*. You speak with too much complexity. It exceeds what listeners can reasonably comprehend. And even if they can comprehend it, remember the marginal net gain model: by adding unnecessary complexity, you raise perceived (and real) marginal costs of listening to you.

So, a sentence like this one, one that has twists and turns – even without big words – and a sentence which extends itself (and includes side-thoughts and related anecdotes in parenthesis) but doesn't concisely center on one idea, possibly including examples of many different ideas under the roof of one sentence, though not tying them back to one – or perhaps two (but not three) – major thematic element or, in the case of more examples, elements plural, won't kill your writing.

It will only bring your writing to the brink of death. It's so incredibly far from ideal writing. But a reader can comprehend it, with a little boost of added effort.

A listener, however, would get lost. Why? Because of all the twists and turns embedded in that sentence. All the tangents. All the parentheticals. All the added pieces of relevant but unnecessary details. All the rumination. All the content that is not tied to one central idea. All the meta-information, or information about information. All the of nonsense.

A moderately persistent reader can overcome those things, but even the most persistent listener would lose you around "and includes side-thoughts and related anecdotes in parenthesis."

Maintain clarity in your communication by avoiding parentheticals more often than not, replacing them with short, punchy, decisive sentences that flow off the tongue.

Much rhetorically beautiful language includes some longer sentences. But only after earning attention with shorter, easy sentences. And even those longer sentences do not try to take on more than they can handle by using hyper-complex structures. The sentences may be long, but the micro-structures embedded in them break up information and ease comprehension.

A spoken parenthetical is not as obvious as a written parenthetical; there are no visible parenthesis symbols. A spoken parenthetical is an attempt to include a sub-point or sub-message in a sentence with a different purpose entirely. And often, a parenthetical is information about information, or meta-information.

Each sentence should have one purpose, accomplish it quickly, decisively, and effortlessly, and then include the sub-point or sub-message in the next sentence if it is so important. Give each sentence a job, do that job in that sentence, and no other job. Leave the rest to other sentences.

Avoid tangents. We speak a sentence with a clear purpose (whether we realize the purpose or not). Another idea flashes into our heads. We jump on the shiny new idea, deviating the path of the sentence and not achieving a synthesis of the original thought. We say something like "and, by the way..." or "which, if we think about it..." and then we deliver the new idea instead of the original one.

He who chases two rabbits catches neither. So, it's already bad at this point; it's already bad the moment you deviate from the precise path of a sentence to stuff in another idea. But it gets worse when we forget to close the original sentence and leave a loose end up in the air.

KEY INSIGHT:

Move Your Message Forward in a Focused, Clear, Logical, Simple, Methodical, Accurate, Intentional Way: From A to B to C to D.

Guard Against Your Tendency to Go Back to B From A, and to D Before C... To Say Too Much, Too Quickly, Too Frantically.

SENTENCE-LEVEL PARANTHETICALS WEAKEN YOUR IMPACT

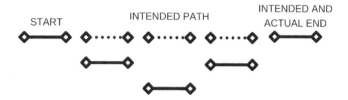

FIGURE 82: Parentheticals are similar to tangents, but loop back into the intended path before the end. They take a less effective path to the same destination.

SENTENCE-LEVEL TANGENTS BLUR YOUR MESSAGE

FIGURE 82: You would like to deliver a message in five sentences. You know exactly where you want to go, and the path to get there. You begin as intended. You deliver your second sentence as intended. However, you get a tempting thought to throw in. You deviate from your initial intended path and follow this red-herring for three more sentences. This is a sentence-level tangent (tangents also occur within sentences), and it kills effective communication like nothing else. As the distance between your intended end and your actual end rises (A), the strength of your communication falls. Keep it tight, focused, and direct. Move in a

straight line. Have a plan and stick to it. You can deliver the red-herring thought after you finished what you started.

STRATEGY #12: PRESENT SHARED VALUES AND BELIEFS

People prize their values and beliefs above all else. The Cold War exemplifies this. Two nations brought the world to the brink of total annihilation because they operated on contrary value systems. This underscores the tremendous importance of values. And when people see you echo their values and beliefs, they will instinctively feel drawn to you. They will instantly perceive a dramatically positive halo of wonderful qualities. Appealing to shared values is one of the most powerful ways to resonate and connect with an audience, while opening them up to all of your subsequent ideas.

Describe things the way they see them. Subtly indicate your opinion is the same as theirs (the key word here is subtly). Enter their minds, see the world through their eyes, identify their values and beliefs, and incorporate these into your communication. This mode of radical empathy allows you to understand their worldview and then echo it.

HALO-EFFECT CONCLUSION

John F. Kennedy opened his address at Rice University by presenting a host of positive qualities. He presented clairvoyance. He presented gratitude. He presented humility. He presented enthusiasm. As a result, the halo effect worked in his favor, granting him a halo of positive qualities he never actually displayed.

..............................Chapter Summary...............................

- The halo effect is our tendency to extrapolate a halo of unshown positive qualities from one observed such quality.
- The halo effect functions through a complex web of cognitive processes that interweave and coalesce.
- The halo effect explains why the common wisdom of the importance of first impressions holds true.
- You use the halo effect in communication by applying strategies that decisively present a positive quality.
- You overcome the halo effect by relying not on intuitive judgements but behavioral records, when available.
- John F. Kennedy used the halo effect by subtly presenting a host of positive qualities at the start of his speech.

HOW TO OVERCOME THE PSYCHOLOGY (PART SIX)

1	**The Availability Bias**
1.1	Gather All Available Statistics Instead of Relying on Ease of Recall
2	**The Anchoring Effect**
2.1	Educate Yourself on the Subject of Evaluation
2.2	Strive to Ignore the First Number You Hear
2.3	Be Cognizant of the Impact of Unrelated Anchors
2.4	Seek Historical Evidence Related to Your Evaluation
2.5	Concentrate Attention on a Self-Supplied Counter-Anchor
3	**Munger's Biases**
3.1	Watch Carefully for Bias-Activating Circumstances
4	**The Contrast Effect**
4.1	Generate Counteracting Contrasting Inputs
5	**Zero-Risk Bias**
5.1	Run Statistical, Empirical, Rational Risk-Reward Calculations
6	**The Halo Effect**
6.1	Rely on Behavioral Records as Opposed to Snap Judgments
7	**Agent Detection Bias**
8	**Attribute Substitution**
9	**Base Rate Neglect**

Claim These Free Resources that Will Help You Unleash the Power of Your Words and Speak with Confidence. Visit www.speakforsuccesshub.com/toolkit for Access.

30 Free Video Lessons

We'll send you one free video lesson every day for 30 days, written and recorded by Peter D. Andrei. Days 1-10 cover authenticity, the prerequisite to confidence and persuasive power. Days 11-20 cover building self-belief and defeating communication anxiety. Days 21-30 cover how to speak with impact and influence, ensuring your words change minds instead of falling flat. Authenticity, self-belief, and impact – this course helps you master three components of confidence, turning even the most high-stakes presentations from obstacles into opportunities.

Claim These Free Resources that Will Help You Unleash the Power of Your Words and Speak with Confidence. Visit www.speakforsuccesshub.com/toolkit for Access.

2 Free Workbooks

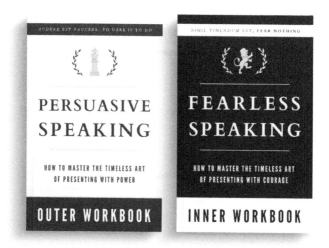

We'll send you two free workbooks, including long-lost excerpts by Dale Carnegie, the mega-bestselling author of *How to Win Friends and Influence People* (5,000,000 copies sold). *Fearless Speaking* guides you in the proven principles of mastering your inner game as a speaker. *Persuasive Speaking* guides you in the time-tested tactics of mastering your outer game by maximizing the power of your words. All of these resources complement the Speak for Success collection.

SPEAK FOR SUCCESS COLLECTION BOOK

I

HOW HIGHLY EFFECTIVE PEOPLE SPEAK CHAPTER

VIII

AGENT DETECTION BIAS:

How People Perceive and Judge Reality

"WE'RE USING UP PRIME TIME. THANK YOU VERY MUCH. THANK YOU VERY MUCH..."

R ONALD REAGAN'S "A TIME FOR CHOOSING" propelled him to the White House. But before he could contend for the Presidency, he had to contend for the Republican nomination. This is the speech he gave when he won that contest. It reconciled the disputes within the party, presented a unified front to the nation, repudiated the strategies of his opponents, and revealed deeper nuances of his views.

> The Republican program for solving economic problems is based on growth and productivity. Large amounts of oil and natural gas lay beneath our land and off our shores, untouched because the present Administration seems to believe the American people would rather see more regulation, more taxes, and more controls than more energy. Coal offers great potential. So does nuclear energy produced under rigorous safety standards. It could supply electricity for thousands of industry [sic] and millions of jobs and homes. It must not be thwarted by a tiny minority opposed to economic growth which often finds friendly ears in regulatory agencies for its obstructionist campaigns. Now, make no mistake. We will not permit the safety of our people or our environmental heritage to be jeopardized, but we are going to reaffirm that the economic prosperity of our people is a fundamental part of our environment. Our problems – Our problems are both acute and chronic, yet all we hear from those in positions of leadership are the same tired proposals for more Government tinkering, more meddling, and more control – all of which led us to this sorry state in the first place. Can anyone look at the record of this Administration and say, "Well done?" Can anyone compare the state of our economy when the Carter Administration took office with where we are today and say, "Keep up the good work?" Can anyone look at our reduced standing in the world today and say, "Let's have four more years of this?" I believe the American people are going to answer these questions, as you've answered them, in the first week in November and their answer will be, "No – we've had enough." And then – And then it will be up to us, beginning next January 20th, to offer an administration and congressional leadership of competence and more than a little courage. We must have the clarity of vision to see the difference between what is essential and what is merely desirable, and then the courage to bring our government back under control.

There is a complex science behind the sequence of questions Reagan posed. In this section, we pull back the curtain, revealing how Reagan painted a wrongdoer to achieve massive influence, repudiating the wrong approach to emphasize his right approach, laying the blame for the economic disaster squarely and unequivocally at the feet of his opponent. Using the same psychology Reagan used in this section offers you immense impact and influence, and ensures your message doesn't fall flat.

WHAT IS THE AGENT DETECTION BIAS?

Humans tend to assume random events in the environment result from living agents acting in certain ways, with clear motive and intent. We quickly assume an intelligent and sentient agent created an observed phenomenon. We don't buy complex, multi-causal explanations. We don't buy uncertain webs of intertwining causal relationships.

AGENT DETECTION BIAS VISUALIZED

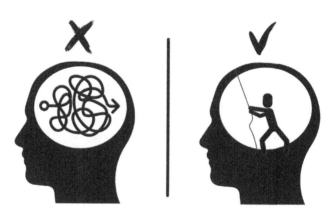

FIGURE 84: The human mind rejects a complex tangle of multiple causal factors. It intuitively accepts a single agent acting with intent and pulling the string.

WHAT IS AN EXAMPLE OF THE AGENT DETECTION BIAS?

When the economy is good, people credit the president. Likewise, when the economy is bad, people blame him. Why? Because agent detection bias pushes them to detect the president – a (hopefully) sentient and intelligent being – as an agent causing the phenomenon. But the truth is that presidents receive too much credit or blame for the economies over which they preside.

What creates a positive economy? Not one agent working with clear motive or intent: an unfathomably large number of agents working with often contrary motives towards often completely opposite ends, and a deeply complicated confluence of random events. So why does the president always get blame or credit when, in truth, they exert little control over the economy? Because of agent detection bias.

It's the burden of leadership: getting blamed for bad things happening even if you can't possibly control them. But it can also be the benefit of leadership: getting praised for good things you can't possibly control.

And this ties into our natural human tendency to create stories where none exist. We should define a new bias: story or narrative bias. We understand information packaged in a story outstandingly well. We find story-molded, narrative-packaged information more truthful. We create narratives where none exist.

Why does this tie to agent detection bias? Because good stories hinge on the actions of two key agents, the protagonist and antagonist. And events in stories are not random: the machinations of these two key agents and their intentional actions produce them.

Where does agent detection bias come from? Scientists theorize it is an evolutionary trait. Why? Because hearing a twig snap in the forest 1,000,000 years ago and assuming an agent caused the disturbance, like a mountain lion, helped us survive. It is better to run 20 times even if 19 times there is no threat than to stick around 20 times. This bias essentially pushed us to err on the side of caution. The problem is that cultural and technological evolution outpaced human psychological evolution, and this bias today leads to frequent misjudgments.

I have a hunch. This is not scientifically validated, as far as my research found, but I believe the agent detection bias also pushes us to perceive a singular agent, who is vivid and specific, as opposed to an abstract and ill-defined group. I draw this from the singularity effect in compassion fade: Our compassion peaks with one victim, and decreases as the number of victims increases. And if a group acts, we tend to identify a single leader as the clear agent, neglecting the possibility of multiple agents, sub-coalitions, or inner-group forces.

Conspiracy theories are another example of agent detection bias at work. I'll leave identifying how this bias empowers conspiracy theories as an exercise for the reader.

HOW DO YOU OVERCOME THE AGENT DETECTION BIAS?

Whenever you identify a causal relationship hinging on a single agent's actions, question yourself. Don't outright falsify it. Just do your due diligence. Double check for multiple agents, random events, or a confluence of factors acting in one direction. It's possible a single agent acting with clear intent caused the bulk of the phenomenon, but the larger the phenomenon, the less likely it is that a single agent caused it. Even powerful agents, like presidents, can't exert a tremendous amount of influence over the aggregate results of human existence at large, like economics.

KEY INSIGHT:

The Human Project: Seek to Explain The (Almost) Unexplainably Complex Causal Webs Surrounding Us.

THE LIKELIHOOD OF AGENT-DETECTION-DRIVEN ERRORS

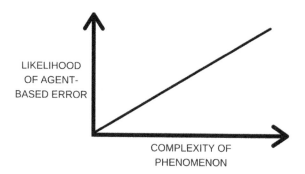

FIGURE 85: As the complexity of the phenomenon in question rises, the likelihood of agent detection bias leading to an erroneous conclusion as opposed to an accurate one rises, as complex phenomena rarely have a single causal agent behind them.

HOW DO YOU USE THE AGENT DETECTION BIAS IN COMMUNICATION?

In *The Science of Selling*, David Hoffeld teaches us that psychological features embedded in humans determine how we make buying decisions, and that the best way to sell is in a manner congruent with these psychological features. Or, more simply, sell the way people buy (Hoffeld, 2016). This echoes a frequent theme of my books. Human psychological characteristics define how we interpret information. Want to convey information? Convey information the way science proves we interpret it. Want to succeed as a communicator? Follow this rule. Want to struggle? Ignore it.

The following strategies activating agent detection bias convey information in a way aligned with how humans interpret it. Thus, they work. It's not my hunch; it's not validated by only my experience; it's not based on rough guess-work. It's scientific.

These strategies are critical to instantly receiving understanding, speaking with influence and persuasion, and getting people to gravitate to your point of view.

STRATEGY #1: PAINT A PERPETRATOR

I previously divulged the Victim-Perpetrator-Benevolence model. Are you discussing a problem? Are you selling a solution to a problem or diagnosing an issue? Are you dealing with harms, struggles, obstacles, pains, or difficulties? Paint a perpetrator; paint a clear, specific actor causing the problems. Why? This validates the problems, making them compelling and captivating centers of attention and thus furthering your persuasive objective. Embedding the problem (the effect) in a cause-and-effect relationship with a clear agent acting as the cause validates the problems because it is intuitive, and it is intuitive because of agent detection bias. We systematically overweigh the value and truth of intuitive arguments.

PAINTING A PERPETRATOR AND AGENT DETECTION

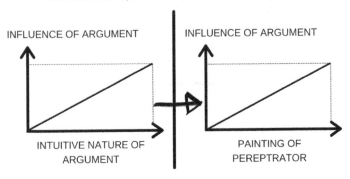

FIGURE 86: As the intuitive nature of your argument rises, so does its influence. As you paint a perpetrator, your influence rises, because it appeals to intuition.

STRATEGY #2: EXPLAIN EVENTS THROUGH HUMAN ACTION

Explain events through narratives of human action. People reject complex, convoluted arguments about extensive arrays of overlapping causal relationships. What do they reflexively accept? Agents acting with intent. And it's not misleading to paint a clear agent causing a phenomenon: you are not saying it's only this agent, you are merely choosing to focus on him.

Why do this? Why select a clear agent and present his actions as causing the salient phenomena? It is intuitive, and we overweigh intuitive information. It is compelling. It appeals to how humans interpret information. And most importantly, it validates the existence of the problem, and you cannot advocate for a solution successfully without elaborating the problem it solves.

Arguments like these exemplify the strategy: A confluence of an unfathomably large number of economic phenomena nearly nobody on this planet completely understands didn't cause income inequality, Reagan did. A tremendously complicated web of thousands of causal relationships dating back 200,000 years, tangled with thousands we created this year isn't causing climate change: A new administration weakening the environmental protection agency in 2020 is causing the climate change observed in 2020. Hillary Clinton lost only because of Donald Trump, not dozens of issues with her own campaign. The agent-oriented explanation isn't false, just incomplete.

STRATEGY #3: EXPLAIN EVENTS AS A STRUGGLE BETWEEN A PROTAGONIST AND ANTAGONIST

Stories persuade us. Stories carry tremendous intuitive appeal by shaping random events into narrative patterns. Mr. Story is your best friend if you want to become a compelling communicator. And stories activate the agent detection bias.

A specific story activates this bias most. Tell stories not as a sequence of events, but as a sequence of actions and counteractions in a conflict between a protagonist and an antagonist, in which the protagonist is your audience or someone they can identify with, and the antagonist is the clear perpetrator – the agent – we discussed earlier. The key is this: Your proposal or idea is what can help the protagonist win the conflict at long last.

STRATEGY #4: VIVIDLY DESCRIBE A COMMON ENEMY

This strategy builds on our previous one. What kind of story do you find most compelling? One where all the focus is placed on defining the protagonist? Or one with a developed antagonist? Developed antagonists make stories more compelling.

Paint a vivid common enemy. The more well-defined your antagonist, the more persuasive your story.

How do we paint a vivid common enemy? Focus on motives, backstory, and characteristics. What do you say about motives? You told us what he's doing and why it's bad – now why does he want to do it? What about backstory? You told us why he wants to do it – now is there a backstory creating the motive? Finally, what are the compelling characteristics standing for the whole? If you could pick three characteristics allowing people to connect the rest of the dots themselves for a fairly full picture, what would they be?

And it is not absolutely necessary to select a particular individual to paint as the perpetrator. You can personify a process, or leave the identity of the perpetrators vaguely defined: "There are those who want you to believe [insert malevolent claim]." It may be inappropriate for you to call out a particular perpetrator, depending on the context of your communication. In this scenario, personify a process, leave the identity of the perpetrators vaguely defined, or even call out a group instead of a particular member of that group.

STRATEGY #5: ANSWER THE "HDHDI?" QUESTION

The art of appealing to agent detection bias is explaining phenomena through the lens of human action. Thus, you must define one key the mechanism of manifestation; you must answer the "HDHDI?" question.

What's the "HDHDI?" question? And when do you use it? Pull out this question when presenting a causal agent behind an event. "How did he do it?" What was the plan a sentient, intelligent agent with clear motives, a clear backstory, and clear characteristics used to manifest his desired results, the undesirable phenomenon you're explaining?

There is another reason why it is so important to appeal to agent detection bias. Solutions seem valid in the presence of a clear agent causing the salient problem. For example, Republicans who don't deny the existence of climate change but deny clear human agents cause it maintain that Congress shouldn't regulate against it. Democrats, on the contrary, believe it is caused not by Earth's natural processes, but by clear agents. This causal story validates a solution, because while we can't always regulate natural processes, we can regulate the actions of intelligent, sentient agents in our purview. Presenting a clear agent creates the kind of causal story validating a solution, which is exactly what you want if you're proposing a solution. Moreover, people assume that since clear agent caused the problem, a clear agent can fix it – you.

STRATEGY #6: PRESENT ACTION-DRIVEN SOLUTIONS

Agent detection bias doesn't just bias us to detect agents for bad events, but good ones too. Orient your presentation around how clear agents can act in clear ways to achieve clear results for clear motives. It works like orienting your explanation of problems around a vivid negative agent, except it is a clearly positive agent acting in clearly positive ways to achieve clearly positive results for clearly positive motives.

STRATEGY #7: REJECT RANDOMNESS

You must reject randomness in your explanation of events. To be clear, in communication theory, I define randomness as a confluence of causal factors so far out of human perception an effect appears to be purely unexplainable.

Reject this. It paralyzes the human mind. It operates against the salient cognitive bias: agent detection bias. It is trying to swim upstream. Paralyzed human minds don't leap to action. Humans don't act in the presence of doubt. Dispel the doubt by presenting a clear agent, not randomness. Flow with the river of human psychology, not against it.

STRATEGY #8: APPLY THE WHO, WHAT, HOW, WHY STRUCTURE

Structure simplifies using the tools revealed in this book. It draws them together in a simple, straightforward, step-by-step process giving you fluency while working the strategies in the same direction at once instead of turning them toward opposite ends.

Want not only to speak with immense influence, but fluency? Not only persuasively, but confidently? Not only impactfully, but with effortless ease?

Want not only to expertly appeal to the hidden, little-known cognitive biases, mental heuristics, and features of human psychology, but with a simple, effective, step-by-step process?

Structure offers you these opportunities. And this section reveals yet another structure for your toolbox. Who did this? What did they do (the phenomenon you're explaining)? How did they do it? Why did they do it?

"Ronald Reagan (who) created income inequality in this country (what) by lowering taxes on the super-wealthy (how) to satisfy his libertarian vision (why)." Remember: Appealing to agent detection bias works with events both positive and negative. After going through these four steps, you can add a fifth, answering either the question "why is this good?" or "why is this bad?" There are four key principles of structures; four laws of structure.

First, the law of expansion. You can stretch the structure out like an accordion and it maintains the same impact on a different scale, as long as all the steps maintain their proportion relative to the whole.

Second, the law of reduction. You can deliver these stories in ten minutes, five minutes, or thirty seconds. Again: If you maintain proportion, the impact retains its inherent quality and persuasive strength. This makes the stories (and all structures) extremely versatile: You can stretch or shorten them to fit any possible timeframe.

Third, the law of precise tracing. You must precisely trace the structure. Don't entrust yourself to one of these structures (or any communication structure) and deviate from it unnecessarily. The steps are sequenced for a reason. Trust them. Follow them.

Fourth, the law of separation of concerns. Don't try to accomplish step five in step one. A structure is a sequence of steps. The sequence generates the impact. And if you don't separate out the steps distinctly, blurring the lines between steps, perhaps by sticking step five anywhere except between four and six, you lose the impact.

THE FOUR IMMUTABLE LAWS OF STRUCTURE

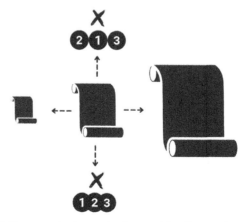

FIGURE 87: You can shorten a structure and it will maintain a proportional impact. You can lengthen it and it will maintain a

proportional impact. You must follow the steps in their exact order. You must not overlap the steps.

STRATEGY #9: REJECT LUCK, GOOD OR BAD

Like rejecting randomness, reject luck, good or bad. It happened because someone somewhere did something with clear intent and a clear motive. Not "we were lucky this quarter," but "we performed well this quarter – particularly because…"

To review, nearly all these strategies hinge on packaging information how people are psychologically biased and irresistibly genetically predisposed to interpret information. How? By introducing agents, not explaining away events as luck.

STRATEGY #10: PRESENT UNRELATED POSITIVE EVENTS

This one is sneaky. It's sophisticated. And it allows you to create the impression you are a phenomenal leader, without taking undue credit, bragging, or otherwise undermining your image of modesty.

People tend to attribute random events to agents. As a leader, you are a visible, salient agent, thus people attribute events largely outside of your control to your merit (or demerit). So, report what happened during your tenure as leader. Without you saying "I did this," people will give you credit for it. Why? Because agent detection bias pushes them to reflexively detect agents as causes of observed effects. In this case, you present the positive observed effects, and you allow agent detection bias to interpret you, the leader, as the cause. Obama famously used this strategy:

To my fellow Americans: Eight years ago, America faced a moment of peril unlike any we'd seen in decades. A spiraling financial crisis threatened to plunge an economy in recession into a deep depression. The very heartbeat of American manufacturing – the American auto industry – was on the brink of collapse. In some communities, nearly one in five Americans were out of work. Nearly 180,000 American troops were serving in harm's way in Iraq and Afghanistan, and the mastermind of the worst terror attack on American soil remained at large. And on challenges from health care to climate change, we'd been kicking the can down the road for way too long. But in the depths of that winter, on January 20, 2009, I stood before you and swore a sacred oath. I told you that day that the challenges we faced would not be met easily or in a short span of time – but they would be met. And after eight busy years, we've met them – because of you. Eight years later, an economy that was shrinking at more than eight percent is now growing at more than three percent. Businesses that were bleeding jobs unleashed the longest streak of job creation on record. The auto industry has roared its way back, saving one million jobs across the country and fueling a manufacturing sector that, after a decade of decline, has added new jobs for the first time since the 1990s. And wages have grown faster over the past few years than at any time in the past forty. Today, thanks to the Affordable Care Act, another 20 million American adults know the financial security and peace of mind that comes with health insurance. Another three million children have gained health insurance. For the first time ever, more than ninety percent of Americans are insured – the highest rate ever. We've seen the slowest growth in the price of health care in fifty years, along with improvements in patient safety that have prevented an estimated 87,000 deaths. Every American with insurance is covered by the strongest set of consumer protections in history – a true Patients' Bill of Rights – and free from the fear that illness or accident will derail your dreams, because America is now a place where discrimination against preexisting conditions is a relic of the past. And the new health insurance marketplace means that if you lose your job, change your job, or start that new business, you'll finally be able to purchase quality, affordable care and the security and peace of mind that comes with it – and that's one reason why entrepreneurship is growing for the second straight year.

He's presenting a list of positive events occurring under his tenure. He's even attributing different agents as their causes: "We've met them – because of you." But he is the leader. He is a salient and visible agent, with significant power, though certainly not enough to do all those things alone. People attribute the positive events to his credit.

This same strategy can work for you when you're in a position of leadership. Present positive events occurring under your tenure, though not necessarily the direct results of your actions, and people will give you credit. And the best part is that you won't need to give yourself credit, which is always a disdainful display.

HOW TO CLAIM CREDIT WITHOUT CLAIMING CREDIT

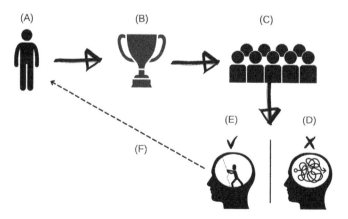

FIGURE 88: When a leader (A) presents positive events or accomplishments (B) to an audience (C), the audience rejects a complex causal web (D) and, due to agent detection bias, affirms a single agent acting with intent (E). As a result, they often attribute the accomplishment to the leader (F).

HOW PERSONIFICATION APPEALS TO HUMAN INTUITION

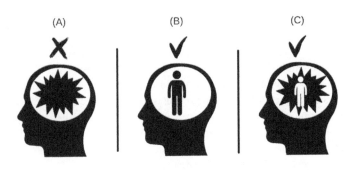

FIGURE 89: People reject complex phenomena occurring without a personal causal agent while reflexively accepting agent-driven explanations. Personification figuratively projects an agent into the phenomenon, presenting it as its own agent.

STRATEGY #12: ANSWER "WHAT DID IT DO?" NOT "WHAT IS IT?"

According to Daniel Kahneman's groundbreaking book, *Thinking, Fast and Slow*, people understand one type of sentence best: one in which something acts on another thing, as opposed to one in which something is another thing. For example, "[insert politician] is unjust," is inferior to "[insert politician] breaks justice." Why? "X acts on Y" beats "X is Y." We understand action-oriented sentences significantly better (Kahneman, 2011).

What strategy emerges? Orient your sentences to answer the question "what did it do?" not "what is it?" And how does this tie into the agent detection bias? Because in the "X acts on Y" sentence, X is an agent. Why does this matter? Because it orients the sentence how our information-interpretation machinery evolved to read it.

STRATEGY #13: PRESENT A CLEAR, VIVID, SINGULAR GROUP OR ACTOR

Present one item, and it gets 100% of your obtained attention (which could be 70%). Present two? All else equal, they each get 50% of your obtained attention. Three? 33% each. And what does this mean for the agent detection bias, and our efforts to activate and appeal to it? You have the choice between fully directing attention to one agent, or diluting it between multiple.

Which wins? 100% attention on one agent, or 33% on each of three? I argue the first. Why? Because a plurality of actors is not neat; it is not organized; it is confusing, convoluted, and complex; it raises cognitive load, which reduces attention yet further. It dilutes the impact of the strategy, blurs your message, and weakens the activation of agent detection. In short: We interpret one actor, or one group, with greater ease than a plurality. How can you cater to this? You can choose the principal actor, or group the plurality of actors into one unifying brand.

AGENT DETECTION BIAS CONCLUSION

Ronald Reagan pinned the entire blame for the poor economy on Jimmy Carter. Of course, much else accounted for the poor economy in reality. Nonetheless, the agent detection bias pushes people to perceive agency, particularly in the form of single, powerful agents, behind visible phenomenon. As a result, the sequence of rhetorical questions pinning the blame on Carter meshed perfectly with human intuition.

..............................Chapter Summary................................

- The agent detection bias is our tendency to attribute observable phenomena to agents acting with intent.
- The agent detection bias may be the byproduct of evolutionary beneficence, causing us to act cautiously.
- The agent detection bias explains why leaders often receive blame or praise for events fully outside of their control.
- You use the agent detection bias in communication by applying strategies that present a clear agent.
- You overcome the agent detection bias by piercing first impressions and studying complex phenomena deeply.
- Ronald Reagan used the agent detection bias by presenting one cause for complex economic events: Jimmy Carter.

KEY INSIGHT:

Put the Blame Where it Belongs. If That's at the Feet of One Person, Agent Detection Agrees. If Not, No Agent Detection for You.

HOW TO OVERCOME THE PSYCHOLOGY (PART SEVEN)

1	The Availability Bias
1.1	Gather All Available Statistics Instead of Relying on Ease of Recall
2	The Anchoring Effect
2.1	Educate Yourself on the Subject of Evaluation
2.2	Strive to Ignore the First Number You Hear
2.3	Be Cognizant of the Impact of Unrelated Anchors
2.4	Seek Historical Evidence Related to Your Evaluation
2.5	Concentrate Attention on a Self-Supplied Counter-Anchor
3	Munger's Biases
3.1	Watch Carefully for Bias-Activating Circumstances
4	The Contrast Effect
4.1	Generate Counteracting Contrasting Inputs
5	Zero-Risk Bias
5.1	Run Statistical, Empirical, Rational Risk-Reward Calculations
6	The Halo Effect
6.1	Rely on Behavioral Records as Opposed to Snap Judgments
7	Agent Detection Bias
7.1	Question Omni-Causal Explanations in Complex Systems
8	Attribute Substitution
9	Base Rate Neglect

Claim These Free Resources that Will Help You Unleash the Power of Your Words and Speak with Confidence. Visit www.speakforsuccesshub.com/toolkit for Access.

18 Free PDF Resources

12 Iron Rules for Captivating Story, 21 Speeches that Changed the World, 341-Point Influence Checklist, 143 Persuasive Cognitive Biases, 17 Ways to Think On Your Feet, 18 Lies About Speaking Well, 137 Deadly Logical Fallacies, 12 Iron Rules For Captivating Slides, 371 Words that Persuade, 63 Truths of Speaking Well, 27 Laws of Empathy, 21 Secrets of Legendary Speeches, 19 Scripts that Persuade, 12 Iron Rules For Captivating Speech, 33 Laws of Charisma, 11 Influence Formulas, 219-Point Speech-Writing Checklist, 21 Eloquence Formulas

SPEAK FOR SUCCESS COLLECTION BOOK

I

HOW HIGHLY EFFECTIVE PEOPLE SPEAK CHAPTER

XI

ATTRIBUTE SUBSTITUTION:

How to Use the Psychology of Mental Shortcuts in Your Favor

"THE AMERICAN PEOPLE HAVE SUMMONED THE CHANGE WE CELEBRATE TODAY..."

B ILL CLINTON'S 1993 INAUGURAL ADDRESS was not only masterfully eloquent, but also deeply persuasive due to the message itself.

> The American people have summoned the change we celebrate today. You have raised your voices in an unmistakable chorus. You have cast your votes in historic numbers. And you have changed the face of Congress, the presidency and the political process itself. Yes, you, my fellow Americans have forced the spring. Now, we must do the work the season demands. To that work I now turn, with all the authority of my office. I ask the Congress to join with me. But no president, no Congress, no government, can undertake this mission alone. My fellow Americans, you, too, must play your part in our renewal. I challenge a new generation of young Americans to a season of service; to act on your idealism by helping troubled children, keeping company with those in need, reconnecting our torn communities. There is so much to be done; enough indeed for millions of others who are still young in spirit to give of themselves in service, too.

He uses a particular strategy in this segment that plays upon attribute substitution. In this section, we reveal the secrets of attribute substitution, and how it offers you drastically more influence. Using attribute substation gently exerts immense influence over the hearts and minds of your audience members, activating yet another powerful cognitive bias in the direction of your choosing. Attribute substitution is a layer deeper than the other cognitive biases. It is more fundamental, more inherent to human psychology, and underscores myriad other features of human cognition. The complex strategies for activating it call for a high level of fluency and expertise.

WHAT IS ATTRIBUTE SUBSTITUTION?

Attribute substitution creates dozens, if not hundreds, of other biases and heuristics. Faced with a complicated, difficult, high-cognitive load question, we substitute an easier question acting as a "good enough" proxy. We do this subconsciously. We answer the easy question, and apply the answer to the hard question. We also do this with attributes. Instead of estimating a hard attribute, we substitute an easy attribute and transfer the evaluation to the hard one.

ATTRIBUTE SUBSTITUTION VISUALIZED

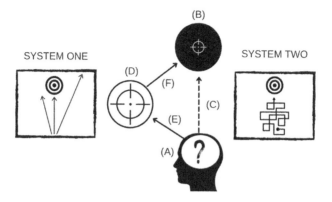

FIGURE 90: Revisit the attribute substitution process. Consider how it undergirds many of the cognitive biases and psychological processes we discussed.

WHAT IS AN EXAMPLE OF ATTRIBUTE SUBSTITUTION?

Logical fallacies fascinate me for one reason in particular: they hint at cognitive biases. If we enumerate a logical fallacy, it means people predictably, systematically, and repetitively make the same logical mistake. Sounds like a cognitive bias, doesn't it? Where we observe a logical fallacy, we can often observe a cognitive bias creating it. We can reverse-engineer logical fallacies to uncover or further validate cognitive biases.

THE CONNECTION BETWEEN FALLACIES, BIASES, AND TRUTH

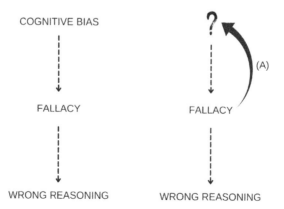

FIGURE 91: Cognitive biases create logical fallacies that lead to wrong reasoning. If you know a fallacy, you can work backward to

illuminate a potential cognitive bias or further exemplify an identified one.

What is the most common logical fallacy? The *ad hominem*, or "at the person" fallacy: attacking the source of the message, not the message itself. And I believe attribute substitution spawns the *ad hominem* because people substitute the easy question, "what do I think of this speaker?" for the hard one: "what do I think of this message?"

THE AD HOMINEM LOGICAL FALLACY VISUALIZED

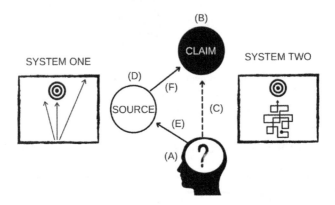

FIGURE 92: The *ad hominem* logical fallacy is a type of cognitive substitution. Prompted with a question (A) about a claim (B), like "whether or not it is true," humans in system one do not evaluate the claim directly (C). Instead, they often commit the ad hominem fallacy, substituting "how I feel about the source" (D), answering this question (E), and transferring it to the claim (F).

If a political figure you despise speaks words you love, science proves you will likely despise the words too. You substitute "what do I think of this speaker?" for "what do I think of these words?" and apply the answer to both questions. The world is insanely complex. You have responsibilities. You have things on your mind. You have threats and dangers to avoid, plus opportunities to seize. You need to limit your cognitive load to conserve enough mental energy for focusing on the important things. That's why you use these shortcuts which, I remind you, often produce correct judgements.

We also refer to mental heuristics as "rules of thumb." And when did the expression "rule of thumb" originate? In the Cold War, if you saw a mushroom cloud, it was in your best interest (to put it mildly) to figure out if you were in the radiation zone, and to do so quickly. Assume you have no Geiger counter or machinery or resources available to help you reach a completely sound judgement. How do you do it? How do you figure out if you're in the radiation zone or not? Like this: Extend your arm at full length, raise your thumb (like a "thumbs up"), and if your thumb completely blocks the cloud, you're probably fine.

Yes, you should leave, but you're not in direct danger yet. If the cloud peaks around the edges of your thumb, get out now. I emphasize one word: probably. If it blocks, you're probably fine, and if it doesn't, you're probably not. Rules of thumb help us make snap judgements when deep, accurate deliberation is infeasible: we don't have the energy, it's not worth it, or we need imperfect speed instead of slow perfection. With rules of thumb, we trade the accuracy of deep deliberation for other goodies: speed, low mental energy strain, and moderately satisfactory accuracy. And often, this is a wise trade.

To summarize attribute substitution, we try to answer a question about a target attribute, like "truth of message," but find it difficult. So, we substitute a heuristic attribute, one easier to evaluate, like "feelings about speaker."

Consider the example of the nuclear cloud. The target attribute is if you are in the radiation zone. The heuristic attribute is the size of your cloud relative to your thumb. And here's the key: When the target attribute highly correlates to the heuristic attribute, attribute substitution is more likely to produce an accurate judgement. And the reverse applies too. Unfortunately, perfect correlations are rare. Room for error plagues almost all substitution, though the extent of that room for error varies according to the correspondence between the heuristic and target attributes. But remember: It's not designed to be perfect. It's designed to be good enough.

HOW DO YOU OVERCOME ATTRIBUTE SUBSTITUTION?

Identify the question you're trying to answer, and enumerate it precisely. Allow no ambiguity about what it asks. You must define the parameters of your inquiry; you must circumscribe the question with precision. This helps you identify when your thoughts deviate to a different question; to a heuristic question. In the absence of a circumscribed question, the ease of substitution tempts our subconscious minds. This evokes the wisdom Jordan B. Peterson shared in his bestseller *12 Rules for Life:* "[Rule 10] Be precise in your speech." By articulating your struggle precisely, you lighten your burden. It is no longer a mountain of potential problems – it could be this, that, the other thing, or all three – but one clearly circumscribed problem (Peterson, 2018).

KEY INSIGHT:

Precise Speech is a Superpower. Better Even to Be Precise Than Persuasive, Although Precision is Persuasive.

PRECISELY ARTICULATE THE QUESTION FOR CLARITY

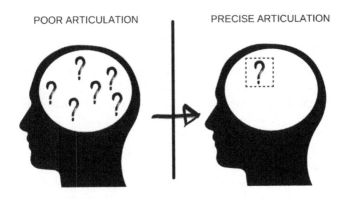

FIGURE 93: Precisely articulating the question cuts away the cloud of abstraction surrounding it; cuts away the cloud of "what the question could be" to focus you on what it is.

HOW TO OVERCOME ATTRIBUTE SUBSTITUTION

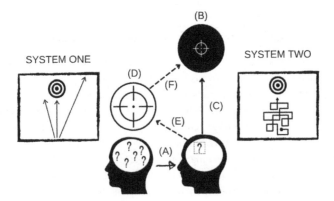

FIGURE 94: By precisely articulating the question (A) you are asking about the target variable (B), you empower yourself to evaluate the target directly (C) instead of substituting a heuristic variable (D) and transferring the answer to the target variable (F).

HOW DO YOU USE ATTRIBUTE SUBSTITUTION IN COMMUNICATION?

What's an algorithm? Google says the following:

A process or set of rules to be followed in calculations or other problem-solving operations, especially by a computer.

You're not a computer. But you are trying to solve a problem: ineffective communication. And here's the secret: I, and many others like me (but mostly me), developed thousands of communication algorithms you can use for phenomenal results. And we package them as repeatable step-by-step processes to make them easy. We can break many of these strategies into algorithmic steps, including conditionals, and all features of computational algorithms.

COMMUNICATION ALGORITHMS VISUALIZED

YOUR
MESSAGE

COMMUNICATION
ALGORITHM

UPGRADED
MESSAGE

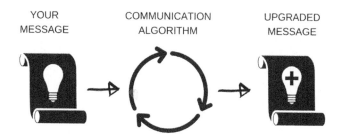

FIGURE 95: A communication algorithm is a step-by-step process for improving your message. You plug it in, execute the steps of the algorithm, and receive an improved message. Most of the strategies revealed in this book can be conceived as communication algorithms.

KEY INSIGHT:

The Habit is the Original Algorithm.
As Aristotle Knew, Habits Make us.

HOW COMMUNICATION ALGORITHMS PRODUCE MASTERY

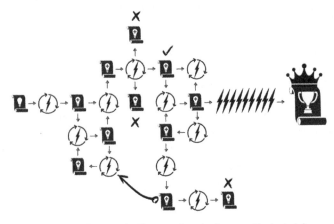

FIGURE 96: Communication mastery is the result of chaining these algorithms together.

We have a communication algorithm on our hands now: the ASA algorithm, or the attribute substitution activation algorithm. What is the step-by-step process? Step one: Identify the question you are trying to answer with your communication. For example, maybe you want to answer the question "is [insert your idea] a good idea?" And you want to answer it with a resounding "yes," not in your mind, but in your audience's minds. Step two: Identify the probable heuristic attributes people will substitute for your target attribute. Step three: Take people from a one to a ten on the spectrum of perception of those heuristic attributes.

Let's say you're selling a car. Step one: The target attribute is "net benefit of the car including opportunity cost of the best alternative forgone." This is complicated and difficult, thus subject to attribute substitution. Step two: Identify the probable heuristic attributes people will substitute for the target attribute: "It looks good; it feels nice; I like the salesperson; I like the company, etc." Step three: Maximize perception not only of the target attribute (which you should still focus on), but also of the heuristic attributes. Why? Because people substitute them for the target attribute, and think they perceive the target attribute if they perceive the heuristic attributes.

We have two more loose ends. How do you identify the probable heuristic attributes? First, some pop up over and over, like emotional and aesthetic appeal. Second, you must fill in the blanks by understanding your audience members. According to world-class sales trainer Jordan Belfort in *The Way of the Wolf:*

We all arrive at any particular moment in time with a history of beliefs and values and opinions and experiences and victories and defeats and insecurities and decision-making strategies – and then based on all of that stuff, our brain, working at near light speed, will instantly relate it to whatever scenario lies before it. Then, based on the result, it will place us at whatever point on the certainty scale it deems appropriate for each of the three tens, and it's from that starting point that we can then be influenced. (Belfort, 2017)

In short: You must develop a compelling, accurate, and complete audience persona. Based on your pre-existing intelligence and what you can gather, develop a "persona" that includes the characteristics Jordan identified. It must describe at least two thirds of your audience. Now you know who you're speaking to.

Are you having trouble creating an audience persona? Maybe you have a broad, diverse audience. What do you do then? Build your persona around their unifying traits. And speak in terms of core human desires, engaging with their self-interest at the level of specificity that unites them all.

But what if you're speaking to a homogenous group of people? What if you can build a clear, complete, and compelling audience persona; one that is distinct, specific, and in-depth? What if you can clearly identify specific and unifying audience needs, beliefs, values, objections, pain points, preconceptions about you, hierarchy of values, past experiences with similar ideas, speakers, and situations? Then this is easy, isn't it? This takes care of the first loose end: identifying probable heuristic attributes.

What about the second loose end? What did I mean by "take people from a one to a ten on the spectrum of perception of those heuristic attributes?" The theory of mental malleability states this: Your communication inputs change your audience's mental states, and for every action you desire, an ideal mental state inspires maximum action, and you can identify and create it. If you want to successfully apply the theory of mental malleability, you have to take one extra step. What is a mental state? Spectrum theory answers this question: We can break the ideal mental state down into a series of qualities, each with a spectrum of magnitude. Thus, with your persuasive inputs, you can move people up and down these spectrums to achieve the desired mental state.

Let's say you're a politician campaigning for votes. What ideal mental state pushes the most people to vote for you? It includes qualities like anger toward the other party, a belief in personal gain if you win, agreement with your values, a feeling of personal connection, and policy agreement. For each quality, your audience can be anywhere on the one-to-ten spectrum. At ten, they fully have the quality. At one, they completely lack it. To achieve persuasive communication, move your audience from wherever they start on these spectrums to wherever you want them to be.

KEY INSIGHT:

Meaningful Discourse Cannot Be Devoid of Emotion, And Shouldn't Be, Provided It Doesn't Drive Out Reason.

HOW THE SPECTRUM MODEL GIVES YOU CLARITY

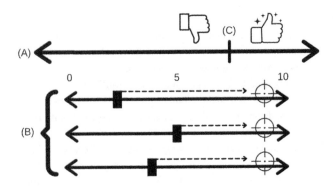

FIGURE 97: The overall spectrum between "success" and "failure" in communication (A) breaks down into a set of more specific spectrums (B). Your audience members occupy "starting states" along these spectrums. Your goal is to move them from these starting states to 10 positions using your communication. You can conceive of your position on the spectrum between success and failure as the average of the positions the audience occupies on the sub-spectrums. There is some theoretical threshold signifying the communication as sufficiently successful (C).

And this is just one simple example of a mental state broken down into a set of qualities. The examples are infinite. I can't possibly predict what the ideal mental state of your audience will be, but I can equip you with the tools to figure it out and use the theory for yourself.

Briefly, the algorithm is as follows: First, identify what you want your audience to think; the target attribute you want them to perceive; the ideal mental state producing the most of your desired action. Second, identify the probable heuristic attributes people will substitute for your target attribute. How? By understanding common substitutes and developing audience personas to predict the others. Third, move people from a one to a ten not only on perception of target attribute, but on perception of heuristic attributes.

KEY INSIGHT:

Every Map is Wrong, But Some Help You Navigate. This is One of Them.

THE "ASA" ALGORITHM VISUALIZED

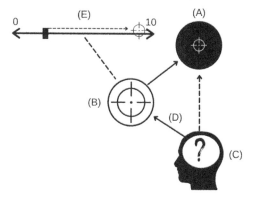

FIGURE 98: Simply put, the attribute substitution activation algorithm is, for the target variable (A), identifying a probable heuristic variable (B) which your audience members (C) substitute for the target variable (D) and raising people from a one-to-ten on "perception of heuristic variable." (E)

STRATEGY #1: MANIPULATE AFFECT

What is the essence of manipulating affect? Raising people from a one to a ten on perception of one of the most common heuristic attributes: affect; feeling; emotion. People substitute the heuristic attribute of "my feelings about X" for the target attribute "the truth of X." We can also say they substitute the heuristic question "how do I feel about X?" with the target question "is X true?"

When people say emotion is key to persuasion, they're right. But why? Because of emotional substitution. If you want to instantly make people love your ideas and proposal, if you want to immediately achieve significantly more influence, and if you want to alter any situation in your favor, you have to do one thing: make people feel a certain way about your proposal.

But how do you make people feel? How do you make people resonate emotionally with your idea? Think of persuasion as invading a castle; the castle of your audience's bias to disconfirm; the castle of your audience's skepticism; the castle of your audience's pain from being lied to over and over again by people who look, sound, and talk just like you.

Logic is just the moat: the channel of water around the castle, designed to keep invaders away from the walls. But emotional resonance will break down the walls and allow your persuasion to penetrate their minds until they are as much on your side as you are.

You have to pass the moat to get to the castle. You have to satisfy their logical "check-box" before they even allow the possibility of emotional resonance working its magic and breaking down their walls. You have to present some evidence, some logic-driven language, and some ethos-building information about your authority and how you have their interests at heart.

But once you do, you need to pull out your emotional resonance. If persuasion-resistance is a tree, emotional resonance is a chainsaw. The thicker the trunk of the tree, the longer you need to keep that chainsaw buzzing.

I took an effective speaking class in college. I was certainly an effective speaker at the time (perhaps one of the most effective in the state of Massachusetts, according to the Massachusetts Speech and Debate League). I just wanted an easy A, and to further immerse myself in the subject I love, while helping some fellow students who needed it. But I'm not going to pretend I didn't learn anything. One of my most vivid memories from the class was the teacher saying something along these lines:

> If I want to persuade someone to stop smoking, I should not just hammer them with statistic after statistic about the risks and dangers associated with smoking. I should tell them a story; an emotional one; a personal one. I should say, 'I've heard all the statistics, but I couldn't stop smoking. I learned the habit from my Grandma. What really pushed me to quit was seeing her in her later years; seeing the sparkle slowly extinguish from her eyes as she lacked the lung capacity to join the family in our favorite activities, like hiking; seeing the emotional toll evident in the way she carried herself, and in her saddened face, the toll of knowing what she had sacrificed due to the habit she nurtured for most of her life; seeing the regret on her face and hearing it in her words, when she told me with tear-rimmed eyes, even as she lit yet another cigarette, that if she could do it all over again, she would never have started, though it was too late for her now.

Matched with his expert emotional delivery, this story hooked and persuaded us all. Why? Because of emotional resonance.

All effective communication connects the speaker to the receiver(s), the receiver(s) to the subject, and the subject to the speaker. The communicator creates this three-way connection (the communication triad) by applying the communication toolbox: words, body language, and vocal tonalities.

Emotionally resonating stories accomplish the communication triad. The personal story connects the speaker to the receivers. The subject of the story becomes intriguing to the receivers, thus connecting them to it in a compelling way. Finally, the personal story connects the speaker to the subject by expressing the speaker's relationship to it.

KEY INSIGHT:

To "Manipulate" Does Not Mean to Deceive, But Merely to Change.

THE FOUNDATION OF ALL EFFECTIVE COMMUNICATION

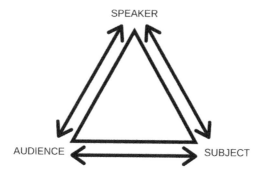

FIGURE 99: Successful communication connects speaker with subject, audience with subject, and speaker with audience, in no particular order.

This is all perfected with emotionally charged words, emotionally charged body language (principally facial expressions, which people emotionally mirror the most), and emotionally charged vocal tonalities. And you must remember, you can only achieve emotional impact in the presence of effective paralanguage; in the presence of impactful vocal modulation and body language. Tell a personal, emotional story with emotional words, emotional body language, and emotional vocal modulation, completing the three connections in the triad for massive emotional resonance.

THE FOUNDATION OF ALL EMOTIONAL PARALANGUAGE

FIGURE 100: Your "public speaking toolbox" or "communication toolbox" consists of the three components of your communication:

your words, body language, and vocal tonalities. Nearly every piece of communication advice relates to improving one of these three tools.

EMOTIONAL PARALANGUAGE AND THE THREE CONNECTIONS

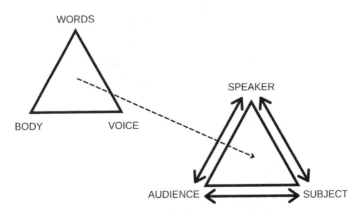

FIGURE 101: You form the three connections in the public speaking triad by using your three languages. You interconnect the speaker, audience, and subject by using your words, body language, and voice. Emotional paralanguage delivering an emotional story forms these connections around pathos.

I just handed you a chainsaw. I just gave you a Trojan Horse. I was talking to a friend who was involved in operating the apparatus of a national political campaign devoted to whipping up votes, support, and donations from my state.

He told me something interesting. He said that when canvassing (going door-to-door to help undecided voters come to the obviously correct conclusion that they should vote for your candidate), you have to use a particular strategy – and it's not what anyone thinks.

I was fascinated, and this confirmed a long-term hunch of mine. It also evoked an image of a Trojan Horse. The Trojan Horse (a personal story) was how the Greek military (your persuasive ideas) invaded the impervious walls of Troy (your audience's persuasion resistance); they built a giant wooden horse, and stuck a small squadron of Greek soldiers in it, before offering it as an olive-branch to Troy.

The Trojans took it in without realizing what it contained. As a result, the Greek soldiers managed to take the city from within after years of brutal and unsuccessful siege combat from outside the walls.

Let me explain the canvassing strategy. What do you *not* do? Go in there and say, "Here's why you should vote for this candidate." That's the intuitive image of persuasion we assume goes down in these door-to-door meetings. It's jumping straight to leading. And that's what the Greeks were doing for years before they got the Trojan Horse idea. The better strategy is to do something entirely different. Something that embeds the elements of persuasion in the sneaky, subtle facade of a personal story. So, instead of saying, "here's why you should vote for this candidate," you're supposed to say, "I was once undecided myself. The reason I am now a supporter of this candidate is that..." and tell the story of your conversion from undecided to decided.

TELLING STORIES THAT WIN HEARTS AND CHANGE MINDS

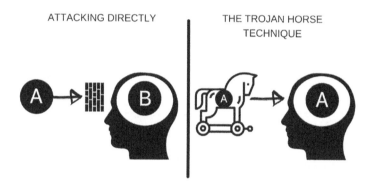

ATTACKING DIRECTLY   THE TROJAN HORSE
                                       TECHNIQUE

FIGURE 102: Instead of approaching your persuasive prospects by flatly stating the core persuasive epiphany you would like them to adopt, embed this persuasive epiphany in a story that will give them the ingredients to experience the belief-shift themselves.

It is a form of pacing and leading. More accurately, it is pacing and leading layered under a story of your conversion. It activates the intuitive bias. It activates countless functions of human psychology that we discussed, all in your favor. It is gentle, and gentle persuasion builds credibility while overt and aggressive persuasion destroys it. It fosters likeability, and people find those they like much more credible. It is conversational and promotes two-way communication, which is attention-grabbing. Attention is a prerequisite for credibility because it is a prerequisite for communication and communication is a prerequisite for credibility. In short, the strategy is this: Embedding persuasive elements in a personal story or the story of someone similar to your audience. Maybe like this: "I used to believe X because... and now I believe Y, because..." Or like this: "I used to believe X. One time I [insert personal story]. This was when I realized that [insert what you want them to believe]." And even this: "I used to be a fervent opponent of X, but after I experienced a particular moment that I will never forget, I realized that maybe it wasn't so bad all along. What happened was [insert personal story]."

The stories should be personal and should foster a connection between you and your audience. This is always true: First connect, then persuade. That is not merely a better way. It is the only way.

But that's just one way of achieving emotional resonance and manipulating affect. The other is with empathy. How do you achieve emotional resonance by way of empathy? By describing in vivid detail your audience's emotional state; expressing their struggle as a shared struggle; presenting body language and vocal tonality that imply the following: "I feel what you feel."

STRATEGY #2: PRESENT SHARED WORLDVIEW

People substitute the easy question, "do I like this speaker?" for the hard one, "is this speaker's message true?" just as easily as substituting emotional affect for any salient target attribute.

How do you use this? How do you put yourself on the right side of the first question, determining their trust in your message? It's simple, and we covered it before: Present a shared world-view.

People love people who see things how they see things. People gravitate toward those reflecting their views. Why? Because hearing dissenting opinions hurts. According to Drew Westin in *The Political Brain*, the same areas of our brain activating when faced with a physical threat also activate when faced with an intellectual threat (Westin, 2007).

And we know people strive to minimize psychological pain. From this, we can infer people gravitate to those who echo their views, forming an intellectual "echo chamber" around themselves. Why? To minimize psychological pain. Still: We don't have to infer this. We can see it. It's self-evident every single day, in so many ways.

WHY INTELLECTUAL CONFLICT REALLY IS VERBAL COMBAT

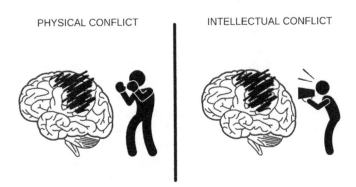

PHYSICAL CONFLICT   INTELLECTUAL CONFLICT

FIGURE 103: The same parts of the brain that light up during physical conflict light up during intellectual conflict.

HOW COMFORT-MAXIMIZATION PRODUCES ECHO CHAMBERS

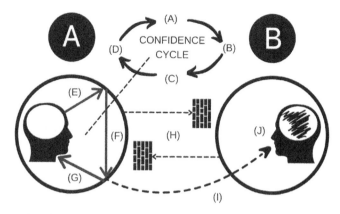

FIGURE 104: There are two intellectual coalitions here: A and B. As a review, the confidence cycle is the cyclical relationship between pride (A), conviction (B), confirmation bias (C), and validation (D). In the echo chambers, members send out messages (E) that bounce around for a while (F) and return, in some form or another, back to the source (G). This step is the "echo." This cycle in the echo chamber produces the confidence cycle. Meanwhile, messages the A and B coalitions send to each other get blocked as people seek to avoid the pain of intellectual conflict (H). However, if a message from one coalition reaches the other (I), it often causes psychological pain and cognitive dissonance (J), making them feel "attacked." This may then contribute to a strengthening of the barriers as a means to protect against further "attacks."

What should you do? Recall your audience persona. Describe the world how they see it. Describe them how they see themselves. Describe events, problems, and ideas with a tone echoing their beliefs. What do you do if you don't know these things? Then ask. "What do you think of [insert relevant subject]? I agree. It's true that [insert echoing statement]."

STRATEGY #3: ELOQUENCE AND RHYME AS REASON

I told you attribute substitution creates countless psychological biases. One of the psychological biases that is likely closely linked to attribute substitution is the rhyme as reason effect: eloquent messages conveying the same ideas are rated more trustworthy.

Another common heuristic attribute is "how the message sounds." Closely tied to this are others, like "how the speaker sounds saying the message," and "how the speaker looks saying the message." What strategy emerges? Apply the principles of eloquence; convey confidence with your vocal tonalities; present open body language. Aside from the inherent benefits, you'll also move your audience closer to tens on the spectrums of how the message sounds, how the speaker looks saying it, how they sounds saying it.

STRATEGY #4: ACHIEVE AESTHETICISM

Remember the distinction between contextual inputs and direct inputs? This is another strategy falling in the contextual domain. What is it? What is the heuristic attribute it maximizes? The attribute of aesthetic appeal.

And these heuristic attributes form a tangled web. We tend to substitute emotional appeal, or affect, for our judgement of a difficult target attribute, just as we do with aesthetic appeal. But at the same time, emotional appeal can create aesthetic appeal, and aesthetic appeal can create an emotional pull.

The strategy is simple. Maximize the aesthetic appeal of your offer. People substitute the easy heuristic question, "does this look good?" and apply the answer the difficult target question, "is it good?" You better hope the answer to the first question is a resounding "yes." Why? Because in the presence of attribute substitution, it determines whether they perceive value in your offering.

How do you maximize the aesthetic appeal of your offer? Remember: Perception of aesthetic appeal is largely contextual, occurring outside your direct inputs. And yet, it communicates a great deal. Let's say you're presenting a brilliant proposal you dreamt up. Are you handing out packets for later review? Package them in nice binders; include beautifully-colored visualized data; make the fonts, visual information hierarchies, and typography excellent. Put attractive images throughout. Consider working with a graphic designer. Make the colors striking and complementary. What about the PowerPoint? No spelling mistakes. No blocks of text. No outlandish colors. Simple, straightforward, clean, and professional; aesthetic. This will produce an outsized persuasive impact when people subconsciously and automatically perform attribute substitution.

STRATEGY #5: ACTIVATE THE SOURCE AND EVIDENCE BIASES

You may notice a theme in these strategies: I present a common attribute substitution, and show you how to maximize the perception of a heuristic attribute and thus the perception of an associated target attribute. This section is no different.

What are the source and evidence biases? Specifically, what are the attribute substitutions they represent? For the source bias, "do I like this source?" substitutes for "is this source and its message(s) reputable?" For the evidence bias, "is there evidence?" substitutes for "is there good evidence?"

I present them together because they relate. What two heuristic attributes should you seek to maximize? Good-will toward the sources you cite in favor of your position (or dislike of sources you cite against your position), and the perception of a mountain of evidence. While the perception of a mountain of evidence is often enough (because people operating on attribute substitution assume it's good), I still advocate finding good evidence.

Why find good evidence of the evidence bias treats the presence of evidence as a heuristic for its quality? Because two sets of cognitive features govern human thought; some intuitive and heuristic-driven, and some based on slow deliberation. These strategies work best when people are in the former state. And if they are not, and they analyze the difficult target attribute (validity of evidence), you need to be ready. Avoid non-sequiturs, logical fallacies in which the proof doesn't actually justify the claim.

Why do politicians seek celebrity endorsements? Celebrities aren't reputable sources of political wisdom. But people feel good-will toward them, and the heuristic attribute, "good-will toward source" substitutes for the target attribute, "authority of source."

What about the evidence bias? Back in my competitive debating days, I noticed a trend: The presence of evidence validated a claim even if it didn't really prove it. Why? Judges and other debaters substituted the heuristic attribute "presence of evidence" for the target attribute "validity of evidence."

THE "EVIDENCE GATE" AND THE TWO SYSTEMS

HOW EVIDENCE INTERACTS WITH THE TWO SYSTEMS

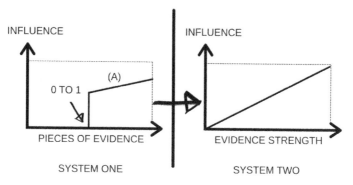

FIGURE 105: In system one, the first piece of evidence you offer satisfies the "is there evidence?" heuristic question, which the audience substituted for "is it good evidence?" As a result, the first piece of evidence you offer raises your influence significantly, and subsequent pieces of evidence do so to a lesser degree (A). In system one, as the amount of your evidence rises, your influence rises. In system two, as the strength of your evidence rises, your influence rises.

STRATEGY #6: ACTIVATE ORGANIZATION BIAS

The target attribute is the "authority and trustworthiness of the speaker." The heuristic attribute is the "authority and trustworthiness of the organization the speaker represents."

Why does this represent a sufficiently effective rule of thumb? Why does this often produce accurate judgements? Because authoritative and trustworthy organizations hire authoritative and trustworthy personnel. In other words, the heuristic attribute and the target attribute correlate moderately strongly. But it's not a perfect correlation, so a chance of error remains.

How do you maximize perception of the heuristic attribute? Maybe you're new in the field and lack lots of personal experience to present as evidence of your authority. Present the accomplishments of your organization. This will morph into perception of your authority. And if an organization with a strong reputation hired you, you probably do have authority and expertise.

STRATEGY #7: ACTIVATE SOCIAL PROOF

Social proof stands as one of the most tremendously influential and powerful cognitive heuristics. I believe behavioral economics will one day synthesize with history, and we'll find that social proof created a massive amount of history's ebbs and flows.

What is the heuristic attribute? "What others are doing." What is the target attribute? "What I should be doing." How do you maximize the perception of the heuristic attribute, and thus inspire beneficial judgements? "70% of people agree with... 96% of small business owners report... 80% of scientists suggest..."

The process underlying every strategy in this chapter follows one theme. Instead of trying to raise perception of the target attribute by battering the target attribute, you can instead identify the heuristic attributes governing estimation of the target attribute, and subtly touch upon those. Of course, you can do both: You can say "you should do this because [insert reason] (hitting the target attribute), which is the same reason 80% of people like you did it (hitting the heuristic attribute)."

I call this bimodal influence, including both system one messaging (appealing to snap judgements, intuitive, bias- and heuristic-driven subconscious cognitive functions) and system two messaging (appealing to deep, deliberate, and effortful cognitive functions). People always live in one of the two. Bimodal influence guarantees your communication hits home with everyone. And it's drastically and dramatically more effective.

System one messaging targets heuristic attributes (which people substitute for the target attribute). System one messaging is three-step persuasion: You hit the heuristic attribute, people substitute the heuristic attribute for the target attribute, and thus people perceive the target attribute. For example, you make your proposal literature aesthetically pleasing, people substitute "good looking" for "good," and thus people find your proposal good.

The focus of this book is mostly system one messaging. I believe, in many cases, maximizing perception of the heuristic attributes people substitute for the target attribute can be a more effective method of raising perception of the target attributes than simply hammering them directly. It's like a persuasive backdoor.

SYSTEM ONE MESSAGING

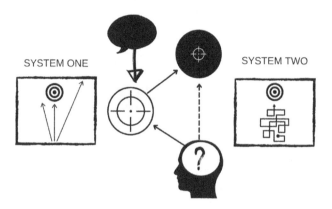

FIGURE 106: System one messaging targets heuristic variables, which act as persuasive backdoors to target variables.

SYSTEM TWO MESSAGING

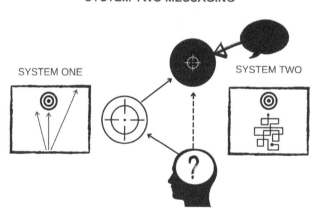

FIGURE 107: System two messaging targets the target variable directly.

BIMODAL INFLUENCE

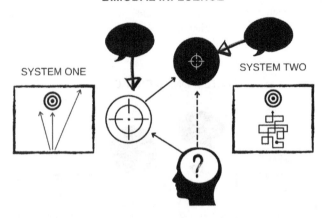

FIGURE 108: Bimodal influence targets both the target variable and the heuristic variables.

Of course, bimodal influence is best: Do them both for most success (I hope I activated the rhyme as reason effect there). I call it a persuasive backdoor partly because of persuasion aversion. People tend to block aggressive persuasive efforts, and react negatively to overt attempts at influence. Keeping it subtle, what system one messaging does, sneaks under the radar of persuasion aversion.

STRATEGY #8: ACTIVATE THE REALITY AND HISTORY BIASES

What is reality bias? People substitute "how will this person behave in the future?" for "how has this person behaved so far?" What about history bias? People substitute "what happened in the past?" for "what will happen in the future?"

How do you appeal to reality bias? Like this: Talk about your big, bold vision for the future, but carry some concrete actions as a token of your credibility. People overweigh what you've already done more than what you promise. You can easily manipulate the latter, but not the former. So, bring some concrete actions to the table: "I know this is just a proposal, but I already put together a prototype showing you... / I already commissioned a research team, which found... / I already compiled a consumer survey unambiguously proving..." Statements of this brand will have an outsized persuasive impact.

How do you appeal to history bias? Like this: Draw support for your predictions from historical mirrors. People substitute "what happened last time?" for "what will happen now?" Pay attention to political debates, and you'll see this in action all the time. "Last time we passed [insert policy], [insert negative results] happened."

YOUR PROPOSED FUTURE MUST MESH WITH THE PAST

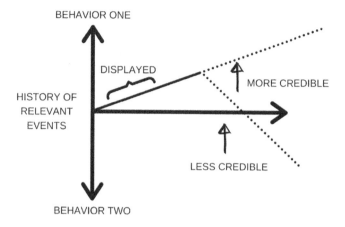

FIGURE 109: Conveying a future that lines up with your history of displayed behavior (or whatever the salient history is) is more credible than one that deviates from it.

STRATEGY #9: FORM YOUR OWN SUBSTITUTIONS

Think about this saying: "If it walks like a duck, looks like a duck, and acts like a duck, it's probably a duck." Think about what it's accomplishing, oddly enough. Isn't it suggesting heuristic attributes to substitute for a target attribute? It substitutes "does it walk like a duck?" and "does it look like a duck?" and "does it act like a duck?" for "is it a duck?" And if this saying can suggest heuristic attributes, why can't you?

How do you suggest heuristic attributes? Like this: "If it is [insert heuristic attribute], it is [insert target attribute]." In saying this, you prime the audience members to perform the substitution. If it is easier to directly prove the heuristic attribute than the target attribute, you can establish this substitution, and indirectly prove the target attribute by proving the heuristic attribute. This is classic system one communication.

Let's say you're a politician who wants to discredit a policy. In other words, you want to make the target attribute "merit of policy" appear as zero. What if it's a new policy area with little substantial associated research? What if it has no negative history? What if it has no substantive matter you can use to discredit it directly (which is system two communication, focusing only on the target attribute)? And let's say you know all about system one communication, but not how to use it in this instance, because you have absolutely no idea what the relevant heuristic attributes are. What's your next move? Identify the target attribute you can't get a persuasive handle on, and present your own heuristic attribute. Give people something to substitute for the target attribute, and something you can easily prove (which is the key advantage here). "If [insert heuristic attribute], then [insert target attribute]."

"If the mushroom cloud is bigger than your thumb, you're in the radiation zone." It's the same idea. "If the monied interests are lobbying heavily for a policy, corrupting government and turning it into another money-making tool (the heuristic attribute), it's probably a bad policy (target attribute), not helping, but hurting the middle class..." Then go on to prove the heuristic attribute (an easy task) and thus prove the target attribute indirectly. Remember: Doing so directly would be a hard task.

And the magnitude of the advantage this strategy yields you hinges on one question: How much easier is proving the heuristic attribute than the target attribute? This strategy removes you from an impossibly difficult situation, from trying to prove a target attribute with no subject matter to wield as your weapon. How? By moving you to a battleground well-supplied with weaponry (the heuristic attribute, which you select), and making the outcome of this battle the outcome of the bigger battle (the target attribute).

HIJACKING A.S. BY FORMING YOUR OWN SUBSTITUTIONS

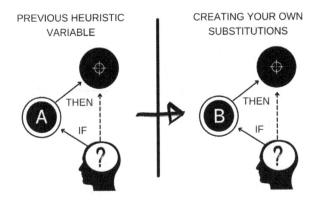

FIGURE 110: You can hijack attribute substitution by injecting your own heuristic variables.

ATTRIBUTE SUBSTITUTION CONCLUSION

Bill Clinton portrayed the immense support behind his administration and agenda. As a result, he activated social proof. He expressed that the crowds are on his side. His audience substituted the question "do people support this?" for the question "should I support this?" When they answered yes to the first question – which they did because of the social proof Clinton presented – they transmuted this answer to the second question.

......................Chapter Summary............................

- Attribute substitution is our tendency to substitute easy "heuristic" variables for difficult "target" variables.
- Attribute substitution emerges from the need to make sufficiently accurate snap-judgements.
- Attribute substation is foundational, explaining many other biases and heuristics, like social proof and consistency.
- You use attribute substitution in communication by applying strategies that target likely heuristic variables.
- You overcome attribute substitution by clearly defining and deliberately focusing on the target question or variable.
- Bill Clinton used social proof, instigating attribute substitution by targeting a common heuristic variable.

KEY INSIGHT:

Assuming "X" Stands For "Y," When it Doesn't is at the Core of Many Systematic Misjudgments.

Thus, Clarity in Thought and Speech Starts with Defining "Y," Deliberately and Unmistakably.

Precision in Speech Leads to Accuracy in Judgment And to Successful Action in Reality.

HOW TO OVERCOME THE PSYCHOLOGY (PART EIGHT)

1	The Availability Bias
1.1	Gather All Available Statistics Instead of Relying on Ease of Recall
2	The Anchoring Effect
2.1	Educate Yourself on the Subject of Evaluation
2.2	Strive to Ignore the First Number You Hear
2.3	Be Cognizant of the Impact of Unrelated Anchors
2.4	Seek Historical Evidence Related to Your Evaluation
2.5	Concentrate Attention on a Self-Supplied Counter-Anchor
3	Munger's Biases
3.1	Watch Carefully for Bias-Activating Circumstances
4	The Contrast Effect
4.1	Generate Counteracting Contrasting Inputs
5	Zero-Risk Bias
5.1	Run Statistical, Empirical, Rational Risk-Reward Calculations
6	The Halo Effect
6.1	Rely on Behavioral Records as Opposed to Snap Judgments
7	Agent Detection Bias
7.1	Question Omni-Causal Explanations in Complex Systems
8	Attribute Substitution
8.1	Specifically Circumscribe the Target Variable; Focus On It
9	Base Rate Neglect

Claim These Free Resources that Will Help You Unleash the Power of Your Words and Speak with Confidence. Visit www.speakforsuccesshub.com/toolkit for Access.

30 Free Video Lessons

We'll send you one free video lesson every day for 30 days, written and recorded by Peter D. Andrei. Days 1-10 cover authenticity, the prerequisite to confidence and persuasive power. Days 11-20 cover building self-belief and defeating communication anxiety. Days 21-30 cover how to speak with impact and influence, ensuring your words change minds instead of falling flat. Authenticity, self-belief, and impact – this course helps you master three components of confidence, turning even the most high-stakes presentations from obstacles into opportunities.

SPEAK FOR SUCCESS COLLECTION BOOK

I

HOW HIGHLY EFFECTIVE PEOPLE SPEAK CHAPTER

BASE RATE NEGLECT:

How to Use the Psychology of Numerical Incompetency

"I THINK WE'RE AGAINST THE HYPOCRISY OF ASSAILING OUR ALLIES BECAUSE HERE AND THERE..."

R ONALD REAGAN, IN "A TIME FOR CHOOSING," presented compelling statistics. But he knew that compelling statistics on their own fall short. He knew the critical ingredient that empowers them.

I think we're for an international organization, where the nations of the world can seek peace. But I think we're against subordinating American interests to an organization that has become so structurally unsound that today you can muster a two-thirds vote on the floor of the General Assembly among nations that represent less than 10 percent of the world's population. I think we're against the hypocrisy of assailing our allies because here and there they cling to a colony, while we engage in a conspiracy of silence and never open our mouths about the millions of people enslaved in the Soviet colonies in the satellite nations. I think we're for aiding our allies by sharing of our material blessings with those nations which share in our fundamental beliefs, but we're against doling out money government to government, creating bureaucracy, if not socialism, all over the world. We set out to help 19 countries. We're helping 107. We've spent 146 billion dollars. With that money, we bought a 2-million-dollar yacht for Haile Selassie. We bought dress suits for Greek undertakers, extra wives for Kenya[n] government officials. We bought a thousand TV sets for a place where they have no electricity. In the last six years, 52 nations have bought 7 billion dollars worth of our gold, and all 52 are receiving foreign aid from this country. No government ever voluntarily reduces itself in size. So governments' programs, once launched, never disappear. Actually, a government bureau is the nearest thing to eternal life we'll ever see on this earth. Federal employees – federal employees number two and a half million; and federal, state, and local, one out of six of the nation's work force employed by government. These proliferating bureaus with their thousands of regulations have cost us many of our constitutional safeguards. How many of us realize that today federal agents can invade a man's property without a warrant? They can impose a fine without a formal hearing, let alone a trial by jury? And they can seize and sell his property at auction to enforce the payment of that fine. In Chico County, Arkansas, James Wier over-planted his rice allotment. The government obtained a 17,000-dollar judgment. And a U.S. marshal sold his 960-acre farm at auction. The government said it was necessary as a warning to others to make the system work.

Ronald Reagan presented compelling quantitative evidence. But then he followed up the numerical evidence with stories, examples, and anecdotes. He talked about the yacht, dress suits, and TV sets for a country with no electricity. He talked about the story of James Wier. In this section, we reveal the psychology of why this is a deeply influential strategy. We reveal why numbers don't work when anecdotes do, and how to use this for easy persuasion.

WHAT IS THE BASE RATE FALLACY?

When asked to evaluate a probability, like the chance someone will behave a certain way, and we learn specific information about the person, and general information about the statistical base rate of the behavior in the population, we tend to neglect the base rate and focus only on the specific information. This is why it is also referred to as base rate neglect. In short: In the presence of general statistical information regarding aggregate data and specific information regarding a specific case, we gravitate to the specific and ignore the statistic.

THE BASE RATE FALLACY VISUALIZED

HOW BASE RATE NEGLECT INTERACTS WITH THE TWO SYSTEMS

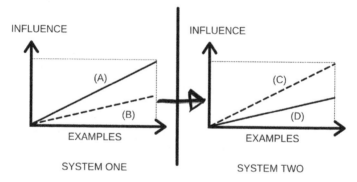

FIGURE 111: In system one, the influence of your message rises as you give specific examples (A) more than it does when you give statistical examples (B). In system two, the influence of your message rises as you give statistical examples (C) more than it does when you give specific examples (D).

WHAT IS AN EXAMPLE OF THE BASE RATE FALLACY?

In one of my first college classes, a seminar on ethical decision-making, I saw base rate neglect at work in a massive way. I recently read about base rate neglect in Daniel Kahneman's *Thinking, Fast and Slow*. And it was thrilling to see such a clear example, so self-evidently expressed.

Have you heard about the Milgram experiment? It tested the limits of what people will do when compelled by an authority figure. Researchers led subjects to believe they were participating in an experiment about negative reinforcement in learning. The subjects, acting as verbal test-givers, would shock the test-taker in the other room when they made a mistake. There was one twist: There was nobody on the receiving end of the shocks. It was just an audio recording. Of course, the subjects didn't know: They thought it was a test-taker, and they thought they were really shocking him. For the experiment to work, the subjects just needed to believe it was real. And they did. The experiment sought to answer this question: Would these perfectly kind people follow the orders of the authority figures in the room – the scientists in their lab coats – and continue to shock the test-taker, despite his desperate pleas, shouts, and screams of pain? Would they follow the orders to raise the voltage, and the pain, after every mistake? Would they continue despite the "lethal voltage" label on the higher-end voltages? And would they continue despite the eerie silence on the line after administering some of these so-called lethal voltages?

We talked about the authority-misinfluence tendency, so this shouldn't surprise you. Nearly everyone followed the orders. I think it was something like 70%. Can you believe it? 70% of subjects continued with the shocks. But this isn't the point. Let's bring it back to my class.

The topic of the day was ethics in research. And here's when I saw the base rate fallacy at work: The professor asked, "How many of you think you would follow the orders in the Milgram experiment? Raise your hands."

Not one hand shot up, except mine. People probably thought I was a little off. But I explained myself. Why should I think I am fundamentally different – in fact, morally superior and more resistant to authority – than 70% of people in the experiment? Think about it: If they knew everything we knew about the experiment, and we asked them the same question, wouldn't they say what we said? "No way! I couldn't do that!"

I said I predicted my probability of doing as the research subjects did and continuing with the voltages at 70%: the base rate. Why? Because they were people with moral intuitions, just like us. But they did it anyway. And just like us, they would vehemently say, "No, I wouldn't do that," if they were dispassionately analyzing the scenario. But they weren't, and if we weren't, we would probably do as they did.

What does this have to do with base rate neglect? Why did every single person in the room feel like they wouldn't have done as 70% of the subjects did? Because they had general information ("70% of them did it"), they had specific information ("I'm a fairly good person, I don't want to hurt others, I strive to act morally," etc.) and they completely ignored the general in favor of the specific. This was a major judgement mistake. This represents base rate neglect at work. And if I didn't recently read about base rate neglect, I would have fallen in their camp too.

Why does it happen? Evolution gave us many gifts, but ill-equipped our minds to munch on statistics and quantitative information. We naturally deal well with vivid, specific, visual information. Are you surprised we overweigh the natural and neglect the unnatural?

And there's another theory about human prediction: We judge the likelihood an item belongs to a category based on how representative it is of the category based on the characteristics we perceive as typical of items in the category. Representativeness acts as another heuristic attribute: attribute substitution strikes again. We substitute the easy heuristic attribute "representativeness of the category" for the difficult target attribute "likelihood it belongs to the category."

HOW DO YOU OVERCOME THE BASE RATE FALLACY?

You shouldn't completely ignore specific information. But you shouldn't overweigh it either. You should place a premium on base rate information. You should strive to emphasize it in your own mind to resist base rate neglect tendency. Here's how to overcome it: Use base rate information, not specific information, as your starting point. Then use the specific information to conservatively adjust from the base rate. In other words, use the base rate as an anchor. This is how you can make significantly more accurate judgements about probabilities. And the power of accurate prediction is a major professional advantage. This is known as Bayesian reasoning.

OVERCOMING THE BASE-RATE FALLACY WITH ANCHORING

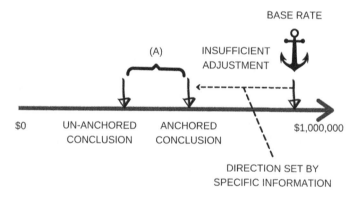

FIGURE 112: The Bayesian reasoning model uses the base rate as an anchor. Specific information then provides the direction of adjustment. In this case, insufficient adjustment is often accurate adjustment. The anchored conclusion arising from Bayesian reasoning counteracts the base rate fallacy. The distance between the un-anchored conclusion and the anchored conclusion (A) is the quantified benefit of this strategy.

HOW DO YOU USE THE BASE RATE FALLACY IN COMMUNICATION?

You use the base rate fallacy in communication by engineering your message to include specific information, as the human mind overweighs it. How will this impact your communication? As firmly system one messaging, it appeals to the subconscious processes dictating snap judgements. Thus, it is subtle, effective, and indirect; it is sophisticated because it appeals to simple, rough heuristics. And this helps you communicate with more clarity and influence.

But what is the second, broader reason it works? It falls under the mantra at the core of this book: By presenting information the way the human mind evolved to interpret it – the way the human mind often cannot resist interpreting it – you communicate with unparalleled power.

STRATEGY #1: USE THE P QUANT QUAL P MODEL

There are two types of evidence, and you need them both for maximum persuasion. As a refresher, you can use quantitative evidence and qualitative evidence. Regard the first as logical, and the second as emotional. Quantitative evidence uses numbers. Quantitative evidence uses stories or examples. And they combine for maximum persuasive power: Quantitative evidence appeals to the logical mind, and builds certainty, while qualitative evidence appeals to the emotional mind, where influence actually occurs.

You need quantitative evidence, but only to coax logical minds into letting their guard down, so you can punch straight at the emotional mind with emotional, qualitative evidence. If you go straight to qualitative, you risk people thinking, "Hold on, I need some real evidence before agreeing." If you skip qualitative and only use quantitative, you risk people thinking, "You just dropped a bunch of numbers on me… what do they even mean? How do I even interpret them?" We are naturally horrible at dealing with statistics and much better at dealing with anecdotes and stories. But for anecdotes and stories to take effect, you need to earn permission with the quantitative.

Let's turn to the P Quant Qual P model. It's another structure. Point: "We need to solve income inequality." Quantitative evidence: "The top 1% made 90% of all new income in the past year." Qualitative evidence: "I spoke with a family in Iowa's fourth district; the father hasn't seen his kids in a week, since he works a night shift at his third job when they go to bed, and the mother had to drop out of school and give up her dreams to make ends, barely, just barely, meet." Point repetition: "It's time to fix income inequality."

This simple model instantly combines the two kinds of evidence in the best possible way. And it persuades bimodally: In case anyone is operating in system two, you address them with the quantitative, and for those operating in system one, you address them with the qualitative.

STRATEGY #2: FIND THE DIAMOND IN THE ROUGH

I read this in a politically liberal publication: McDonalds' CEO received roughly $8 million in total compensation in 2014. This was bemoaning the disparity in compensation between CEOs and other labor. I did the math: Redistributing the entirety of the CEO's salary to the rest of the workforce would give them all a raise just shy of $10. Not hourly, yearly. McDonalds employs 840,000. So, is targeting this form of inequality really worth it? Does the CEO's pay really take anything away from the workforce? Let's say you only want to redistribute it to workers earning minimum wage. I'll take a conservative estimate and pretend McDonalds employs 100,000 such employees. They would each get around $80 extra a year. But the number is likely much larger than 100,000.

To be clear, this is not a discussion of my personal politics. I keep those under wraps. Why? Because all I've ever become as I learned more is more confused; more unsure; more perplexed by the mountain of nuance and complexity, with layers so deep I can't even begin to comprehend it all. And I don't think now is the time to even begin to express it.

So, if not my personal politics, what are we discussing? Finding the diamond in the rough; finding one piece of evidence so persuasive in its specificity it defeats any amount of general information.

For the sake of example, let's say I identify as economically conservative. Let's say I oppose the political targeting of exorbitant compensation packages for CEOs. I would use this McDonalds example. And what does this have to do with base rate neglect? When people consider the question "does exorbitant CEO compensation negatively impact workers?" they will inevitably overweigh specific information, like this example answering "no, not at all – only by $10 a year." And in the presence of this specific example, they will neglect base rate information, perhaps telling a completely different story; perhaps showing us McDonalds is the exception, not the rule.

A DIAMOND IN THE ROUGH INFLUENCES THE AUDIENCE

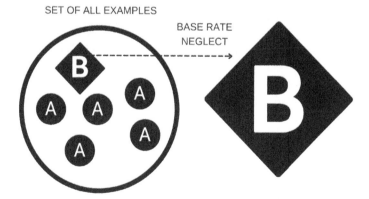

FIGURE 113: Base rate neglect explains why presenting a "diamond in the rough" in the set of all examples will cause human cognition to blow the specific example out of proportion, giving it an outsized impact on their judgment, even if the character of the set at large patently contradicts the implication of the specific example.

Find a story proving your point. Dig deep. Investigate. Peel back the layers. Make it interesting. Make it compelling. Make it intuitive. Make it absurdly undeniable as a standalone example. Base rate neglect fallacy will take care of the rest. You won't need to make people see this diamond in the rough as representative of the whole: base rate neglect will. You just have to present this specific example, and in the presence of general information and this specific information, they'll ignore the general. Of course, you can present both: use the P Quant Qual P model. This strategy simply dictates what you use as the Qual step.

STRATEGY #3: MAKE IT REPRESENTATIVE

Want to convince people an item belongs in a category? I'm sure you do. You want people to place your idea in the "good idea" category, don't you? And how can you do this? Present qualities of the item representing the category.

It's system one work: maximizing perception of an attribute heuristic ("representativeness of category") substituted for a target attribute ("likelihood it belongs to category"), thus indirectly maximizing perception of the target attribute.

Use this to place items in good categories. Want to advance your ideas? Want your proposals to succeed? Want people to take your initiatives seriously? Apply this strategy: Make your idea representative of the most salient positive category.

Want to make an idea stop dead in its tracks? Want to discredit an opposing proposal? Want to persuade people against something? Make it representative of the most salient negative category.

This strategy confuses people, and they tend to lack fluency in using it. So, I'll form a step-by-step algorithm to simplify it. Step one: Identify whether you want to argue for or against an idea. Step two: Identify the most salient relevant category of positive or negative items, based on whether you are arguing for or against it. Step three: Identify the qualities of the positive or negative category. Step four: Express those qualities in the item at hand.

Let's say you want to discredit a presidential candidate. Step one: You want to argue against his candidacy. Step two: What salient relevant categories make a presidential candidate appear like a poor choice? Let's say you perceive pressing public anger toward corruption. Use the negative category "corrupt politicians." Step three: Identify the qualities of this category. For example, "inaccessible, always meeting with monied interests, opinion fluctuating based on the desires of Wall-Street, lots of unanswered questions and vague responses to questions, etc." Step four: Present specific facts about the candidate proving these qualities, making him appear representative of the negative category, and due to the representativeness heuristic, a part of it. Should we vote for corrupt politicians? Of course not. This is a perfect example of system one, indirect, subtle, back-door persuasion.

In the 2020 Democratic primary cycle, something like this happened to Pete Buttigieg. He went to a closed-door fundraiser with a $2,500 minimum donation for access. That's not even the worst part. It was in an exclusive "wine cave" retreat. It just seemed, to many, corrupt. And political pundits seeking to discredit his candidacy loved drawing attention to the "wine cave incident." I'm surprise they didn't call it wine-cave-gate.

So, let's trace the four-step process. Step one: "We want to make Buttigieg appear like someone they shouldn't vote for." Step two: "People don't want to vote for corrupt politicians." Step three: "Corrupt politicians are exclusively accessible to wealthy donors." Step four: "Pete Buttigieg went to an exclusive fundraiser with a $2,500 minimum donation at a wine cave." Of course, they only stated this final step.

What happened next? Base rate neglect tossed aside the truth; base rate neglect ignored the fact that he drew the vast majority of his campaign funds from average Americans. Even though he presented the general, quantitative data about his campaign finances, base rate neglect ignored the general information and overweighed this specific, vivid, visual, and representative instance of behavior suggesting membership in the "corrupt politicians" category: wine-cave-gate.

HIJACKING SNAP-CATEGORIZATION TO SHAPE PERCEPTION

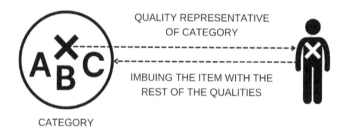

FIGURE 114: Imbuing an item with a quality representative of a category will indirectly imbue the item with the rest of the qualities of the items in the category.

I want to present one of Aesop's fables, called The Fable of the Wind and the Sun:

The North Wind and the Sun had a quarrel about which of them was the stronger. While they were disputing with much heat and bluster, a Traveler passed along the road wrapped in a cloak. "Let us agree," said the Sun, "that he is the stronger who can strip that Traveler of his cloak." "Very well," growled the North Wind, and at once sent a cold, howling blast against the Traveler. With the first gust of wind the ends of the cloak whipped about the Traveler's body. But he immediately wrapped it closely around him, and the harder the Wind blew, the tighter he held it to him. The North Wind tore angrily at the cloak, but all his efforts were in vain. Then the Sun began to shine. At first his beams were gentle, and in the pleasant warmth after the bitter cold of the North Wind, the Traveler unfastened his cloak and let it hang loosely from his shoulders. The Sun's rays grew warmer and warmer. The man took off his cap and mopped his brow. At last he became so heated that he pulled off his cloak, and, to escape the blazing sunshine, threw himself down in the welcome shade of a tree by the roadside. Gentleness and kind persuasion win where force and bluster fail.

When people operate in system one, their default system, trying to address a target attribute directly is like being the wind. Instead, meet their minds where they are: firmly and subconsciously focused on heuristic attributes. What would the sun do? Either system one or bimodal messaging: focusing partially (bimodal) or completely (system one) on heuristic attributes (in this case, representativeness), and letting the subconscious, automatic, predictable, systematic, reliable, psychologically irresistible processes of human cognition fill in the blanks, like the traveler taking off his own coat.

THE WISDOM OF THE FABLE OF THE WIND AND THE SUN

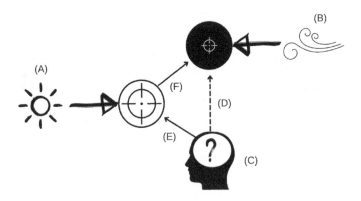

FIGURE 115: The sun (A) targets the heuristic variable; the wind (B) tries to influence the prospect (C) by targeting the target variable (D). The sun relies on the backdoor of substitution, evaluation (E), and transference (F).

In this manner of speaking, you're not injecting the idea into their mind directly; you're not telling them the target attribute is fulfilled; you're not saying "Pete Buttigieg is corrupt." What are you doing? You're sneaking the ingredients into their mind. What ingredients? The ones they need to form the idea themselves: the heuristic attributes. You're being the warm, gentle, subtle sun, not the blustering wind.

STRATEGY #4: SPEAK SPECIFICALLY, NOT STATISTICALLY

Specificity persuades. Use statistics. Don't only use statistics. Statistics lack specificity. Most statistics describe aggregate proportions: "X% of Y are Z." But people neglect base rates in the presence of specific information.

Stories. Anecdotes. Examples. These are the tools of effective communicators. And they go hand in hand with statistics. Statistics lend the stories credibility. But the stories persuade. The stories touch our hearts and minds. And science undeniably, unambiguously, unequivocally proves one thing: we overweigh them.

This is a broader idea, more a guiding principle than a strategy: Specificity sells. Specificity persuades with effortless ease where statistic after statistic fails. Zoom in. Pick a case. Explain it in detail.

Not only do we overweigh this type of information; it also captivates us. Stories grab attention. Details grab attention. Specificity grabs attention. Are you trying to persuade from the cloud of abstraction? Stop yourself. Plan your return to the concrete world.

And I remind you: Abstraction is not bad, and statistics are not bad. They hold critical importance. But they fall flat in the absence of specificity. Likewise, specificity lacks logical strength in the absence of statistics. But in a battle between the two, like in a debate, people judging probabilities overweigh specific information over general information.

STRATEGY #5: USE EXEMPLARY EXAMPLES

Remember the story of Ronald Reagan's push to cut welfare programs? Remember how he zoomed in on one example of a "welfare queen," and the result of this persuasive strategy? What was he really doing? He was using an exemplary example: one particularly compelling piece of information packaged as a narrative – as a story – standing as an example of his message.

You can present aggregate information about the statistics at large, but you can also zoom in and describe one extremely vivid story in deep detail with immense clarity. And let's say the statistics aren't on your side. Presenting an exemplary example often wins because of base rate neglect. In the presence of your specific example, people neglect the general statistic, even though it informs much more.

STRATEGY #6: CREATE ANECDOTES

Anecdotes work. Now you understand why. But how do you create an incredibly powerful anecdote? Present a personal story describing witnessing proof of your point, including your inner dialogue in the moment.

I'll give you a personal story of me using a personal story in my competitive debating days. What was the topic of the tournament? Food and food insecurity. What was the topic of this particular round? Something about fast food and food-related illness; I can't remember exactly. But I do remember making a point about how fast-food sites aggressively proliferate in low-income communities, an exacerbating factor of their below-average health.

What personal story did I use? I knew I could present statistic after statistic – and I did – but I also knew an exemplary anecdote, not another number, would provide my real persuasive punch. So, what was the story? I recently went to New York by bus. Leaving the city on a highway overpass, I saw a sprawling low-income community. Congested, cracked, and crumbling roads; boarded-up windows; all the imaginable markers of economic struggle. What was, without fail, situated on every single street corner? A McDonalds. I probably saw twenty. Not to mention the other fast-food sites littered around the neighborhood. In this moment, I realized the truth. And what was the truth? What I argued in the round, of course.

STRATEGY #7: FILL IN DETAILS EVOKING THE WHOLE

When you paint a picture of someone or something, certain keystone details create the most vivid image by implying the base, fundamental nature of the item at hand, and allowing the audience to fill in the blanks. Think of your description as dots people can connect to form the full image. Now imagine some of them are special: if you present these dots to your audience members, they can connect the others. And show, don't tell, these details. Identify the details standing for the whole, and then show them.

Let's say I wanted to create a vivid scene of what I saw from the highway overpass. What are three keystone details standing for the whole and allowing the audience to fill in the rest? The human despair and anger, the decay, and the omnipotence of the fast-food restaurants. I finished step one: identifying the salient details. Now, I could just say this: "People were angry, people despaired, the town was decaying, and on every street-corner was a fast-food chain." But this wouldn't show the details, would it? Such an anecdote falls flat. Why? Because it only satisfies one of the two keys. It paints details implying the general state of the subject, but tells them. For maximum impact, I must show the details; I must give people the ingredients to come to their own conclusion about the details. How? "Two men were in a vicious shouting match in front of a broken flea-market window, almost coming to blows (anger). The other pedestrians just walked by, tired eyes down, feet shuffling (despair). Further down the street, sticking out of an alley, was an overflowing dumpster, with trash strewn about on the cracked concrete (decay). What was above the flea market? A glowing McDonalds sign. If the pedestrians waiting at the cross-walk up ahead looked up, they would have seen a Wendy's sign. And the dumpster was leaning up against a Five-Guys (omnipotence of fast food). That's when I realized... [insert my point]."

IDENTIFY THE REPRESENTATIVE DETAILS

FIGURE 116: Representative details allow you to fill in the rest of the picture on your own. Non-representative details do not. Can you find the representative details in the example above?

SHOW, DON'T TELL, THE REPRESENTATIVE DETAILS

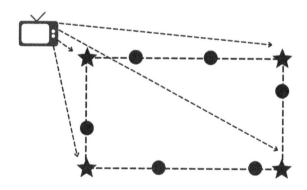

FIGURE 117: Show, don't tell, the representative details standing for the whole of the picture you seek to paint.

STRATEGY #8: USE ARCHETYPAL PERSONALITIES

The Wikipedia article on archetypes provides four definitions for the word:

One: A statement, pattern of behavior, a prototype, a 'first' form or a main model which other statements, patterns of behavior, and objects copy, emulate or "merge" into. (Frequently used informal synonyms for this usage include 'standard example,' "basic example," and the longer form 'archetypal example.' Mathematical archetypes often appear as 'canonical example.') Two: A Platonic philosophical idea referring to pure forms which embody the fundamental characteristics of a thing in Platonism. Three: A collectively-inherited unconscious idea, pattern of thought, image, etc., that is universally present, in individual psyches, as in Jungian psychology. Four: A constantly recurring symbol or motif in literature, painting, or mythology (this usage of the term draws from both comparative anthropology and from Jungian archetypal theory). In various seemingly unrelated cases in classic storytelling, media, etc., characters or ideas sharing similar traits recur. ("Archetype," n.d.)

We'll unpack this shortly. What's the most interesting part? How archetypes function:

> Usage of archetypes in writing is a holistic approach, which can help the writing win universal acceptance. This is because readers can relate to and identify with the characters and the situation, both socially and culturally. By deploying common archetypes contextually, a writer aims to impart realism to their work. According to many literary critics, archetypes have a standard and recurring depiction in a particular human culture or the whole human race that ultimately lays concrete pillars and can shape the whole structure in a literary work. ("Archetype," n.d.)

Further, In Jung's *Man and His Symbols*, he states the following:

> My views about the 'archaic remnants,' which I call 'archetypes' or 'primordial images,' have been constantly criticized by people who lack sufficient knowledge of the psychology of dreams and of mythology. The term 'archetype' is often misunderstood as meaning certain definite mythological images or motifs, but these are nothing more than conscious representations. Such variable representations cannot be inherited. The archetype is a tendency to form such representations of a motif – representations that can vary a great deal in detail without losing their basic pattern. (Jung, 1964)

In *The Seven Basic Plots: Why We Tell Stories*, Christopher Booker presents the following archetypal stories:

> Overcoming the Monster, Rags to Riches, The Quest, Voyage and Return, Comedy, Tragedy, Rebirth. (Booker, 2004)

Finally, in my book *How Legendary Leaders Speak*, I present how archetypes tie into communication:

> Participants in a study had to explain what was happening in a video. The video showed an "interaction" between three triangles. First, there are only two triangles. They move around a little. The people overwhelmingly say one triangle is bullying

the other. Then, the third one comes in. It joins forces with the victim triangle and beats back the bully triangle. The people overwhelmingly say that the third triangle saved the victim triangle. Do you see how deeply ingrained in our minds certain concepts, certain archetypes, and certain personalities are? We have such a high propensity to describe the world in terms of a set of concepts that we even see them played out in the movements of a bunch of triangles on a screen. We might actually be born with an understanding of certain concepts. These are archetypes. Archetypes are easily understood and projected onto the world as we perceive it. God(s), maternal forces, paternal forces, danger, fate, cause and effect, are just some examples of archetypes. Let's have a brief overview. We have evolved with predispositions to easily understand the world through the lens of a set of personalities. The nurturer, the threat, the predator, the prey, the opportunity, the challenge; these are just some archetypes that our minds can effortlessly handle. And know this: stories have been around since language has been around. The cultural evolution of stories and archetypes are closely intertwined. And know this too: most archetypes are characters. Characters and archetypes are often one and the same. Think about the ranks of stock characters that are ever-reoccurring in our stories. What are they? Archetypal personalities.

Let's briefly summarize everything we just learned about archetypes. Archetypes represent repeated patterns of thoughts, actions, events, etc., not in an individual, but in all of humanity. An archetypal item embodies the fundamental characteristics of items in its category. Archetypes tie to ideas, thoughts, and images unconsciously ingrained in each of our individual psyches. Archetypes constantly reoccurred in literature and mythology over the past 4,000 years in completely out-of-contact cultures. Archetypes lend writing realism and make it innately understandable to all. Archetypes stem from a psychological tendency to see the world through their lens. Archetypes advance story patterns we find innately relatable, understandable, and satisfying. Archetypes are images, ideas, and patterns we inherently project onto the world around us. In short: Archetypes are intuitive.

Carl Jung said that "The collective unconscious consists of the sum of the instincts and their correlates, the archetypes. Just as everybody possesses instincts, so he also possesses a stock of archetypal images."

Maynard James Keenan said that "Most religious stories and mythologies have some sort of similar root, some sort of global archetypes." Remember the mantra of this book? Convey information the way human minds interpret it. What could fall more under the mandate of this mantra than archetypal communication? Little.

But how do you produce archetypal communication? Let's pick one of Booker's story archetypes. Out of "overcoming the monster, rags to riches, the quest, voyage and return, comedy, tragedy, rebirth," let's examine how we could use the archetypal "rags to riches" narrative. This is an archetype: It reoccurs in the chronicles of human literature, it is intuitive, and it captivates our consciousness.

WHY ARCHETYPES ARE DEEPLY INTUITIVE

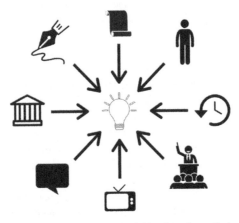

FIGURE 118: Archetypes are essential basic patterns that reoccur across different art forms, forms of communication, times, places, and cultures. They are embedded deep in the collective unconscious and offer you massive intuitive appeal.

How do you use it in communication? Build upon the other strategies in this section by presenting your anecdote or specific example as a rags to riches story. How? To add such an archetypal anecdote to my previous example, I could follow my personal story with a story of potential solutions. I could key in on one specific example of a similar low-income town making a "rags to riches" rebirth and lowering rates of food-related illness. See how I can easily reorient my communication to satisfy the archetype?

LAYERING JUNGIAN ARCHETYPES ON MILLER'S STORY MOLD

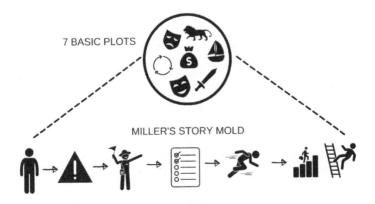

FIGURE 119: An immensely powerful strategy is formulating Miller's story mold to satisfy one or more of the seven basic plots.

But what is the impact? How does this help your communication? We know people neglect general statistics in the presence of specific information. And we also know the sheer extent of our proclivity to project archetypes onto the world. This strategy makes your message outweigh aggregate data and psychologically defeat even the most disconfirming statistics. And this strategy immediately makes your message intuitive and memorable due to the functions of archetypes.

STRATEGY #9: UNDERSTAND SEEMING TRUE VERSUS BEING TRUE

False statements often seem true. And even in the presence of disconfirming evidence, the truer it seems, the more we believe it. Frequently, to our psyches, seeming true equates to being true, and the more it seems true, the more we turn a blind eye to disconfirming evidence. All these strategies hinge on one key: They make your position seem true. They help you orient your communication properly, coaxing captivated minds to toss aside disconfirming evidence until everyone is on your side.

BASE RATE FALLACY CONCLUSION

Ronald Reagan presented compelling pieces of numerical evidence, but followed it with specific stories illustrating the numerical data. He spoke statistically, and then specifically. Due to the base rate fallacy, the specific information had an outsized persuasive impact. The statistics on their own would have lacked the same punch.

.............................Chapter Summary................................

- Base rate neglect is our tendency to overweigh specific information over statistics and base rate information.
- Base rate neglect is a manifestation of our incompetency at dealing with numbers and statistics intuitively.
- Base rate neglect explains why people believe aggregate statistical information doesn't apply to them.
- You use base rate neglect in communication by presenting information both statistically and specifically.
- You overcome base rate neglect by applying the process of Bayesian reasoning: using the base probability as an anchor.
- Ronald Reagan used base rate neglect by following statistical information with specific, punchy, anecdotal examples.

HOW TO OVERCOME THE PSYCHOLOGY (PART NINE)

1	The Availability Bias
1.1	Gather All Available Statistics Instead of Relying on Ease of Recall
2	The Anchoring Effect
2.1	Educate Yourself on the Subject of Evaluation
2.2	Strive to Ignore the First Number You Hear
2.3	Be Cognizant of the Impact of Unrelated Anchors
2.4	Seek Historical Evidence Related to Your Evaluation
2.5	Concentrate Attention on a Self-Supplied Counter-Anchor
3	Munger's Biases
3.1	Watch Carefully for Bias-Activating Circumstances
4	The Contrast Effect
4.1	Generate Counteracting Contrasting Inputs
5	Zero-Risk Bias
5.1	Run Statistical, Empirical, Rational Risk-Reward Calculations
6	The Halo Effect
6.1	Rely on Behavioral Records as Opposed to Snap Judgments
7	Agent Detection Bias
7.1	Question Omni-Causal Explanations in Complex Systems
8	Attribute Substitution
8.1	Specifically Circumscribe the Target Variable; Focus on It
9	Base Rate Neglect
9.1	Apply Bayesian Statistical Reasoning, Anchoring to the Base Rate

Claim These Free Resources that Will Help You Unleash the Power of Your Words and Speak with Confidence. Visit www.speakforsuccesshub.com/toolkit for Access.

2 Free Workbooks

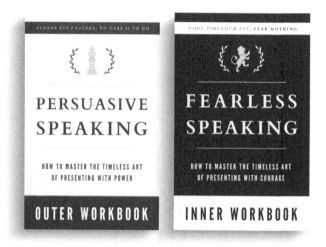

We'll send you two free workbooks, including long-lost excerpts by Dale Carnegie, the mega-bestselling author of *How to Win Friends and Influence People* (5,000,000 copies sold). *Fearless Speaking* guides you in the proven principles of mastering your inner game as a speaker. *Persuasive Speaking* guides you in the time-tested tactics of mastering your outer game by maximizing the power of your words. All of these resources complement the Speak for Success collection.

SOMETHING WAS MISSING. THIS IS IT.

D ECEMBER OF 2021, I COMPLETED the new editions of the 15 books in the Speak for Success collection, after months of work, and many 16-hour-long writing marathons. The collection is over 1,000,000 words long and includes over 1,700 handcrafted diagrams. It is *the* complete communication encyclopedia. But instead of feeling relieved and excited, I felt uneasy and anxious. Why? Well, I know now. After writing over 1,000,000 words on communication across 15 books, it slowly dawned on me that I had missed the most important set of ideas about good communication. What does it *really* mean to be a good speaker? This is my answer.

THERE ARE THREE DIMENSIONS OF SUCCESS

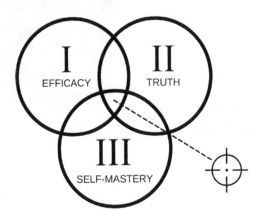

FIGURE I: A good speaker is not only rhetorically effective. They speak the truth, and they are students of self-mastery who experience peace, calm, and deep equanimity as they speak. These three domains are mutually reinforcing.

THE THREE AXES, IN DIFFERENT WORDS

Domain One	Domain Two	Domain Three
Efficacy	Truth	Self-Mastery
Rhetoric	Research	Inner-Peace
Master of Words	Seeker of Truth	Captain of Your Soul
Aristotle's "Pathos"	Aristotle's "Logos"	Aristotle's "Ethos"
Impact	Insight	Integrity
Presence of Power	Proper Perspective	Power of Presence
Inter-Subjective	Objective	Subjective
Competency	Credibility	Character
External-Internal	External	Internal
Verbal Mastery	Subject Mastery	Mental Mastery
Behavioral	Cognitive	Emotional

I realized I left out much about truth and self-mastery, focusing instead on the first domain. On page 27, the practical guide is devoted to domain I. On page 34, the ethical guide is devoted to domain II. We will shortly turn to domain III with an internal guide.

WHAT A GOOD SPEAKER LOOKS LIKE

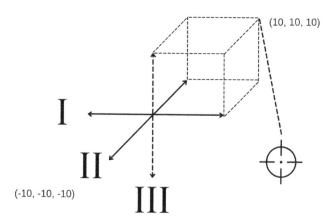

FIGURE II: We can conceptualize the three domains of success as an (X, Y, Z) coordinate plane, with each axis extending between -10 and 10. Your job is to become a (10, 10, 10). A (-10, 10, 10) speaks the truth and has attained self-mastery, but is deeply ineffective. A (10, -10, 10), speaks brilliantly and is at peace, but is somehow severely misleading others. A (10, 10, -10), speaks the truth well, but lives in an extremely negative inner state.

THE THREE AXES VIEWED DIFFERENTLY

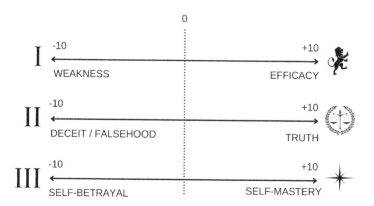

FIGURE III: We can also untangle the dimensions of improvement from representation as a coordinate plane, and instead lay them out flat, as spectrums of progress. A (+10, -10, -10) is a true monster, eloquent but evil. A (10, 10, 10) is a Martin Luther King. A more realistic example is (4, -3, 0): This person is moderately persuasive, bends truth a little too much for comfort (but not horribly), and is mildly anxious about speaking but far from falling apart. Every speaker exists at some point along these axes.

THE EXTERNAL MASTERY PROCESS IS INTERNAL TOO

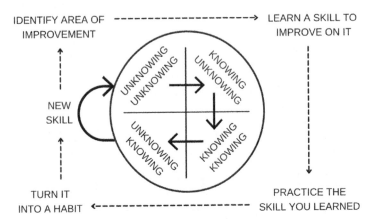

FIGURE IV: The same process presented earlier as a way to achieve rhetorical mastery will also help you achieve self-mastery. Just replace the word "skill" with "thought" or "thought-pattern," and the same cyclical method works.

THE POWER OF LANGUAGE

Language has generative power. This is why many creation stories include language as a primordial agent playing a crucial role in crafting reality. "In the beginning was the Word, and the Word was with God (John 1:1)."

Every problem we face has a story written about its future, whether explicit or implicit, conscious or subconscious. Generative language can rewrite a story that leads downward, turning it into one that aims us toward heaven, and then it can inspire us to realize this story. It can remove the cloud of ignorance from noble possibilities.

And this is good. You can orient your own future upward. That's certainly good for you. You can orient the future upward for yourself and for your family. That's better. And for your friends. That's better. And for your organization, your community, your city, and your country. That's better still. And for your enemies, and for people yet unborn; for all people, at all times, from now until the end of time.

And it doesn't get better than that.

Sound daunting? It is. It is the burden of human life. It is also the mechanism of moral progress. But start wherever you can, wherever you are. Start by acing your upcoming presentation.

But above all, remember this: all progress begins with truth.

Convey truth beautifully. And know thyself, so you can guard against your own proclivity for malevolence, and so you can strive toward self-mastery. Without self-mastery, it's hard, if not nearly impossible, to do the first part; to convey truth beautifully.

Truth, so you do good, not bad; impact, so people believe you; and self-mastery, as an essential precondition for truth and impact. Imagine what the world would be like if everyone were a triple-ten on our three axes. Imagine what good, what beauty, what bliss would define our existence. Imagine what good, what beauty, what bliss *could* define our existence, here and now.

It's up to you.

THE INNER GAME OF SPEAKING

R EFER BACK TO THIS INTERNAL GUIDE as needed. These humble suggestions have helped me deliver high-stakes speeches with inner peace, calm, and equanimity. They are foundational, and the most important words I ever put to paper. I hope these ideas help you as much as they helped me.

MASTER BOTH GAMES. Seek to master the outer game, but also the inner game. The self-mastery game comes before the word-mastery game, and even the world-mastery game. In fact, if you treat *any* game as a way to further your self-mastery, setting this as your "game above all games," you can never lose.

ADOPT THREE FOUNDATIONS. Humility: "The other people here probably know something I don't. They could probably teach me something. I could be overlooking something. I could be wrong. They have something to contribute" Passion: "Conveying truth accurately and convincingly is one of the most important things I'll ever do." Objectivity: "If I'm wrong, I change course. I am open to reason. I want to *be* right; I don't just want to seem right or convince others I am."

STRIVE FOR THESE SUPERLATIVES. Be the kindest, most compassionate, most honest, most attentive, most well-researched, and most confident in the room. Be the one who cares most, who most seeks to uplift others, who is most prepared, and who is most thoughtful about the reason and logic and evidence behind the claims.

START BY CULTIVATING THE HIGHEST VIRTUES IN YOURSELF: love for your audience, love for truth, humility, a deep and abiding desire to make the world a better place, the desire to both be heard and to hear, and the desire to both teach and learn. You will find peace, purpose, clarity, confidence, and persuasive power.

START BY AVOIDING THESE TEMPTING MOTIVES. Avoid the desire to "outsmart" people, to overwhelm and dominate with your rhetorical strength, to embarrass your detractors, to win on the basis of cleverness alone, and to use words to attain power for its own sake. Don't set personal victory as your goal. Strive to achieve a victory for truth. And if you discover you are wrong, change course.

LISTEN TO YOURSELF TALK. (Peterson, 2018). See if what you are saying makes you feel stronger, physically, or weaker. If it makes you feel weaker, stop saying it. Reformulate your speech until you feel the ground under you solidifying.

SPEAK FROM A PLACE OF LOVE. It beats speaking from a desire to dominate. Our motivation and purpose in persuasion must be love. It's ethical *and* effective.

LOVE YOUR ENEMIES (OR HAVE NONE). If people stand against you, do not inflame the situation with resentment or anger. It does no good, least of all for you.

AVOID THESE CORRUPTING EMOTIONS: resistance, resentment, and anger. Against them, set acceptance, forgiveness, and love for all, even your enemies.

PLACE YOUR ATTENTION HERE, NOW. Be where you are. Attend to the moment. Forget the past. Forget the future. Nothing is more important than this.

FOCUS ON YOURSELF, BUT NOW. Speaking gurus will tell you to focus solely on your audience. Yes, that works. But so does focusing on yourself, as long as you focus on yourself *now*. Let this focus root you in the present. Don't pursue a mental commentary on what you see. Instead, just watch. Here. Now. No judgment.

ACCEPT YOUR FEAR. Everyone fears something. If you fear speaking, don't fear your fear of speaking too. Don't reprimand yourself for it. Accept it. Embrace it, even. Courage isn't action without fear. Courage is action despite fear.

STARE DOWN YOUR FEAR. To diminish your fear, stare at the object of your fear (and the fear itself), the way a boxer faces off with his opponent before the fight. Hold it in your mind, signaling to your own psyche that you can face your fear.

CHIP AWAY AT YOUR FEAR. The path out of fear is to take small, voluntary steps toward what you fear. Gradual exposure dissolves fear as rain carves stone.

LET THE OUTER SHAPE THE INNER. Your thoughts impact your actions. But your actions also impact your thoughts. To control fear, seek to manage its outward manifestations, and your calm exterior will shape your interior accordingly.

KNOW THAT EGO IS THE ENEMY. Ego is a black storm cloud blocking the warm sunlight of your true self. Ego is the creation of a false self that masquerades as your true self and demands gratification (which often manifests as the destruction of something good). The allure of arrogance is the siren-song of every good speaker. With it comes pride and the pursuit of power; a placing of the outer game before the inner. Don't fall for the empty promises of ego-gratification. Humility is power.

DON'T IDENTIFY WITH YOUR POSITIONS. Don't turn your positions into your psychological possessions. Don't imbue them with a sense of self.

NOTICE TOXIC AVATARS. When person A speaks to person B, they often craft a false idea, a false avatar, of both themselves and their interlocuter: A1 and B1. So does person B: B2 and A2. The resulting communication is a dance of false avatars; A1, B1, B2, and A2 communicate, but not person A and B. A false idea of one's self speaks to a false idea of someone else, who then does the same. This may be why George Bernard Shaw said "the greatest problem in communication is the illusion that it has been accomplished." How do you avoid this dance of false avatars? This conversation between concepts but not people?

Be present. Don't prematurely judge. Let go of your *sense* of self, for just a moment, so your real self can shine forth.

MINE THE RICHES OF YOUR MIND. Look for what you need within yourself; your strengths and virtues. But also acknowledge and make peace with your own capacity for malevolence. Don't zealously assume the purity of your own motives.

RISE ABOVE YOUR MIND. The ability to think critically, reason, self-analyze, and self-criticize is far more important than being able to communicate, write, and speak. Introspect before you extrospect. Do not identify as your mind, but as the awareness eternally watching your mind. Do not be in your mind, but above it.

CLEAR THE FOG FROM YOUR PSYCHE. Know what you believe. Know your failures. Know your successes. Know your weaknesses. Know your strengths. Know what you fear. Know what you seek. Know your mind. Know yourself. Know your capacity for malevolence and evil. Know your capacity for goodness and greatness. Don't hide any part of yourself from yourself. Don't even try.

KNOW YOUR LOGOS. In 500 B.C. Heraclitus defined Logos as "that universal principle which animates and rules the world." What is your Logos? Meditate on it. Sit with it. Hold it up to the light, as a jeweler does with a gem, examining all angles.

KNOW YOUR LIMITS. The more you delineate and define the actions you consider unethical, the more likely you are to resist when they seem expedient.

REMEMBER THAT EVERYTHING MATTERS. There is no insignificant job, duty, role, mission, or speech. Everything matters. Everything seeks to beat back chaos in some way and create order. A laundromat doesn't deal in clean clothes, nor a trash disposal contractor in clean streets. They deal in order. In civilization. In human dignity. Don't ignore the reservoir of meaning and mattering upon which you stand. And remember that it is there, no matter where you stand.

GIVE THE GIFT OF MEANING. The greatest gift you can give to an audience is the gift of meaning; the knowledge that they matter, that they are irreplaceable.

HONOR YOUR INHERITANCE. You are the heir to thousands of years of human moralizing. Our world is shaped by the words of long-dead philosophers, and the gifts they gave us: gems of wisdom, which strengthen us against the dread and chaos of the world. We stand atop the pillars of 4,000 years of myth and meaning. Our arguments and moral compasses are not like planks of driftwood in a raging sea, but branches nourished by an inestimably old tree. Don't forget it.

BE THE PERSON YOU WANT TO BE SEEN AS. How do you want to be seen by your audience? How can you actually be that way, rather than just seeming to be?

HAVE TRUE ETHOS. Ethos is the audience's perception that the speaker has their best interests at heart. It's your job to make sure this perception is accurate.

CHANGE PLACES WITH YOUR AUDIENCE. Put yourself in their shoes, and then be the speaker you would want to listen to, the speaker worthy of your trust.

ACT AS THOUGH THE WHOLE WORLD IS WATCHING. Or as though a newspaper will publish a record of your actions. Or as though you're writing your autobiography with every action, every word, and even every thought. (You are.)

ACT WITH AUDACIOUS HONOR. As did John McCain when he called Obama, his political opponent, "a decent family man, [and] citizen, that I just happen to have disagreements with." As did Socrates and Galileo when they refused to betray truth.

ADOPT A MECHANIC'S MENTALITY. Face your challenges the way a mechanic faces a broken engine; not drowning in emotion, but with objectivity and clarity. Identify the problem. Analyze the problem. Determine the solution. Execute the solution. If it works, celebrate. If not, repeat the cycle. This is true for both your inner and outer worlds: your fear of speaking, for example, is a specific problem with a specific fix, as are your destructive external rhetorical habits.

APPLY THE MASTERY PROCESS INTERNALLY. The four-step mastery process is not only for mastering your rhetoric, but also for striving toward internal mastery.

MARSHAL YOURSELF ALONG THE THREE AXES. To marshal means to place in proper rank or position – as in marshaling the troops – and to bring together and order in the most effective way. It is a sort of preparation. It begins with taking complete stock of what is available. Then, you order it. So, marshal yourself along three axes: the rhetorical axis (your points, arguments, rhetorical techniques, key phrases, etc.), the internal axis (your peace of mind, your internal principles, your mental climate, etc.), and the truth axis (your research, your facts, your logic, etc.).

PRACTICE ONE PUNCH 10,000 TIMES. As the martial arts adage says, "I fear not the man who practiced 10,000 punches once, but the man who practiced one punch 10,000 times." So it is with speaking skills and rhetorical techniques.

MULTIPLY YOUR PREPARATION BY TEN. Do you need to read a manuscript ten times to memorize it? Aim to read it 100 times. Do you need to research for one hour to grasp the subject of your speech? Aim to research for ten.

REMEMBER THE HIGHEST PRINCIPLE OF COMMUNICATION: the connection between speaker and audience – here, now – in this moment, in this place.

KNOW THERE'S NO SUCH THING AS A "SPEECH." All good communication is just conversation, with varying degrees of formality heaped on top. It's all just connection between consciousnesses. Every "difference" is merely superficial.

SEE YOURSELF IN OTHERS. What are you, truly? Rene Descartes came close to an answer in 1637, when he said "cogito, ego sum," I think therefore I am. The answer this seems to suggest is that your thoughts are most truly you. But your thoughts (and your character) change all the time. Something that never changes, arguably even during deep sleep, is awareness. Awareness is also the precondition for thought. A computer performs operations on information, but we don't say the computer "thinks." Why? Because it lacks awareness. So, I believe what makes you "you," most fundamentally, is your awareness, your consciousness. And if you accept this claim – which is by no means a mystical or religious one – then you must also see yourself in others. Because while the contents of everyone's consciousness is different, the consciousness itself is identical. How could it be otherwise?

FORGIVE. Yourself. Your mistakes. Your detractors. The past. The future. All.

FREE YOUR MIND. Many of the most challenging obstacles we face are thoughts living in our own minds. Identify these thoughts, and treat them like weeds in a garden. Restore the pristine poise of your mind, and return to equanimity.

LET. Let what has been be and what will be be. Most importantly, let what is be what is. Work to do what good you can do, and accept the outcome.

FLOW. Wikipedia defines a flow state as such: "a flow state, also known colloquially as being in the zone, is the mental state in which a person performing some activity is fully immersed in a feeling of energized focus, full involvement, and enjoyment in the process of the activity. In essence, flow is characterized by the complete absorption in what one does, and a resulting transformation in one's sense of time." Speaking in a flow state transports you and your audience outside of space and time. When I entered deep flow states during my speeches and debates, audience members would tell me that "it felt like time stopped." It felt that way for me too. Speaking in a flow state is a form of meditation. And it both leads to and results from these guidelines. Adhering to them leads to flow, and flow helps you adhere to them.

MEDITATE. Meditation brings your attention to the "here and now." It creates flow. Practice silence meditation, sitting in still silence and focusing on the motions of your mind, but knowing yourself as the entity watching the mind, not the mind itself. Practice aiming meditation, centering your noble aim in your mind, and focusing on the resulting feelings. (Also, speaking in flow is its own meditation).

EMBARK ON THE GRAND ADVENTURE. Take a place wherever you are. Develop influence and impact. Improve your status. Take on responsibility. Develop capacity and ability. Do scary things. Dare to leap into a high-stakes speech with no preparation if you must. Dare to trust your instincts. Dare to strive. Dare to lead. Dare to speak the truth freely, no matter how brutal it is. Be bold. Risk failure. Throw out your notes. The greatest human actions – those that capture our hearts and minds – occur on the border between chaos and order, where someone is daring to act and taking a chance when they know they could fall off the tightrope with no net below. Training wheels kill the sense of adventure. Use them if you need to, but only to lose them as soon as you can. Speak from the heart and trust yourself. Put yourself out there. Let people see the gears turning in your mind, let them see you grappling with your message in real time, taking an exploration in the moment. This is not an automaton doing a routine. It's not robotic or mechanical. That's too much order. It's also not unstructured nonsense. That's too much chaos. There is a risk of failure, mitigated not by training wheels, but by preparation. It is not a perfectly practiced routine, but someone pushing themselves just beyond their comfort zone, right at the cutting-edge of what they are capable of. It's not prescriptive. It's not safe either. The possibility that you could falter and fall in real-time calls out the best from you, and is gripping for the audience. It is also a thrilling adventure. Have faith in yourself, faith that you will say the right words when you need to. Don't think ahead, or backward. Simply experience the moment.

BREAK THE SEVEN LAWS OF WEAKNESS. If your goal is weakness, follow these rules. Seek to control what you can't control. Seek praise and admiration from others. Bend the truth to achieve your goals. Treat people as instruments in your game. Only commit to outer goals, not inner goals. Seek power for its own sake. Let anger and dissatisfaction fuel you in your pursuits, and pursue them frantically.

FAIL. Losses lead to lessons. Lessons lead to wins. If there's no chance of failure in your present task, you aren't challenging yourself. And if you aren't challenging yourself, you aren't growing. And that's the deepest and most enduring failure.

DON'T BETRAY YOURSELF. To know the truth and not say the truth is to betray the truth and to betray yourself. To know the truth, seek the truth, love the truth, and to speak the truth and speak it well, with poise and precision and power… this is to honor the truth, and to honor yourself. The choice is yours.

FOLLOW YOUR INNER LIGHT. As the Roman emperor and stoic philosopher Marcus Aurelius wrote in his private journal, "If thou findest in human life anything better than justice, truth, temperance, fortitude, and, in a word, anything better than thy own mind's self-satisfaction in the things which it enables thee to do according to right reason, and in the condition that is assigned to thee without thy own choice; if, I say, thou seest anything better than this, turn to it with all thy soul, and enjoy that which thou hast found to be the best. But if nothing appears to be better than [this], give place to nothing else." And as Kant said, treat humans as ends, not means.

JUDGE THEIR JUDGMENT. People *are* thinking of you. They *are* judging you. But what is their judgment to you? Nothing. (Compared to your self-judgment).

BREAK LESSER RULES IN THE NAME OF HIGHER RULES. Our values and moral priorities nest in a hierarchy, where they exist in relation to one another. Some are more important than others. If life compels a tradeoff between two moral principles, as it often does, this means there is a right choice. Let go the lesser of the two.

DON'T AVOID CONFLICT. Necessary conflict avoided is an impending conflict exacerbated. Slay the hydra when it has two heads, not twenty.

SEE THE WHOLE BOARD. Become wise in the ways of the world, and learned in the games of power and privilege people have been playing for tens of thousands of years. See the status-struggles and dominance-shuffling around you. See the chess board. But then opt to play a different game; a more noble game. The game of self-mastery. The game that transcends all other games. The worthiest game.

SERVE SOMETHING. Everyone has a master. Everyone serves something. Freedom is not the absence of service. Freedom is the ability to choose your service. What, to you, is worth serving? With your work and with your words?

TAKE RESPONSIBILITY FOR YOUR RIPPLE EFFECT. If you interact with 1,000 people, and they each interact with 1,000 more who also do the same, you are three degrees away from one billion people. Remember that compassion is contagious.

ONLY SPEAK WHEN YOUR WORDS ARE BETTER THAN SILENCE. And only write when your words are better than a blank page.

KNOW THERE IS THAT WHICH YOU DON'T KNOW YOU DON'T KNOW. Of course, there's that you know you don't know too. Recognize the existence of both of these domains of knowledge, which are inaccessible to you in your present state.

REMEMBER THAT AS WITHIN, SO (IT APPEARS) WITHOUT. If you orient your aim toward goals fueled by emotions like insecurity, jealousy, or vengeance, the world manifests itself as a difficult warzone. If you orient your aim toward goals fueled by emotions like universal compassion and positive ambition, the beneficence of the world manifests itself to you. Your aim and your values alter your perception.

ORIENT YOUR AIM PROPERLY. Actions flow from thought. Actions flow from *motives*. If you orient your aim properly – if you aim at the greatest good for the greatest number, at acting forthrightly and honorably – then this motive will fuel right actions, subconsciously, automatically, and without any forethought.

STOP TRYING TO USE SPEECH TO GET WHAT YOU WANT. Try to articulate what you believe to be true as carefully as possible, and then accept the outcome.

USE THE MOST POWERFUL "RHETORICAL" TACTIC. There is no rhetorical tool more powerful than the overwhelming moral force of the unvarnished truth.

INJECT YOUR EXPERIENCE INTO YOUR SPEECH. Speak of what you know and testify of what you have seen. Attach your philosophizing and persuading and arguing to something real, some story you lived through, something you've seen.

DETACH FROM OUTCOME. As Stoic philosopher Epictetus said: "There is only one way to happiness and that is to cease worrying about things which are beyond the power of our will. Make the best use of what is in your power, and take the rest as it happens. The essence of philosophy is that a man should so live that his happiness shall depend as little as possible on external things. Remember to conduct yourself in life as if at a banquet. As something being passed around comes to you, reach out your hand and take a moderate helping. Does it pass you? Don't stop it. It hasn't yet come? Don't burn in desire for it, but wait until it arrives in front of you."

FOCUS ON WHAT YOU CONTROL. As Epictetus said, "It's not what happens to you, but how you react to it that matters. You may be always victorious if you will never enter into any contest where the issue does not wholly depend upon yourself. Some things are in our control and others not. Things in our control are opinion, pursuit, desire, aversion, and, in a word, whatever are our own actions. Things not in our control are body, property, reputation, command, and, in one word, whatever are not our own actions. Men are disturbed not by things, but by the view which they take of them. God has entrusted me with myself. Do not with that all things will go well with you, but that you will go well with all things." Before a high-stakes speech or event, I always tell myself this: "All I want from this, all I aim at, is to conduct what I control, my thoughts and actions, to the best of my ability. Any external benefit I earn is merely a bonus."

VIEW YOURSELF AS A VESSEL. Conduct yourself as something through which truth, brilliantly articulated, flows into the world; not as a self-serving entity, but a conduit for something higher. Speak not for your glory, but for the glory of good.

Email Peter D. Andrei, the author of the Speak for Success collection and the President of Speak Truth Well LLC directly.

pandreibusiness@gmail.com

Made in the USA
Monee, IL
31 October 2022

16870687R00164